Changing Paths

*Travels and Meditations in
Alaska's Arctic Wilderness*

BILL SHERWONIT

UNIVERSITY OF ALASKA PRESS
Fairbanks

University of Alaska Press
P.O. Box 756240
Fairbanks, AK 99775-6240

Portions of this book have appeared, in slightly different form, in *Alaska*; *Alaska Airlines Magazine*; *Appalachia*; *American Nature Writing 2001*; *Anchorage Press*; *Connecticut Woodlands*; and *Living with Wildness: An Alaskan Odyssey*.

Printed in China

This publication was printed on paper that meets the minimum requirements for ANSI/NISO Z39.48-1992 (Permanence of Paper).

Library of Congress Cataloging-in-Publication Data

Sherwonit, Bill, 1950–
    Changing paths : travels and meditations in Alaska's Arctic wilderness / Bill Sherwonit.
        p. cm.
    Includes bibliographical references.
    ISBN 978-1-60223-060-6 (pbk. : alk. paper)
    1. Brooks Range (Alaska)—Description and travel. 2. Sherwonit, Bill, 1950–   I. Title.
    F912.B75S54 2009
    917.98'70452—dc22

                                        2009012132

Cover image by Bill Sherwonit. Named by Robert Marshall after his 1929 expedition into the Central Brooks Range, Mount Doonerak is one of the grandest landforms in Gates of the Arctic National Park and Preserve, a dark, towering spire that looms over the surrounding landscape. To the right of Doonerak are Bombardment Creek and a second sheer giant (the latter only partly visible), Hanging Glacier Mountain.

Image of Bill Sherwonit on cover flap is by Helene Feiner.

Contents

For Helene

Acknowledgments

I HAVE REACHED THAT POINT IN MY LIFE WHERE I CAN LOOK back and see patterns where there once seemed little more than chance, coincidence, and even chaos. While at times my life seemed to make no sense at all, the many and varied paths I've taken in nearly six decades of living now seem to connect in a way that somehow makes wonderful sense. I may be deluding myself in this regard, but I don't think so. As I note within this narrative, few if any of my childhood friends or family members would have guessed that the small, shy, sensitive boy of long ago had the potential to become an author, wilderness lover, and activist, or that I would some day live in our nation's "Last Frontier" and trek alone across miles of untrailed arctic wilderness. I never imagined it myself. Yet here I am, living in Alaska, eking out a living as a freelance nature writer, being an advocate for wildness in its various forms, and still occasionally exploring one of our continent's wildest and most remote landscapes. For all of that, I am extremely and humbly grateful. I am also thankful, beyond words, for the many people who've guided, nudged, and inspired me along the way. Here I recognize and thank the people who are most closely tied to the story I share in these pages, but there are likely some I have forgotten to mention and I apologize to any I have overlooked.

I'll start at the beginning, with thanks to my dad and mom. Ed and Torie Sherwonit raised three kids who turned out to be pretty decent adults, which speaks well for their parenting and love. Thanks to my siblings, Karen and Dave, each of whom I admire. My brother, especially, has a love for nature that matches my own and that passion has become a special bond as we've moved along largely disparate paths. And thanks to the "other" Sherwonit family, which lived only a short walk from my own: Uncle Peach and Aunt Evie and their three children, Jim, John, and Bev. Because two brothers (Ed and Peach Sherwonit) married two sisters (Torie and Evie Schmollinger), our families were doubly close. In the context of this story, I owe a special debt of gratitude to Uncle Peach, my first "outdoors" mentor, whose love of fishing—and life—shaped many of my own attitudes and values.

Also influential, in their own ways, were my neighborhood buddies, especially the Wallace twins, Barry and Brian. I have fond memories of our long rambles through the Woods that were such an important refuge during my boyhood. It has been a joy to reconnect with Barry and Brian in recent years after more than three decades apart. At different times, each of us has marveled that all three have become writers who deeply love the wider, wilder world.

Of the many teachers who inspired me across the years, one deserves special acknowledgment here: Donna Anderson, my earth science teacher at Trumbull High School. In her own gentle and encouraging way, Miss Anderson was something of a guardian angel—or at least a beacon of light—during a particularly dark time in my life. Thanks also to my Bates College geology advisor, Dr. Robert Morrison, for suggesting that I "go west" to study geology in graduate school. His good advice led me to Arizona, which in turn led to Alaska.

In graduate school and for several years after, my closest friends were geologists. Though I've lost touch with nearly all of them, with great fondness I recall my friends and former colleagues and the experiences we shared at the University of Arizona and in the Alaska wilds: Tom Andrews, Charlie Barnwell, Jason Bressler, Jim Cappa, Gaylord Cleveland, Terry Cookro, Chris Croft, Rick Frederickson, Sue Karl, Lothar "Kling" Klingmuller, Jim Lessman, Brett Liming, Richard McGehee, Joe Ruzicka, John Schloderer, Joel Stratman, and the head of the Anchorage office of WGM, Riz Bigelow. Others deserving special mention from my geology days are the members of the homesteading Fickus family, who were such a delightful part of my first summer in the Brooks Range, in 1974: Bill, Lil, Debbie, Matt, Linda, and Tim.

Thanks to those who've explored the Central Brooks Range with me since my return to Alaska in 1982, reincarnated as a writer. Mike Burgess and Neil Fidelman joined me in the Arrigetch Peaks in 1984, my first backpacking expedition into Gates of the Arctic National Park. More recently I've shared the good company of William Ashton, Ellen Bielawski, Dulcy Boehle, Chip and Bucky Dennerlein, Dale Gardner, Michael Keroski, Dave Mills, and Steve Ulvi.

Numerous writers and editors were essential to the shaping and polishing of this narrative. Jim Adams, William Ashton, Ellen Bielawski, Nancy Deschu, Jon Nickles, and Andromeda Romano-Lax gave helpful advice on early versions of the story, while Wendell Berry and Kathleen Dean Moore offered insights on later drafts. Above all, Scott Russell Sanders was able to read a portion of the story and imagine an approach that inspired the narrative as presented in these pages, as a story in three parts. Many, many thanks for that, Scott. I also owe a special debt of gratitude to University of Alaska Press managing editor Elisabeth Dabney, who wholeheartedly embraced this book and shepherded it through the acquisition process. I thank the outside reviewers, including Scott Slovic (the other remained anonymous), whose comments strengthened and focused the narrative; the press's advisory board; and others instrumental in turning my manuscript into a book: University of Alaska Press production editor Sue Mitchell; copyeditor and interior designer Rachel Fudge; proofreader Josie Marks; mapmaker and cover designer Dixon Jones; and Jobe Chakuchin of the National Park Service for the map of the entire park.

Many writers, activists, philosophers, and historians informed and inspired the ideas presented in these pages. Chief among them was explorer and wilderness advocate Robert Marshall, whose book *Alaska Wilderness* entered my life not long after I first entered the Central Brooks Range and whose writings about wilderness helped shift the direction of my life. Others meriting special mention include Joseph Campbell, Theodore Catton, Loren Eiseley, Matthew Fox, John Kauffman, Roderick Nash, Gary Snyder, Jack Turner, and Sam Wright. I am also grateful to the Alaskan writers who are strong advocates for Alaska's wild landscapes and wildlife, especially Jeff Fair, Kim Heacox, Marybeth Holleman, Seth Kantner, Nick Jans, Hank Lentfer, Nancy Lord, Richard Nelson, Eva Saulitis, Carolyn Servid, Sherry Simpson, and Tom Walker. You inspire me with your work. Also deserving a sincere thank-you are those whose vision and work led to Gates of the Arctic National Park and Preserve, from Bob Marshall to Olaus and Mardy Murie, John Kauffman, President Jimmy Carter, and others involved in the passage of the Alaska Lands Act.

Deep gratitude to those who took the time to talk with me about the Central Brooks Range in my effort to better understand the place and its people, including Mike Haubert, Dave Mills, Raymond Paneak, Rachel Riley, Steve Ulvi, and Vera Weber.

Finally, I wish to extend my love and appreciation to the women who remain central to my life: my daughter, Tiaré Neill, who lives in faraway Southern California but is always in my heart; my mother, Torie, who lives with me here in Anchorage; and my beloved sweetheart, Helene Feiner. To Helene, many, many thanks for your support of this project specifically and my writing life generally. I eagerly anticipate our first adventure in the Central Brooks Range, a place I love dearly and one that's been so important to my life.

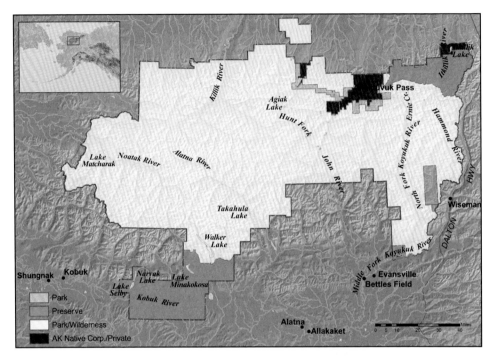

Map of Gates of the Arctic Park and Preserve, courtesy Jobe Chakuchin,
National Park Service.

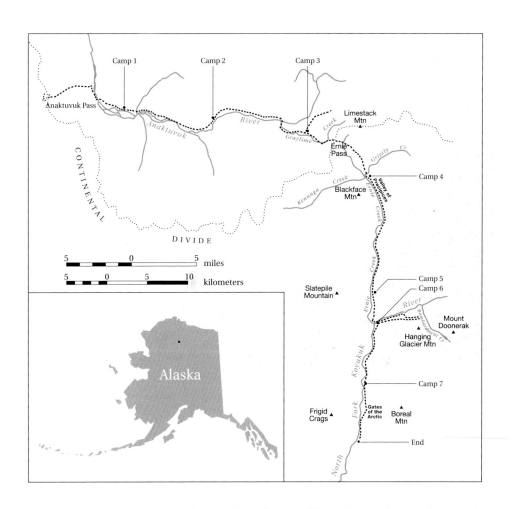

Camp 1   Camp 2   Camp 3

Anaktuvuk Pass

Limestack
Mtn

Anaktuvuk   River   Graylime   Creek

Ernie
Pass

CONTINENTAL

Grizzly Cr

Camp 4

Kenunga   Creek   Blackface
Mtn

Valley of Precipices

Ernie Creek

DIVIDE

5   0   5 miles
5   0   5   10 kilometers

Slatepile
Mountain

Camp 5
Camp 6

River

Ernie Creek

Mount
Doonerak

Hanging
Glacier Mtn

Monument Cr

Alaska

Koyukuk

Camp 7

Frigid
Crags

Fork

Gates
of the
Arctic

Boreal
Mtn

End

North

This map shows the author's route from Anaktuvuk Pass to his rendezvous site near the Gates, in Gates of the Arctic National Park. Also included are his seven campsites and notable landmarks along the way, most of them named by Robert Marshall.

PART ONE

ATV tracks lead from the village of Anaktuvuk Pass up the
Anaktuvuk River valley.

ONE

Entering New Terrain

LATE JULY IN ALASKA'S CENTRAL BROOKS RANGE. CAMPED ALONE a few miles from the Arctic Divide, I huddle in my sleeping bag while wind-driven sheets of rain soak the landscape, pelt my tent. It's been raining like this, off and on, for at least ten hours. Five of the trip's first seven days have now been mostly rainy and overcast. Strange weather, it seems, for a so-called "Arctic desert." Depressing.

I began the day with ambitious goals. But plans to scramble up a nearby mountain were themselves scrambled by prolonged downpours that quickly waterlogged my aging and not-so-water-resistant rain gear. Being a flexible sort with no strict schedule to keep, I retreated to my dry and snug shelter, which has so far proved marvelously rainproof. Instead of ridge walking, I've napped, reread parts of Robert Marshall's classic book about the Brooks Range, *Alaska Wilderness*, written copiously in my journal, and fretted about my journey.

I hate to admit it, but Dad apparently was right: I am a worrywart. "Just like your mother," he'd hasten to add if he were here with me. Too much time spent holed up in a tent, especially when alone, inevitably leads to too much thinking and consequent anxieties. I worry that I haven't brought sufficient food and fuel for my two-week trip. I worry that animals—ground squirrels as much a grizzlies—may discover and invade my food stash. I worry that my blistered feet will worsen. But mostly I worry about the difficulties of fording the rain-swollen North Fork of the Koyukuk, a major river crossing that is still four days away.

Bob Marshall, I'm certain, wouldn't be plagued by such uncertainties. In fact, he would probably be out exploring this valley right now, soaking wet or not.

Thoughts of Marshall are interrupted by muted conversation that drifts into my tent with the splash of rain. I've already heard human voices, or something like them, a number of times while marching alone through these mountains, so I figure my imagination is acting up again. Until I hear shouts.

Craning my neck, I peek out the tent's mosquito netting and glimpse four ghostly shapes approaching from the south, an amazing sight. They seem to be zeroed in on me. "Hey," one yells, "anybody in there?" A couple of minutes later, four bedraggled guys stand beside the tent. Normally I feel let down when meeting other parties in remote wilderness, my desire for solitude compromised. Not tonight, though. I'm intrigued by any group of trekkers who'd be traveling on a stormy night like this. And these guys seem a good-natured, jovial bunch, even in their drenching.

Poking my upper body through the partly unzipped door, I introduce myself, then ask their names and where they've come from, where they're bound. The answer shocks me: Thor Tingey, Phillip Weidner, Sam Newbury, and Dan Dryden are in the midst of a five-hundred-mile, forty-six-day expedition. They began their Brooks Range crossing July 3 at the Arctic National Wildlife Refuge's Canning River and will end it August 19 at the Eskimo village of Kobuk, far to the west. Led by Thor, a recent college grad, the group aims to see lots of country while going light and fast. "We're taking what you might call a minimalist approach to gear," he explains. "And we want to see how fast we can push ourselves." A series of food drops allows them to carry forty-to-sixty-pound packs, loads that include small pack rafts and two firearms. My gear, to start, totaled nearly seventy pounds, minus any raft or gun.

Backpacking and sometimes floating rivers, they're moving eight to ten hours a day, averaging twelve miles. With few rest days in its schedule, the group doesn't have the flexibility to sit out storm-wracked days (or nights), unless conditions become severe. Even then, it depends on how you define *severe*. Tonight, for instance, is pretty darn miserable, but these spirited twentysomething guys are shrugging it off. I'm impressed. And delighted I don't have to be anywhere else in this downpour.

We compare notes, exchange tips. I tell them what I know about the Anaktuvuk River Valley, which they'll reach just a couple miles from here. They tell me not to fret about the North Fork; there's a braided section where the river didn't come much above their knees, even after several days of rain.

A half hour quickly passes. Now cooled and shivering, they're eager to get moving again. I watch them merge into rain and fog, four phantom figures walking slowly, stoically, side-by-side, bundled up against the storm. Finally they top a rise and drop out of sight, as if swallowed by the gloom and wilderness. Something akin to an eerie, haunting loneliness rises in me as they disappear. We've had a momentary crossing of paths, then resumed our separate journeys and destinies. Yet I feel a kinship with them. As I contemplate these notions, mythologist Joseph Campbell comes to mind, particularly his descriptions of "the hero's journey" and the quest for a Holy Grail. There is something heroic in what those four are doing.

My quest is modest by comparison, though it poses its own set of challenges and risks. At fifty years old, I am doing the longest backpack of my life: fifty miles in two weeks, across mostly untrailed wilderness, much of it wet and tussocky. And I'm doing it entirely alone. Never have I gone so long without human company (though once, in graduate school, I considered becoming a hermit). So I'm pushing personal borders, entering new terrain. The landscape is new to me, too, although I've previously flown over these hills and valleys and spent time in neighboring drainages. Much of my route roughly retraces Bob Marshall's explorations through the Graylime Creek, Ernie Creek, and North Fork valleys in 1929 and 1930, with one key difference: I'm approaching from the opposite direction, moving north to south. Marshall began his travels at Wiseman, an early 1900s gold-boom town along the Koyukuk River's Middle Fork. My starting point, the Nunamiut Eskimo village of Anaktuvuk Pass, didn't even exist then.

Marshall is one of the big reasons I've come here, along with a desire for solitude and adventure, and a wish to explore new ground within my favorite mountain wilderness. Located entirely above the Arctic Circle, the Brooks is Alaska's northernmost mountain chain. It is also one of North America's grandest ranges, stretching seven hundred miles from the Chukchi Sea east to Canada's Yukon Territory. In its east-west reach across Alaska, the Brooks Range acts as a grand divide, separating the state's vast Interior region from the North Slope, which tilts gently toward the Arctic Ocean.

Some have called the Brooks Range the continent's "ultimate mountains," with good reason. Largely because of their remote, far north location, these mountains are among the most lightly touched by humans. For most of their history, they've been beyond the reach of most people, except for the hardiest of explorers and treasure seekers and even hardier indigenous tribes. And since 1980 their wild character has been protected by a string of parks, preserves, and refuges that encompass many millions of acres of wilderness lands and waters.

Though I've explored its eastern and western portions, I feel most closely connected to Central Brooks Range, made famous by Marshall's writings and wilderness advocacy. This is where I first entered the range and where I fell in love with far north landscapes, with Alaska. On this trip I will see for the first time many of the places that Marshall mapped, named, and so vividly described in *Alaska Wilderness*, a book that helped to reshape my life so many years ago: the Valley of Precipices, Mount Doonerak, Boreal Mountain, Frigid Crags.

Born and raised in New York City in the early 1900s, Bob Marshall was an exuberant, people-loving person who felt a lifelong pull to wild, unpeopled, and unexplored places. He came north to the Central Brooks Range in 1929, drawn, he wrote, by "what seemed on the map to be the most unknown section of Alaska." The Brooks Range fulfilled and inspired him while deepening his vision for wilderness preservation, a vision that greatly influenced America's twentieth-century environmental movement.

The route I'm following passes through the heart of Marshall country, now one of the grandest areas within the 8.2-million-acre Gates of the Arctic National Park and Preserve, widely considered the preeminent wilderness of our nation's system of parklands by those who've come to know it. If I am to fully appreciate the magnificence of Gates, I can hardly ignore Marshall's "Koyukuk country."

There are other reasons I've come here, less easy to articulate. Just as it did with Marshall, and arguably more so, the Central Brooks Range has played a pivotal role in my life. In a way, this landscape turned my life around, set me on a new and unexpected path, while crystallizing for me the importance—and power—of raw, immense wilderness. Over the past quarter century, it has remained a source of hope and inspiration and challenge. So this journey is both something of a celebration and a quest for greater understanding. I want to better comprehend why wilderness matters so much to me and other like-minded (and -hearted) souls. And, immersed in wildness, I hope to better know my own wild nature.

When Marshall came here, few people had ever set foot in these valleys. Those who did were usually Nunamiut hunters or solitary prospectors, sometimes never heard from again. Nowadays, scores of wilderness adventurers pass this way each year; though that's a small number by Lower 48 standards, it's heavy usage for the Alaskan Arctic. Many begin their travels at Anaktuvuk Pass, backpack to the North Fork, and then fly or float to Bettles, a remote outpost and regional transportation hub south of the range. But even along this well-established route, it's possible to go days without seeing another person. The four who passed through my camp tonight were the first humans I've encountered in a week of trekking. Now, once again, I'm alone with my thoughts and notes and questions. Alone, deep in the wilderness. For all my earlier worries, that simple thought now calms me.

TWO

The Question

REWIND TO JULY 17. AFTER A ONE-HOUR FLIGHT FROM ANCHORAGE to Fairbanks, I grab a taxi to the Wright Air terminal, where I'll catch the early-afternoon plane to Anaktuvuk Pass. I'm two hours early and the place is nearly deserted except for staff, and I wonder if any other trekkers or river runners will be on my flight to Anaktuvuk. The Nunamiut Eskimo village is a popular starting or ending point for Central Brooks Range adventurers because commuter flights from Fairbanks go there daily in summer. The cost is comparatively cheap, compared to those of charter planes that fly into the range: this year's going rate is less than $400 round-trip—unless you're carrying huge loads. Anything above forty pounds is excess baggage, charged at seventy-five cents a pound.

Yikes! I think, when my gear weighs in at seventy-five pounds, including a gallon can of fuel. That will drop a few pounds before I head into the wilderness, but it's still the heaviest load I've ever carried on my back. Even when climbing 20,320-foot Denali in 1987, I split my load between pack and sled while making double hauls between camps. I've tweaked my lower back a couple times in recent years, so I'm praying it holds up under the strain.

I grab a seat in the waiting area, which is spare but neat, with carpet, sofas, and cushioned chairs, and pass the time by reading the newspaper, studying maps, rechecking my gear list. Over the next couple hours, a steady if small stream of people flows in and out of the building and the terminal gradually fills with bodies and talk. A nearby couple mentions Anaktuvuk Pass; my curiosity piqued, I learn from their conversation that the arctic summer was late arriving and has remained cool. Just two days ago it snowed at the pass, and today's early-morning temperatures were in the forties. Snow, in mid-July. Ugh. Well, at least that should help keep the mosquito population down.

At last we're called to board the plane. The flight is a bumpy one, first across vast Interior lowlands of boreal forest and marshy tundra wetlands speckled with legions of unnamed ponds and lakes, then between somber foothills and mountains wreathed in clouds. Our final approach takes us up the John River Valley, a major drainage that cuts a broad north–south arc through the range. One of eight passengers squeezed into the plane with boxes, packs, and duffel bags, I peer out the aircraft's right-hand side, searching for familiar landmarks. I have flown this valley many times before, but not in fifteen years.

There's one feature in particular that I'm hoping to see, so I keep looking through the fogged window, though the bouncing plane is jumbling my stomach. Finally I spot the place. Located along a rushing clearwater stream, it's defined by a narrow dirt strip, some cleared, squarish fields, and a few log buildings. Easily missed in the immensity of the mountains, Crevice Creek ranch is the homestead of Bill and Lil Fickus and the place where my relationship with the Brooks Range began in June 1974.

Like Bob Marshall, I came north to Alaska while in my twenties, bringing a scientific background and a desire for adventure. But there were great differences, too. A geologist fresh out of graduate school, I knew nothing about the Brooks Range or Marshall and, unlike him, I had no special hunger to visit the Arctic. Yet I would spend most of my first summer, and three field seasons after that, exploring the same mountain landscape that Marshall had walked and mapped decades earlier. Within days, I fell in love with the immense wildness of America's northernmost mountain chain. The wildness was manifested in wave after wave of knife-edged ridges that stretched to the horizon and beyond; in glacially carved basins that grew lush in midsummer with the rich greens of tundra meadows and rainbow hues of alpine wildflowers; in wolves, caribou, bears, and wolverines; in a largely unpeopled landscape where one could travel for days, perhaps even weeks, without seeing any obvious signs of humans.

It was while working in the Brooks Range in 1974 that I discovered Marshall's inspired—and inspiring—writings. It was also then that I met my first wild bear. A chocolate-colored grizzly, the animal stood several hundred yards away, busily digging into the tundra for roots or perhaps ground squirrels, while I collected rock and sediment specimens from a mountain creek. I was deeply stirred by the bear's presence. Though what moved me initially was the grizzly itself, I think I intuitively understood that the animal's presence implied something special about this arctic wilderness and the other landscapes it inhabited, usually vast and wild. A fuller understanding of those implications would come over time, in bits and pieces.

* * *

HERE'S A CURIOUS FACT, given my decades-long romance with Alaska: until my final months of grad school, I had never fantasized about traveling to America's "Last Frontier." At age twenty-four I knew almost nothing about Alaska, except for the usual stereotypes: that it was a land of Eskimos, polar bears, vast wilderness, and Mount McKinley. Then, a few weeks from completing my studies, Tom Andrews popped the question.

His question was a simple, straightforward one, yet it held far deeper implications than I could have imagined in the spring of 1974: "Would you like to work in Alaska this summer?"

Tom had worked seasonally in Alaska before, searching the northern landscape for mineral deposits that might be developed into copper, silver, or gold mines. Now, about to get an MS degree in economic geology, he'd been hired full time by an Anchorage consulting company. His first assignment: round up summer help. A friend and classmate of Tom's at the University of Arizona, I happened to be in the right place at the right time. Back then, I would have considered this to be a happy coincidence, a stroke of good luck. Now I'm not so sure. The older I get, the less I believe in the notion of coincidences. Things happen for a reason, I like to tell friends. There are no accidents, I say, though not totally certain that's what I believe either.

Whatever put me at UA in 1974—fate, chance, some guiding power, or grand plan—I answered Tom with an emphatic "Yes!" And with that response, I took an unexpected fork in the trail.

In replying yes, I consciously knew only one thing for certain: a great adventure lay ahead. Now I suspect that some deeper, wiser part of me knew a doorway was opening to more than a summer's adventure. In some curious and inexplicable way, I would be coming home, to a place whose wild spirit would touch my own like no other had since my boyhood days in Connecticut.

After a brief, whirlwind stay in Anchorage filled with last-minute gear purchases, packing, and miscellaneous gofer duties, my crewmates and I flew north to Bettles. Established on forested flats near one of the Koyukuk River's innumerable horseshoe-shaped bends, this arctic outpost twenty miles south of the mountains is a major staging point for flights into the Central Brooks Range. Then, transferred to smaller planes, we continued on to Crevice Creek, to be greeted by Lil and Bill Fickus and their four kids: Debbie, Matt, Linda, and Timmy, all between the ages of twelve and five.

Bill Fickus had come north to Alaska in the mid-1950s, seeking a new life of frontier adventure. Initially the transplanted Pennsylvanian settled in the Fairbanks area and found work as a machinist. Also a pilot, he went flying in his spare time. While the flights provided a relaxing break from his job, they had a more serious intent. Longing for a simpler lifestyle, Bill wanted to build a home deep in the backcountry, be self-reliant, live off the land. He found that place in the southern hills of the Brooks Range, some thirty-five miles north of Bettles, two hundred miles from Fairbanks, and more than ten miles from his nearest neighbors.

Bill moved to Crevice Creek in the early sixties, joined by Lil, an Athabascan raised in the village of Fort Yukon, and their two small children. To support the family, Bill mined for gold in the summer and trapped lynx, marten, and wolves in the winter. He ran the trapline with a dog team for more than a decade, finally replacing it in 1975 with a snowmachine. With Lil as his assistant, Bill also worked as a registered guide, leading clients on trophy hunts for grizzlies, Dall sheep, and moose. To help with the packing, the Fickuses purchased several horses, thus establishing the farthest-north horse herd in Alaska, and perhaps the continent. Years later, when interviewed by the Alaska Trappers Association, Bill would admit that keeping horses year-round in the Arctic had been a tough challenge, but worth the trouble: "[I'd] had enough of packing gear and meat on my back."

The Fickuses's horses and huge vegetable garden shocked me. Both seemed out of place in these arctic mountains. Equally surprising was the weather that greeted us that first summer: days and days of warm sunshine, temperatures sometimes reaching into the seventies or even higher. This was not the Arctic I had imagined. Still, remnant snowfields in mountain basins and large patches of overflow ice in Crevice Creek served as a reminder of winter's harsh hold on the land. Even in June, the layered, pale-blue crystalline sheets near our camp were several feet thick, keeping the creek flowing below and beside them icy cold.

We set up camp on cleared land beside the runway. We slept, ate meals, and did our data compilation in large guacamole-green tents, commanded by a stern, mustachioed geologist whose heavy accent and stoic demeanor betrayed his Germanic roots: Lothar Klingmuller, Kling for short. Jane, his wife, was the cook, and a Vietnam veteran named Joe was our helicopter pilot. None of my grad-school buddies were on the crew, which except for Kling and his second-in-command was filled with geologists new to mineral exploration. To break us in, Kling took a few days to teach us the sampling and mapping methods preferred by our employer, the consulting firm WGM, and to test us on local rock types and our target minerals.

It wasn't long before we were scouring the landscape for metals. We spent long days in the field, seven days a week. After getting our assignments, we'd fly out in the helicopter and be dropped on ridges or in valley bottoms. Mostly we walked our stream traverses alone, usually armed with only a radio to give the pilot our locations when he came for pickup. A few people carried guns; but then, like now, I considered firearms a bigger problem than bears. Plus I didn't want the extra weight.

Though some people preferred having partners, I didn't mind working on my own. In fact I embraced it. Going alone I could keep my own schedule, be with my thoughts, and more easily get swallowed by the vastness of these mountains.

LOOKING BACK, that summer's work is mostly a blur of collecting and hauling stream sediment samples, hammering rocks, and compiling field data. But certain places and events stand out, most of them having nothing directly to do with geology. Among my most vivid memories are encounters with the Arctic's wild inhabitants.

During one long afternoon hike in energy-sapping heat, two Dall sheep appeared atop a ledge, like some far north mirage. Less than fifty feet above me, the short-spiked ewes seemed more curious than wary as I passed slowly beneath them. And why not? I may have been the first human they'd ever seen, just as they were my first wild sheep.

Another day, while sampling a creek, I heard loud rustling in a nearby patch of lowland black-spruce forest. Afraid it was a bear, I backed away several feet while looking for a tree to climb. All were too stunted and scraggly to even merit an attempt, so I stood frozen in place, unsure what to do. Running crossed my mind, but the advice *never run from a bear* echoed through my head. *It's the worst thing you can do.* Moments later my high anxiety released itself in laughter, when a porcupine waddled onto the banks of the creek bed where I waited.

Later that summer, a second close encounter charged my body with adrenaline. After dinner one evening, I grabbed my fishing gear and headed toward the John River, a short hike from camp through birch-spruce forest. Not far from the river's banks, something rattled the bushes. Looking up, I spotted a small, dark animal moving like a shadow among the willows. The animal disappeared an instant later. And an instant after that it hit me: bear cub! Though I didn't yet know a lot about bears, I did know this: the worst thing you can do (besides running from a bear) is get between a mom and her cubs. I swirled around, half expecting to see a grizzly bounding toward me. Then, backing away and fighting the urge to run, I looked for a nearby tree to climb. Body tensed, head swiveling back and forth, I reached some birches. But my instincts told me to continue my retreat, to leave the area. Only when I was within sight of camp did I begin to relax and breathe easily again.

I've wondered, off and on, if I could have been mistaken. If the animal I spotted was a cub, then why didn't I see or hear its mother? Despite any lingering doubts, something ineffable in my memory leads me to the same conclusion whenever I replay that evening: my senses and intuitions were right. I stood near the threshold of grave danger and, thankfully, backed away.

My first sighting of an adult bear wasn't nearly as unnerving (thank goodness), but it was powerful in its own way. Circling into my assigned work area, a tributary of Sixtymile Creek, the helicopter pilot spotted a large grizzly, almost certainly a male, in the valley I'd be traversing. The bear was in an upper basin, several hundred yards from my starting point, and neither of us felt the animal to be a danger. Still, Joe asked if I'd prefer that he drive the grizzly even farther away. No, I decided. Any "herding" seemed unnecessarily disruptive and might only serve to agitate the grizzly, perhaps leading to unanticipated problems. I was the last geologist to be dropped off that morning, and Joe didn't have to be any place else for a few hours, so he parked his helicopter nearby after setting me down. If the bear began to move in my direction, he would start the chopper up (the noise itself likely enough to keep the grizzly away) and, if necessary, retrieve me.

There was something special about sharing the valley with the grizzly, who looked up from his grazing when the helicopter flew over in its initial pass, but then hardly seemed to notice us. His attention was given to more pressing matters: bulking up on roots and newly sprouting plants in a valley still more brown than green and heavily streaked with the whites of melting snowfields.

The grizzly's presence changed my relationship with the landscape. Part of that was the element of danger, even with the helicopter on call. The sense of peril was deepened by the many bear-attack stories I'd heard and read—stories, I would later learn, that were often overblown or taken out of context, and which presented only a narrow aspect of the bear's complex nature. The grizzly certainly looked capable of wreaking havoc if he chose to. Likely enlarged by my imagination, the bear looked both muscular and huge, though even the biggest male grizzlies that roam the Brooks Range weigh "only" four hundred to five hundred pounds in early summer (and up to one and a half times as much when they enter their dens in the fall). Brown bears, the coastal cousins of grizzlies, may weigh twice that because of more-abundant and higher-calorie foods, particularly salmon.

But there was more to the experience than just some vague sense of danger, real or imagined. Grizzlies had not been part of any other landscape I'd inhabited. Their rarity across the Lower 48 spoke volumes about the special nature of this valley and mountain range, where they, not humans, largely remained the dominant species. More than fear, I felt a buzz of excitement, a lifting of spirit. As the years passed, I would more fully appreciate the power of their presence, which demands that we humans pay deeper attention to our surroundings whenever passing through bear country, if we're to avoid sudden, dangerous encounters with beings much fiercer and more powerful than ourselves. Beyond even that, bears in general, and grizzlies in particular, would become a symbol of my deepening connection to both the Brooks Range and larger wilderness, and a totem of my own inherent wildness.

I wasn't the only one to feel the power of bear's presence. Any grizzly sighting, no matter how distant, was shared in camp. Inevitably, each report got us talking. And remembering other stories. Everyone had close-encounter stories to tell, but nearly all were second- or thirdhand, at best. Many came from magazines or books. Others had been told and retold by more experienced field geologists. Some of the most gruesome tales were those shared by Bill Fickus, who'd encountered lots of bears and heard even more stories during his many years as a big-game guide. Whether told by Bill or by one of my teammates, the stories usually painted bears—especially grizzlies—as one-dimensional bloodthirsty critters that would tear a person up, given half a chance. Even then I wondered how much of what I was learning about bears was fact, how much was fiction. Or imaginations run wild.

As much as grizzlies, and arguably more so, wolves demand vast sweeps of wilderness to thrive. So they too suffered immense losses as Euro-Americans spread across North America; even greater losses than grizzlies, in fact, because wolves (as many pioneers, historians, and scientists have documented) were believed to be both dangerous and vermin. With my own home territories previously limited to New England and Arizona, the Brooks Range presented my first chance to see—or hear—wolves in the wild.

As with *Ursus arctos*, I knew little about the natural history of *Canis lupus* when I came north to Alaska. I hadn't yet read Farley Mowat's controversial but enthralling *Never Cry Wolf*, and Barry Lopez was still working on his seminal book, *Of Wolves and Men*. Both would greatly influence my understanding of wolves and spark me, in time, to challenge Alaska's predator-control programs, an outdated form of wildlife "management" that amazingly still occurs across broad swaths of the state. But even before encountering Lopez's and Mowat's influential works, I carried less fear than fascination for the animal. Alas, I would see no wolves that entire summer. But I would discover their tracks and scat. And toward the end of the field season, I would hear their cries.

Decades later, a faint chill passes through my body as I call up the memory, which is dreamlike yet remarkably vivid. On a gloomy and raw September day, with fresh snow powdering the higher mountaintops and the field season nearly ended, I leave my tent and take a short walk. The air is still and no one else is stirring in camp or outside the Fickus cabin, so the fog-shrouded valley is absolutely silent. That makes it possible for the faraway conversation to reach my ears.

The first voice I hear sounds like a sort of moan, and it comes from the forested lowlands north of the homestead. Turning toward it, I lean against a fence railing. And I listen. Minutes pass before the deep, bass howl sounds again, this time joined by another, of higher pitch. The howls are so faint I have to concentrate to hear them. Because of the complex way that wolves commingle their voices, I can't be sure how many of them I hear, just as I can't easily explain why each time the howls reach me, I break into a smile. Is it the beauty of their song? Or the realization of my good fortune, after a season of hoping? I have no idea how long I remain in this trance, just me and a distant wolf pack connected by the string of their notes as they move across the John River Valley. The word *haunting* comes to mind as I recall that time, but it's the loveliest sort of haunting you can imagine.

THOUGH NOT A HUNTER, I'd been an avid fisherman since my Uncle Peach first took me fishing at age eleven, and I came to the Brooks Range in 1974 outfitted with spinning reel and rod and lures. My main targets that summer were arctic grayling, small but beautifully sleek fish that inhabit streams and lakes throughout much of Alaska. Grayling have iridescent greenish-gray sides speckled by black spots, but their most uniquely attractive attribute is an overly large dorsal fin, dotted red and green.

Crevice Creek's grayling rarely reached a foot in length, but the John River held some lunkers fifteen to twenty inches long. When the river wasn't running dirty, I would often go there in the evening for an hour or two of fishing. Mostly I practiced catch and release, but occasionally I brought some back for the Fickuses or my crewmates to eat.

Among my biggest—and most exciting—surprises of the summer occurred in July, while fishing the John for grayling. Feeling a strike, I set the hook. And suddenly the fish on the end of my line was streaking upstream and ripping out line. Loosening the drag on my reel so the line wouldn't snap, I chased the fish upriver and down while wondering what the heck I might have hooked. My lightweight gear required that I be patient in working the fish toward shore and I let it tire itself out in the fast-running current. Fifteen or twenty minutes later, I stood above the biggest fish I'd ever landed, a giant compared to the grayling beside it. And I had no idea what it was. Vaguely troutlike in appearance, the fish had a sharply hooked nose, a mouth filled with large, crooked teeth, and greenish-gray sides marked with ragged vertical bars of purple and dark green. Instinctively I killed my catch. Then, feeling a bit like I did upon catching my first brown trout thirteen years earlier, I lugged the fish to Bill and Lil.

"Oh, you caught a dog," Lil laughed, as she opened her door.

"A what?"

"A dog salmon. Some people call 'em chum, but we call them dogs. They're not so good tasting to people, especially when they've been in freshwater as long as that one, but dogs like 'em. A lot of people catch 'em for their dog teams."

Now embarrassed by my gift, I regretted killing the salmon, but Lil graciously accepted the fish. That was the last I saw of my "trophy" and I suppose that she fed it to the family's dogs.

Much tastier than that spawning-ready chum were the northern pike that we caught in Kidney Lake, a few miles from camp. A bunch of us joined Lil and her four kids on a trek to the lake during one of our crew's rare days off. Not much more than a big pond, really, the lake was filled with pike. In keeping with their voracious-predator image, they struck just about anything we cast into the water with our three or four poles (two of them belonging to the Fickuses). Within a short time, we'd caught our fill, most of them two and four feet long, with overly large "hammer heads" accentuated by long, flat snouts and huge mouths bursting with razor-sharp teeth. Back at the ranch, Lil fried up a bunch of the pike's white meat and we had a fish feast. The breaded, golf ball–sized pieces of fish she made for us were surprisingly tender and delicious, hardly what I'd expected of such monster fish.

THE GEOLOGY DIDN'T grab me the way the Arctic's wildlife and fishing did, but the work had its moments of surprise and delight. The same valley where I saw my first grizzly produced one of our crew's best prospects that long-ago summer. Though I hadn't noticed any striking minerals during my traverse, several of the sediment samples came back from the lab red-hot in lead and zinc. (We employed a geochemical color code on our maps to help us identify areas for more detailed work: brown lines marked stream segments that were lowest in the metals we sought; then up the scale we went to blue, green, yellow, orange, red.) Kling accompanied me back to the valley and while breaking some rocks in the "hot zone" we discovered bits of sphalerite and galena: zinc sulfide and lead sulfide, respectively. Kling congratulated me on my find and the bosses back in Anchorage also seemed impressed. But I was embarrassed that I'd missed the minerals my first time through. Perhaps I'd paid too much attention to that bear.

We tracked the mineralized zone to a nearby hill and found enough lead, zinc, and copper sulfides on the ground to claim the area for our company and client. More detailed prospecting and mapping and even some drilling and geophysical surveys followed the staking. Though excited to be part of a discovery—and to earn the praises of my bosses—I never sensed that this deposit was enough, on its own, to merit development. Perhaps that's why I didn't seriously consider the possibility that the valley where I'd spotted my first grizzly might some day become an industrial site.

My intuition proved right. We found no evidence that the rocks here might have economic potential. Still, my employers considered it a hopeful sign, a hint that larger riches might await us. Being a grunt, I wasn't privy to the bigger picture. More than anything, my "discovery" gave me the chance to do some serious rock hounding, to search for silvery pockets of galena and dark, shining reddish-brown veins of sphalerite. I much preferred to study sulfide-bearing rocks than to fill bag after bag with sand and silt for lab techs to analyze.

We found other traces and hints of sulfide deposits through the summer, but nothing quite as stirring, economically speaking. The landscape, though: now that was stirring, in an entirely different way. That's not to say the mountains we explored were spectacular, at least in the way that most people use that word. In fact, by Alaskan standards they were rather ordinary hills. Most topped out below five thousand feet and their comparatively gentle snow- and ice-free slopes could be hiked without any technical gear. But that was part of their appeal.

In midsummer you could walk among the range's high places in jeans and short-sleeved jersey without worrying about avalanches or crevasses or falling off cliff faces. And from the tops of almost any of those hills, you could spin your body 360 degrees and see nothing but other mountains and river valleys, stretching to the horizon without end. I had never seen—or imagined—such vast, open spaces with an acutely primordial feel, as if I were somehow transported to a distant epoch before machines and cities, pencils and maps. Before humans. Arizona's deserts, the Grand Canyon, the Rocky Mountains—none of them matched this.

Since leaving the profession, I have often thought that geology's chief gift to me was the opportunity to immerse myself in some of Alaska's grandest wild places, especially the Brooks Range, and in doing so, to discover firsthand the glories and fragility of this and other wilderness landscapes. Much like a first kiss, I got a taste of something that stirred new—or perhaps renewed—passions that first summer in the Arctic. Many more would follow. For that gift, geology and my geology-enamored friends and bosses continue to hold a place in my wild, wild heart.

THREE

The Nunamiut

I'M SLIGHTLY NAUSEATED—AND RELIEVED—WHEN WE FINALLY
touch down on Anaktuvuk's airstrip, which is large enough to accommo-
date the huge cargo planes that haul in fuel, machinery, and building supplies.

Especially from a distance, the village of Anaktuvuk Pass appears out of place.
It's as if the community's outsized runway, gravel streets and gravel pits, rusting
trucks, and prefab houses have somehow been mistakenly plopped onto a high tundra plain in the middle of a vast and otherwise uninhabited mountain landscape.
(To most modern Americans, this would be the ultimate "middle of nowhere.")
Indeed, there's no other village remotely like it in Alaska. At twenty-three hundred feet, Anaktuvuk Pass is the only community located on a high mountain pass
along the Arctic Divide and the only one inside the borders of Gates of the Arctic National Park and Preserve. It's also the only remaining settlement of Alaska's
Nunamiut people, a tribe of inland Eskimos whose nomadic ancestors followed
migratory herds of caribou across the western Arctic.

Ethnographers tell us that the Nunamiut immigrated to the Brooks Range from
the coast only 150 to 550 years ago (though there's evidence that different "cultural traditions" of indigenous peoples traveled through its hills and mountains
for thousands of years). Upon entering the mountains, they battled and eventually replaced Athabascan Indian groups already there. But the tribe's own oral traditions say that the Nunamiut people are firmly rooted in these mountains. One
story tells of a kindly giant, *Aiyagomahala*, who lived near the headwaters of the
Alatna River, a southeast-flowing mountain stream that springs from the Arctic
Divide eighty miles west of Anaktuvuk Pass. The giant created the Nunamiut, the

"people of the land." He then taught the tribe how to survive the harsh arctic environment by hunting, fishing, and gathering plants.

To make sure the people would remember him, Aiyagomahala took off one of his gloves and transformed it into a group of towering mountains. These are the spectacular granite spires and walls that thrust into the sky west of the Alatna River. Known as the Arrigetch Peaks, they are the "fingers of the hand, outstretched." Other stories recall a later time, when huge glaciers formed in the mountains and drove the Nunamiut to the coast. There they stayed until the glaciers' retreat permitted a return to ancient homelands.

The Nunamiut maintained a seminomadic lifestyle deep into the twentieth century, tracking wild game through the northern Brooks Range in extended-family groups of thirty to a hundred people. No animal was more important to their lives than the caribou. At certain times of the year, these northern members of the deer family made up 90 percent of the Nunamiut's diet. They also provided skins for clothing and shelter, bone and antlers for tools, and sinew for sewing.

Because caribou herds migrated between winter and summer ranges, the people had to move too. Of course not even the most skilled human hunters could keep pace with the original "nomads of the north," whose bodies are highly adapted to moving across snow and spongy tundra. So the Nunamiut learned the caribou's primary migration routes. They would then intercept the herd, and take their share, as the animals swept past. Unfortunately, the herds' movements couldn't easily be predicted. Though they favored certain valleys over others, the caribou's migration routes sometimes varied from year to year. Or weather shifts changed the timing of their migration. To miss their passage entirely meant disaster, so hunters who proved themselves especially skilled in finding the caribou rose to the position of *umialik*, or headman.

To improve their odds, the Nunamiut identified the caribou's primary, most reliable routes and stationed scouts at strategic points, where they could spot any approaching herd from afar and then alert other members of the band. Using large rocks or mounds of tundra sod, they also built cairns and placed them in rows. Atop the piled rocks they put willows bearing strips of rawhide, which would wave in the wind, much like humans might do if signaling their presence. Such "surrounds" helped the Nunamiut steer the caribou toward places where real hunters waited. Some hills and valleys still bear the stone guards, or *inuksuk*, built generations ago to help the Eskimo bands survive.

At their peak, as many as a thousand Nunamiut may have roamed these mountains. But their numbers dropped close to zero in the early 1900s, following a cyclical crash of the Western Arctic Caribou Herd. Without caribou, the inland Eskimos had no choice but to move to the coast. Over a period of one or two decades, nearly all left the mountains; by the 1920s, some anthropologists argue, it's likely that no Nunamiut inhabited the Brooks Range. But during the Depression years of the 1930s, as fur prices fell and trading posts shut down along the Arctic Coast, the mountain people began returning to their ancestral home. By the end of that decade, hundreds of Nunamiut had resettled into their original ways, following the resurgent caribou herd across the Western and Central Brooks Range. William Brown describes that reinhabitation in *History of the Central Brooks Range*:

> Remnants of the old bands trickle back to their ancestral territories—Killik River, Chandler Lake, Ulu Valley. For a decade or more, their lives revert to an approximation of traditional times....They are more rather than less dependent on the old ways and the old landscapes and resources. They are still doing some communal hunting, storing their meat in the old caches, roaming the known places. Until the mid-1940s they see few white men, at least in their home territories.

Only in 1949, nudged along by bush pilot Sig Wien's promise of air service plus the possibility of schooling for their children, did the Nunamiut permanently settle at Anaktuvuk Pass, "place of caribou droppings." As the English translation suggests, the village lies in the middle of a major caribou migration route. So despite first appearances, the village is strategically placed.

A CROWD GREETS our plane and several young Eskimo boys on bicycles approach as I heft my weighty pack. After an exchange of names, they enthusiastically guide me to the National Park Service's local office. Before heading into the wilderness, I want to learn more about this village, its people, and Nunamiut life, both past and present. Seasonal ranger Mike Haubert is letting me stay a couple nights in the park's bunkhouse and acting as something of a host and go-between during my visit. Mike is a lean, lanky guy with pale eyes, whiskered face, unruly but thinning hair, and sharp, hawklike nose. He's calm and welcoming, with a quiet intensity that occasionally bubbles up as he enthusiastically describes his job and life here in the arctic wilds. Wilderness lured Mike here in 1996 and he admits to still being more interested in landscape than local culture, but he's gradually learning about both. How long he'll stay is anybody's guess, but for now he feels at home.

Mike likes to be direct about things, but he's learned that too much directness doesn't always mesh comfortably with Eskimo ways, as when confronting some locals about park-related issues. So he's learned to approach sensitive topics in a more roundabout way, which has actually made his job easier. Less confrontation has led to more cooperation. At the same time, he's become less of an outside authority figure, more of a neighbor. And student.

One of his friends and teachers is Raymond Paneak, a village elder born in 1940. Short and wiry, with a creased, dark brown face and graying hair beneath his baseball cap, he has bright, sparkling eyes, an easy smile, and a sprightly demeanor that make him seem considerably younger than his years. "Raymond is sort of a diplomat to visitors," says Mike, "like his father used to be. He's taught me lots, and over time we've earned each other's trust." Raymond, in turn, calls Mike "the best ranger we ever had here. I like to tease him, but he's a good guy."

Raymond agrees to help me understand local ways and traditions. For a price. Here, as in a growing number of communities across rural Alaska, Native residents have become less and less willing to freely share their stories with outsiders who show up unannounced, stay a short while, then abruptly leave. They've seen too many white folks take their memories, mythic tales, and family histories and, with not much more than a hurried thank-you, incorporate those stories into their own books, magazines, or tapes. Missionaries, anthropologists, journalists, and novelists have all contributed to this sense that outsiders are getting rich from Native stories they've collected. Though that's rarely the case, it is indeed true that people like me have profited in one way or another from indigenous tales. It's not just storytellers, of course. From totem poles to shaman's masks, ivory carvings, and seal-gut parkas, Westerners have taken—and sometimes stolen—indigenous cultural treasures, from the Arctic to the tropics and everywhere in between.

Having learned over time how others have benefited from their culture's stories, many Natives now demand to be paid when interviewed. I'd been warned that this might happen, so I've brought my checkbook. The journalist in me rebels just a bit, but the larger part of me, including the evolving creative writer, understands why Natives might feel that they are being ripped off once again. And already I'm certain that the Nunamiut will have some place in the stories I write about my trek through the range.

Raymond and I quickly settle on terms agreeable to us both: $50 for two hours. If I need or want more of his time, we'll renegotiate. Because I'm a freelancer who's not on assignment, I can't afford much more than one or two of these formal, face-to-face interviews, but back in Anchorage I'll also talk briefly by phone with a few other Nunamiut elders.

We begin with Raymond's own story. One of ten siblings, he was born along the Killik River, a clear-water stream on the north side of the range now increasingly popular with recreational river floaters. In summer, his band of four to five families would set up a seasonal base camp along a lake. From there they fished and hunted wild game. Some years they stayed at Chandler Lake, about twenty miles from Anaktuvuk Pass; other years, at Tulugak Lake, also north of the divide. Both are places seasonally inhabited by generations of arctic peoples. Hunting parties would seek out snowfields in the hills, where caribou congregate to escape mosquitoes and parasitic flies. If they found a group not far from camp, the hunters would drive the caribou into the lake. "My dad used to harpoon them from his kayak," Raymond recalls. "He got quite a few that way." As winter approached the band would take down camp, split into smaller groups, and follow the migrating herd as it moved through the mountains.

"We've always had a special connection with caribou," Raymond reminds me. "Back then we hunted caribou year-round, just like now, but it was a lot more work. Fall is the best time, because they're fat. In summer we only take bulls [because cows are nursing calves]. In winter, after the rut, we switch to cows, because the bulls get skinny and their meat tastes bad."

Raymond pauses, as if recalling some memory. "Back then we didn't have no grocery store, so we had to hunt every day. If we couldn't find caribou, we'd take moose or sheep or whatever we could find." Starvation was an ever-present danger, shadowing the Nunamiut as they stalked the caribou.

To get ammunition or Western staples such as tea or salt, the Nunamiut would travel long distances, sometimes to Bettles, other times to Athabascan villages along the Koyukuk River south of the Brooks Range, or Eskimo villages along the Kobuk River or the Chukchi Sea coast. In their nomadic days, and even after settling at Anaktuvuk Pass, they depended heavily on dogs, hitching them to sleds in winter and working them as pack animals in summer. Only in the mid-seventies would dogs largely be replaced by snowmachines.

Except for the few years that he left the Arctic to attend school, Raymond has lived in the Brooks Range his entire life. His father both understood and spoke some English, which he'd learned from white traders along the coast. But he rarely, if ever, spoke it around his family, so Raymond didn't learn the language until he was eight or nine. Nowadays, he regularly speaks both, "about fifty-fifty. I think I might speak better English if I didn't speak Eskimo so much," he says with a laugh.

Even before settling at Anaktuvuk Pass, his people used to hang out here, both to hunt caribou and to escape mosquitoes and biting flies. "It's windy in summer," he explains, "so the bugs don't bother you so much." Caribou continue to use the pass during their seasonal migrations, despite the Nunamiut's year-round presence and the noise generated by snowmachines, ATVs, and planes. Their close passage makes hunting as easy as stepping outside, but residents continue to follow certain traditions from the distant past. For instance, they always let the herd's leading edge pass through unharmed. Those behind will then follow their trail, ensuring good hunting for up to a week or more as the herd trickles through.

Mike sits in and mostly listens, but now and then Raymond invites him into the conversation. Between the two of them, I learn that some three hundred people now live in Anaktuvuk. All but a couple dozen are Nunamiut. Nearly everyone depends on subsistence harvesting—hunting, fishing, trapping, berry picking—to some degree, with caribou still at the center of it all. No longer do residents need caribou for tools and shelter, but the animals remain a chief source of food. Some people still use caribou parts for clothing: boots, parkas, gloves, hats.

"Even though we don't have to hunt every day, we still need caribou in our diet," Raymond explains. "We don't do so good without it. And we never get tired of that caribou meat. [Dall] sheep we can't eat every day; but caribou, we sure do."

Even more than settling down, perhaps, modern conveniences have fundamentally changed the way the Nunamiut live. The influx of cable TV, phones, a grocery store and laundromat, a local school, computers and the Internet, commuter airlines, snowmachines, and ATVs have made life easier. But Western ways and technologies have also brought their share of problems: a disconnection from traditional ways of being with the land, new dependencies, drugs of various sorts, increased violence. And new economics.

"Living is better overall, but everything costs way too much money," Raymond sighs. "When we were living off the land, we didn't need any money. Now almost everything you do needs money, even hunting. The changes are both good and bad, but I feel hopeful about where the community is headed. I think we're learning how to deal with things. We're an adaptable people."

As our conversation closes, Raymond suggests I visit Anaktuvuk's Simon Paneak Museum, whose displays illustrate the evolving relationship of caribou and Nunamiut from prehistoric times to the present. The museum is named after his deceased father, a well-respected community leader who played a key role in the settling of Anaktuvuk Pass and the passage of the Alaska Native Claims Settlement Act in 1971.

The headman of a wandering band that numbered thirty to forty people in the mid-1940s, Simon Paneak was also an exceedingly adaptable and visionary man who successfully navigated the fierce collision of indigenous and Western worlds. He, more than any other Nunamiut, seemed to recognize that a more settled and modern lifestyle would ultimately benefit his family and community. But he also knew that such a change would present enormous challenges to a people who still lived in skin tents and moved through the landscape with the seasons. In 1947, Simon approached Sig Wien, a bush pilot who'd been hauling supplies (ammunition, salt, flour, coffee, and other basic Western staples) to the Nunamiut for several years. Two years later, with the help of Sig and others, several dozen people from Simon's band and others put down roots at Anaktuvuk Pass in the collective hope it would lead to an easier, and ultimately better, life.

In 1950, at the suggestion of a census taker named Ethel Ross Oliver, Simon began to document his people's transition. His journal entries and letters to her (now kept in the Rasmuson Library at the University of Alaska Fairbanks) present a uniquely Native perspective on those times. Historian Theodore Catton notes that

> Paneak's writings provide us with an indigenous view of Nunamiut affairs and a point of reference for the descriptions left by anthropologists and other visitors. If one theme may be distilled from Paneak's writings, it is that there was no shame in his people wanting to shuck off some of the hardness of their lives and acquire commodities—from modern education and medicine to snowmachines and oil-heated homes. At the same time, Paneak wanted to maintain the cohesiveness of the families and the group and pass down the traditional knowledge and skills that were basic to his people's identity.

Simon's leadership role, combined with his intimate knowledge of the Brooks Range, made him popular with researchers who came into the region. "They would seek him out," recalls his son Raymond, "and hire him as a guide. He helped a lot of scientists, showed them around."

The museum is open to the public only a few hours a day, but my timing is good and a young, attractive Nunamiut woman wearing glasses and a smile invites me in. I move slowly around the small building, taking copious notes at each of the exhibits, which document the people's origins and their path to the present. After my tour, I interview Vera Weber, cocurator of Alaska's "farthest north museum." Perhaps because she's on the job, or belongs to a younger generation, she doesn't say a word about getting paid.

When I mention that I've already talked with Raymond Paneak, Vera tells me that her mother, Ada, grew up with him. Later, while visiting Barrow, Ada met Gilbert Lincoln, a skilled Eskimo drummer. The two married and settled in Alaska's northernmost community, and started a family. When Vera was nine, the Lincolns traveled to Anaktuvuk Pass so that Ada could see her parents, whom she missed greatly. The visit was supposed to last only two weeks, but "we never went back," Vera says. Like Raymond, she has always lived in the Arctic except for time spent away at school. She too sees both good and bad in the Nunamiut's rapidly changing world. The new technologies and educational opportunities are "really good," but she's saddened by the gradual loss of her people's language, which "seems to be dropping away." Still, she sees signs that her people are determined to hold onto their culture and says, "we're fortunate to live both ways of life."

Partway through our conversation, the soft-spoken mother of two young children confides, "I'm just now learning how to hunt." She says it in a way that suggests a mix of embarrassment and pride. In the past Vera has helped with the butchering and hauling of meat, but only now will she finally participate in the killing, as her mother and grandmother before her. "We hunt caribou year-round," she adds. "A lot of people work regular jobs during the week, then leave Friday afternoon to go hunting."

The Nunamiut, like rural Native residents throughout Alaska, have adapted new technologies to their hunting ways. Here, snowmachines long ago replaced dog teams for winter travel. And heavy-duty, four-wheeled all-terrain vehicles are used during the few months that the tundra is bare. ATV trails lead out from the village like spokes from a wheel; some extend fifteen miles or more, finally petering out where Native land gives way to parkland. Where the tundra is soft and wet, the tracks become deeply rutted and muddied. In places, they are also littered with machine parts and trash.

To an unsuspecting wilderness adventurer, the trails and their debris can be a shocking eyesore. Still, the Nunamiut's motorized habits didn't draw much attention until Gates of the Arctic was established in 1980.

THE PRESENCE OF the Nunamiut inside Gates, and particularly their long-standing and continued year-round dependence on the park's landscape and its animals and plants, is at odds with the idea of wilderness as our modern Western culture usually imagines it: a place where humans are merely visitors. In historian Theodore Catton's words, Gates of the Arctic (like some other Alaska parklands) is an "inhabited wilderness." Or, as former Gates subsistence and wilderness specialist Steve Ulvi puts it, the park is a centuries-old homeland to the region's Native inhabitants.

The Nunamiut aren't the only locals dependent on Gates's natural resources. Iñupiat Eskimo, Athabascan, and non-Native residents of ten small communities in and around the park possess "resident zone" status and have subsistence rights to hunt, trap, fish, and harvest plants within its boundaries. But no group of people is as dependent on Gates as the residents of Anaktuvuk Pass. "Clearly," says Ulvi, "the Nunamiut have a special relationship with this landscape. So not only does Gates ensure that this wilderness remains intact, it also ensures that an indigenous culture remains intact. That combination is unique to this park."

In his book *Inhabited Wilderness*, Catton points out that the preservation of subsistence lifestyles and cultures within several of Alaska's premier parklands (Denali, Gates, and Wrangell–St. Elias among them) forced the National Park Service—and wilderness advocates—to reevaluate the long-held tenet that parks should preserve a more "primitive" America. In Alaska, the cultural past in some key aspects remains present in a way that it doesn't in the Lower 48. Here, the idea of parks as "historical vignettes" doesn't work very well. As strange as it sounds, the 1980 Alaska National Interest Lands Conservation Act that established Gates forced our culture to accept the fact—or at least the idea—that humans are indeed a part of wild nature, something that more primitive, earth-friendly cultures intuitively understand, but which seems revolutionary to many of us modern Westerners.

Catton also looks, in considerable detail, at the Nunamiut's connection to the Brooks Range, conflicts that arose once the larger, white culture "discovered" these inland Eskimos, and their importance to the creation of the surrounding park. "That these people had an ancestral claim to the area was never in dispute," he writes, while accepting the Western view that their "claim" extends back only five hundred to six hundred years. Furthermore, anthropologists believe that the Nunamiut didn't move into the range's central section until perhaps the early nineteenth century.

While their lives in precontact days remained largely the same for generations, the twentieth century brought swift and enormous changes, and that's the period that most interests Catton. Among the greatest shifts were the influx of Western technologies that changed the Nunamiut's relationship with caribou and the decision to settle at Anaktuvuk Pass. That latter change was "an epochal event in the cultural evolution of the Nunamiut people," Catton writes. Partly that's because they had ended centuries of nomadic living, but also because

> for the first time, the outside world learned of the existence of these primitive caribou hunters....The Nunamiuts' early visitors [chiefly researchers and bureaucrats] came to Anaktuvuk Pass expecting to find the Eskimos as pristine as the wilderness that they inhabited...while the Nunamiuts tried to define themselves as a distinctive though essentially American people, those who visited and wrote about their village insisted on making the Nunamiuts an exotic people, a people of nature.

How sad it is, that our own culture would consider people who are more fully a part of nature to be somehow foreign.

Two starkly different interpretations of the newly "modern" Nunamiut culture emerged. According to Catton, some whites, including wilderness advocates, romanticized them "as the keepers of an ancient land wisdom." Others, chiefly wildlife conservationists, argued that the Nunamiut, like other Native groups, had become wildlife wasters rather than respectful stewards, slaughtering the available game because technology had made hunting so easy. State and federal hunting laws that conflicted with traditional harvest patterns and techniques accentuated that latter image. Zealous law-enforcement officers sometimes cited

Native hunters for taking too many game birds or mammals, or harvesting them "out of season."

Though the Nunamiut had inhabited this wild arctic landscape for centuries, their new settlement also conflicted with many conservationists' image of "pure" wilderness, which envisions a place untainted by human touch. Only a few years after the Nunamiut settled at Anaktuvuk Pass, Congress would be guided by that fundamentally white-American vision while debating and eventually passing the Wilderness Act of 1964, which explicitly states that wilderness is "an area where the earth and its community of life are untrammeled by man, where man himself is a visitor who does not remain." The act created a system of designated wilderness lands to include those landscapes deemed sufficiently grand, pristine, and otherwise worthy of special protections from human activities, particularly habitation and development.

As might be expected, the Nunamiut considered such contradictory images of themselves—also applied to many other Native Alaskan tribes—both humorous and disturbing. As conflicts increased, they worked at creating their own image for Western consumption, based on two main ideas: first, Native peoples do not waste wild foods; second, hunting (and fishing) laws unfairly persecuted them.

The often-tense relationship between Nunamiut and whites intensified during the winter of 1968–69, when Governor Walter Hickel ordered the state's transportation department to build a temporary winter road up the John River Valley and through Anaktuvuk Pass, to the newly discovered Prudhoe Bay oilfields. Catton succinctly summarizes the impacts, initially reported at a science conference hosted by the University of Alaska Fairbanks: "For the six weeks that the road was in operation, the Nunamiuts were exposed to a rough, hard-drinking class of truckers. Twelve thousand dollars in cash went through the village like a flash flood. The Nunamiuts were sickened by the sight of animals being hunted from helicopters and animals' carcasses mutilated and displayed alongside the road for no explicable reason."

Preservationists, too, were upset and angered by the now-notorious "Hickel Highway." Arctic homesteader and author Sam Wright seemed to sum up the sentiments of many when he warned, "The arrival of the road at Anaktuvuk Pass signals not only the end of a way of life for the Nunamiut but for the wilderness itself."

All of this set the stage for an unlikely alliance, as Congress began work on legislation to protect much of Alaska's wildlands and waters, during the 1970s. Though they were not entirely trusting of the preservationist/environmental community, memories of the Hickel Highway debacle worried the Nunamiut people much more, while spurring visions of other unwanted development. In the mid-1970s, they and other Arctic Eskimos supported the creation of a Nunamiut National Wildlands, to be cooperatively managed by the National Park Service and Eskimos. To the east and west of it would be Gates of the Arctic National Wilderness Park.

Though initially intrigued by the idea, the Park Service's top planner for the Arctic, John Kauffman, eventually backed away from it. The Nunamiut National Wildlands "would drive an ominous wedge between the two [Gates] park units," he explained, " a wedge where management could well become more permissive, allowing developments and uses that could change the primitive character of the central Brooks Range."

Eventually, a compromise was reached. There would be no Nunamiut Wildlands, but the village of Anaktuvuk Pass would be granted significant inholdings within Gates of the Arctic National Park and they would be allowed to continue their subsistence activities.

After Gates was officially established in 1980, however, the Nunamiut felt betrayed by Park Service interpretations of what activities were permissible, and where. With their village placed inside the new park's boundaries, Anaktuvuk residents inevitably clashed with park managers over ATVs, which locals had been using for years. Gates staff worried that the vehicles were tearing up surrounding wilderness lands, so they restricted them to narrow corridors. Locals, in turn, felt cut off from traditional hunting grounds. By the mid-1980s, with tensions over ATV use flaring, Anaktuvuk seemed on the verge of a rebellion. Rachel Riley, an elder who remembers the days when her people moved about the landscape with the seasons, bluntly says, "We hated the Park Service. They were taking over our place, the place where we would always go hunting."

To keep things from blowing out of control, park staff and Nunamiut leaders began discussing a land exchange in 1984. Negotiations were complex and sometimes contentious, but both sides realized the issue of ATV use for hunting had to be resolved. They culminated in November 1996 with a massive—and, in some quarters, controversial—land exchange that Steve Ulvi called "a unique solution to a unique place; one of those rare deals where everybody benefits."

Among the positive spin-offs: Anaktuvuk residents are free to continue their traditional hunt for caribou, using modern technology; in return, the Nunamiut agreed to restrict development on their lands and allow public recreational access. Park managers, meanwhile, promoted goodwill with their neighbors and established a working relationship with the Nunamiut.

"That land exchange worked out real good," Rachel Riley recalls, "because now we can hunt where we've always hunted. What they did was wonderful. People felt much better about them Park Service people."

* * *

AS MY STAY in Anaktuvuk Pass winds down, my talks with Mike eventually—
and perhaps inevitably—turn to grizzlies and philosophies about carrying firearms in the backcountry. "The residents of Anaktuvuk think you're a fool if you
don't carry a gun. For them it's an essential piece of gear, as much as a tent or fuel,"
Mike says, then adds, "I'm no expert, but I wouldn't carry a gun if I wasn't required
to as a ranger. People want assurances, they want easy answers. I tell them, don't
take my advice, read up on bears; there's a lot of good information out there. Then
make your own choice."

My choice, as always, is to go without a gun. I'm not a firearms expert and
have no desire to be. Guns, I'm convinced, change the way a person relates to wild
places and wild creatures. They offer security, but they also can prompt people
to take chances they ordinarily wouldn't, sometimes resulting in confrontations
with bears that might have been avoided. The usual result is injury or death, most
often (by far) for the bear.

It's often said that bears, like people, are individuals. Each one is different, unpredictable, and you can never know when you might meet a rogue bear. Back in the
late eighties, I stood near a friend who was knocked down by an enraged female grizzly protecting her cubs. Fortunately, neither human nor bear was harmed.

For a while after that attack, I questioned my philosophy and gave serious
thought to the words of Richard Nelson, an Alaskan writer, anthropologist, and
naturalist whom I greatly respect. As Nelson reflects in *The Island Within*, "All it
takes is once in a lifetime, the wrong bear in the wrong place. Without a rifle (and
the knowledge of when and how to use it), the rest of the story would be entirely
up to the bear....It's my way of self-preservation, as the hawk has its talons, the
heron its piercing beak, the bear its claws...." But as time has passed, I've become
more convinced than ever that it is right, for me, to walk unarmed in Alaska's
backcountry. It would be different, perhaps, if grizzlies or black bears preyed on
people. But they rarely do. And for all the talk of bears' unpredictability, grizzly
behavior is largely predictable to those who've invested the time to learn about the
animals. When passing through grizzly country, a backcountry traveler can take
measures that greatly diminish the odds of an attack.

Certainly it's important to respect bears and recognize they are wild carnivores
equipped to kill other large mammals. But it's equally important to understand that
bears are complex animals, not one-dimensional, bloodthirsty killers. Bears rarely
attack humans, except when surprised at close range. Feeling threatened, with no
time to assess the situation, they have to make a split-second decision: flee or fight?

In a sense, my choice is a symbolic gesture of respect to the animal and its world. I'm only a visitor in the bear's realm, passing through and intending no harm. Instead of a gun, I choose common sense and a knowledge of bear behavior as my primary defenses. I also carry "bear repellent," which some highly respected bear researchers have concluded can provide a more effective defense against bear attacks than firearms. Still, I've always believed my can of pepper spray to be more of a psychological comfort than a practical defense, a last-resort tool useful only in close quarters—for instance, if a bear decided to enter my tent at night.

After trading some bear stories, Mike shares one about another ferocious arctic beast, the mosquito. "A year ago," he recalls, "a guy from New Jersey came through Anaktuvuk, intending to do a solo, ten-day trip. Why he chose this place for his first solo-backpacking trip I don't know. He was worried about bears, but what got to him were the mosquitoes. He spent one night out there and came back. The mosquitoes were unlike anything he'd imagined. They drove him crazy. Just one night and he couldn't take it anymore."

Cool temperatures and a steady, brisk breeze have kept the mosquitoes at bay during my village stopover. But July is the peak of the Arctic's mosquito season and I'll soon be reminded just how maddening they can be.

The weather has been wet as well as windy. A heavy rain poured out of the sky my first night in Anaktuvuk and rain continues to fall—sometimes heavily, sometimes as a light mist—for most of the next day and night. It's still raining the morning I'm scheduled to leave the village. This is unusual for July, says Mike, more typical of August. But the weather has been strange all summer, so nothing surprises him anymore.

It's hard to begin my trek knowing I'll soon be drenched. Plus there's a stream crossing to consider: only a few miles from the village I have to ford the Anaktuvuk River. With all this rain, water levels are sure to be high. So I procrastinate. At midmorning, Mike goes online and calls up a statewide weather map on his computer. It shows a small low-pressure system with rain showers to the east of us and a larger low to the south. Tomorrow a high-pressure system is expected to move in.

Bob Marshall never had the benefit of such high-tech aids. My guess is that he would already be miles down the trail, plowing full-speed ahead. Yet I hesitate. Should I wait for tomorrow's clearing skies? Mike says that stream levels in the Central Brooks Range both rise and fall quickly, usually within an eight-to-ten-hour period. The prospect of drier weather and lower stream flow is seductive. But what if the rain continues? How long will I wait? My wish for comfort is gradually losing the battle with my desire to be started, to make some miles and deal with the stream crossing. I step outside, where the temperature is forty-nine degrees. The air has a palpable physical presence: heavy, wet, chilling.

With only a light mist falling, I prepare to leave Anaktuvuk shortly after noon on July 19. Mike Haubert lifts my pack and says, "Not bad for two weeks." I'm not sure exactly what he means, but take it as a compliment. Then, for the second time, Mike asks, "So, you have everything you need?"

I suspect he's inquiring, in a roundabout way, if I'm taking a bear-resistant food container, or BRFC. Made of dense, durable, space-age plastics, BRFCs are black, cylindrical contraptions, about eight inches in diameter. Besides being crushproof, they have locking tops that bears haven't figured out. Though bulky and awkward and heavy, BRFCs are the only sure way to keep grizzlies (and smaller critters) out of food supplies where there are no trees. Another shortcoming is that they don't hold much food, maybe four or five days' worth for one person. Certainly not enough for a two-week trip. Yet as Mike has pointed out, you can at least store some emergency rations in the container. In the unlikely event a bear does get into a backpacker's food cache, at least some will be protected.

BRFCs aren't mandatory here as at Denali National Park (though they will become so, several years after my solo trek) but park staff highly recommends their use. We carried them in 1998, when I explored Gates with superintendent Dave Mills. After all, NPS employees must set a good example. I'm not taking one on this trip, though. To be honest, I don't think I could cram one into my already-overstuffed pack. And I certainly don't need the extra weight.

Despite my pack-weight concerns, I've added a couple extra pounds by carrying an aviation handheld radio for emergencies. I balked at the idea initially, wishing to be as self-sufficient as possible, but there's no good reason—aside from weight—not to take the extra precaution, especially if it eases family anxieties. And if a radio could mean the difference between life and death, why not?

Again I think of Marshall. Would he have brought such a radio into the wilderness? If he'd had access to today's abundance of high-tech gizmos, would he have become a gearhead? I also wonder just how much modern electronics—GPS systems, radios, cell phones—affect our relationship to wilderness. Do they make wildlands less wild? Does the knowledge that I can radio a plane or jetliner somehow diminish my experience?

Electronic gadgets make things easier, but so do modern foods and stoves and packs, synthetic clothing, the space-age fabrics used in tents and sleeping bags and boots. Even without a radio, I have advantages that Marshall likely never imagined. Does that mean his wilderness experience was richer than mine? And what about the Nunamiut? Have high-powered rifles, binoculars, and ATVs diminished their relationship with the landscape and its animals?

A bigger question, perhaps, is this: to what degree do radios or cell phones diminish backcountry travelers' self-sufficiency? There's plenty of evidence that some modern adventurers take unnecessary risks—or too easily request help—because rescue is only a call away. In recent years, Alaska's newspapers have reported numerous rescues launched in response to cell-phone calls for help. In some instances, people had been lulled into complacency or gotten themselves into jams at least partly because they had cell phones to bail them out. In other cases, people called for help when they likely could have saved themselves, needlessly exposing rescuers to danger. Still, there's no denying that modern communications have saved lives and prevented prolonged suffering. Thor Tingey can vouch for that. Thor's teenage sister Daphne had joined his group at the Haul Road for part of their trek through the Brooks Range. But those plans were scrambled when she injured an Achilles tendon. Contacted by radio, a pilot flew in, made an emergency landing, and then hauled Daphne out of the mountains.

FOUR

A River to Cross

LEAVING THE VILLAGE, I FOLLOW AN ATV TRAIL AROUND ELEANOR
Lake then cut northeast across saturated, boggy tundra toward the Anaktuvuk River. Because I already know the story of these tracks, they don't shock
my wilderness-seeking spirit. Besides, the trails are not entirely loathsome: in
drier areas, their hard-packed surfaces can be preferable to tussock stumbling,
particularly when starting an expedition lugging a seventy-pound pack that
weighs mightily on a not-yet-tundra-toughened body. In a sense, the trails offer a
relatively smooth and short transition from twenty-first-century Native culture to
unspoiled wildlands. There's also the fact that I'm using trails made by the locals
on their lands. It's not pristine wilderness for miles outside the village, and hasn't
been for years. Or am I just rationalizing here?

I'd be among the last to advocate a trail system through Gates, yet I freely admit
to following one out of Anaktuvuk. I suppose that leaves me open to charges of
hypocrisy. At the very least, it's one of those troubling contradictions, like owning
a car—or taking a commuter flight into the mountains—while being opposed to
further oil development in the Arctic National Wildlife Refuge and other wilderness areas, as I am. Or what about the carbon footprint of my flights from Anchorage to Fairbanks and then Anaktuvuk Pass in this age of global warming? It could
be argued that we modern, fossil fuel–dependent wilderness explorers are threaten-
ing the very landscapes we so passionately wish to protect—and visit. We humans
have a hard time saying no to conveniences that make life easier (and adventures
like this possible) even when those conveniences challenge our values.

It seems the Nunamiut and other Eskimo peoples experience little or none of my high-tech angst. Practical people, they consider ATVs and snowmobiles new tools that make life easier. In reflecting upon his relationship with an Inupiat Eskimo friend, author and longtime arctic resident Nick Jans writes,

> The aesthetics of chasing down animals with machines doesn't concern Clarence, and I wish it did; but he didn't invent the machines nor our [modern, Euro-American] concepts of fair chase and conservation. If I broached the subject he'd consider me a fool. The new technology is just another means toward an ancient end. Eskimos have embraced snowmobiles and semiautomatic rifles so that the seams between cultures are scarcely visible.

Where the ATV trails pass through wet areas, their deep ruts are pooled with water, forcing me to work my way through sedge-tussock tundra. The stuff of arctic legend—and the bane of backpackers—tussocks begin as narrow clumps of sedges that grow outward as well as upward. Their mushroom shape and wobbly nature make these grassy mounds highly unstable to walk upon; any step slightly off center makes them lean this way or that. It's possible to walk between the tussocks, but the boggy ground between them quickly soaks boots.

My boots stay reasonably dry for the first hour or two. Then, skirting a swamp, I slip off a tussock and plunge into a deep mudhole. Shockingly cold water pours into one boot, then the other. Given recent rains, my feet were doomed to eventual sogginess, but I wished to postpone the inevitable for as long as possible. No longer obsessed with the impossibility of keeping my feet dry, I slosh toward the Anaktuvuk River.

The rain has stopped, which is good. I feel warm sunlight on my body for the first time since my arrival. But the wind too has died. And that's lousy. As overhead cloud masses pull apart to reveal streaks of blue, other clouds rise from the tundra. Soon legions of mosquitoes voraciously attack my steaming body, sweat dripping heavily from first-day exertions. I coat and recoat my flesh and clothes with DEET-laden bug repellent, but that is only a temporary fix. Continued harassment by these frenzied bloodsuckers forces me to take an extreme step: I don a head net.

I hate head nets. They make me claustrophobic. But today the head net is a blessing. It keeps the mosquitoes off my face and neck, though they continue their maddening buzz around my ears and bounce off the head net's mesh. The mosquitoes are clearly excited by my arrival, but I could do without such an enthusiastic welcome.

Still searching for a place to cross the Anaktuvuk, I walk upstream toward a braided section. I've forded streams before and know the rules for safe crossings. But I also know the basics for safe travel in bear country, yet once managed to surprise a bear and get charged. So knowledge of what's "right" is no guarantee of safety. Besides, I've never attempted a river as large and fast as this one. And now, to do it alone—the prospect sets my stomach churning.

River crossings are a bigger worry than anything else I'll likely face in my wanderings through Gates, including grizzlies. For good reason: Alaska's ice-fed rivers kill far more backcountry travelers than bears do.

Even in mid-July, parts of the Anaktuvuk River are spanned by remnant fields of pale blue aufeis, the thick, banded overflow ice that forms as rivers freeze in winter. The ice is an inviting bridge, but potentially a deadly trap. Still several feet thick, it looks solid enough, but is likely rotten in places and could collapse if walked upon, particularly where undercut by the main river channel.

A half hour of hiking the river's edge brings me to a wide, braided, and ice-free stretch. This looks like the spot. The stream, as expected, is running muddy and high. How high, is the question. I look for riffles, which indicate shallow water, while slowly picking a route. The first few channels go easily. Then I come to the main one. A few steps in, the water is mid-thigh deep and my walking pole suggests deeper water ahead, so I back off. Leaving my pack on a gravel bar, I test alternate routes and, after several dead ends, trace out a path that seems doable.

Pack once more on my back, I instinctively mumble, "ok, do-or-die time," then wince at the words. My body shivers with cold and adrenaline, heart ka-thumps inside my chest, back and shoulders ache with weight and feet ache with cold as I reenter the stream—and also enter a state of focused awareness. I angle upstream, every step measured. I stumble once, but aided by my trekking pole I quickly regain balance. Reading the riffles, I think I've found a place to cross but the bottom suddenly drops off and the water quickly rises: midshin to knee to midthigh. Feeling the river's increased tug I back off, try another path.

I know it's not wise to rush, but my feet and lower legs are growing numb in the frigid, ice-fed waters. I don't know how much longer I can stand this, yet retreat seems unimaginable now. I reassure myself. Then, urging patience, I wade farther into the channel, make certain that every step is firmly placed before advancing.

Step by aching step, I weave my way through the river, which pulls at my legs, urging me downstream. A little more than halfway across the last channel, at about the point of no return, the water again edges above my knees. A pause, to calm myself, then another step. And the river drops a bit. One more step and the water is back down to my knees. The river stays knee-deep until only a few yards remain. Water now down to my shins, I happily splash the final few feet. I'm across! It's taken me an hour to reconnoiter and then cross a half-dozen braids and several hundred yards of chilling, fast-moving water.

Collapsing to the ground I take several deep breaths, then remove my pack, dump water from my boots, and wring out my socks. I'm exhausted and my feet are lumps of numb flesh. But I've passed my first and, I hope, biggest test, though one major crossing remains, across the Koyukuk's North Fork.

My first day ends after six hours and six and a half miles of hard, foot-drenching packing. There's no question the Nunamiut's trails eased my passage in places, but they were little or no help wherever the route dipped into marshy lowlands and I spent much of the afternoon stumbling among tussocks.

Clouds build as I'm setting up the tent, and I cook and eat in a light rainshower. Prepared on a backpacking stove that is lightweight but burns noisily as it consumes white gas, my first backcountry meal is chicken-and-noodles, with decaf coffee and two squares of semisweet chocolate. Chocolate, coffee, and various types of pastas will be my dinner mainstays throughout the trek, sometimes supplemented by freeze-dried green beans or corn. I eat slowly, savoring each bite, stretching out a meal that doesn't fully satisfy my hunger. For all the weight I'm carrying, I've had to skimp a bit on food, one of the small hardships—or at least challenges—of traveling alone for two weeks. Nutritious, high-calorie food (at least the kind that's palatable to me) is both heavy and bulky. I've filled my pack until it's bursting, and about as heavy as I can endure.

Part of the problem is that I prefer to carry gear that I'm sure will keep me dry and warm in an emergency. So I carry a larger tent, heavier stove and sleeping bag, and more fuel, water, and clothes (for instance, two extra pairs of socks, extra long- and short-sleeved shirts) than other "go light" outdoors types would consider necessary. Plus I have camera gear, journals, some reading material, a small tarp, and that aviation radio. All of that, in turn, requires a bigger and heavier pack.

The bottom line is that I'm burning more calories than I'm taking in. By trek's end I'll lose ten to fifteen pounds, maybe more. Thor Tingey, on the other hand, won't lose any weight in forty-six days, thanks to resupplies.

There's only a light breeze, so a crowd of mosquitoes joins me for dinner. For some reason they're not as aggressive as earlier in the day. They form a halo around me, but don't attack. I'm grateful, but also curious to know why. Can it be the rain? Cooler temperatures?

Though it keeps me damp, the evening shower leads to my first glorious moment: a double rainbow to the east, spanning the Anaktuvuk River valley and enclosing hills of gray limestone. Deep, warm hues arc against a darkly ominous sky and walls of mountains. There's also a short burst of intense evening sunlight that turns the tundra into a golden, glowing presence. These are beautiful, peaceful moments to end a tough, worrisome, and sometimes frustrating day. I take the light displays as a good omen. And a more pleasing sort of welcome to the arctic wilderness.

After dinner, I take inventory of my body. Shoulders and lower back are seriously achy, hips less so. And I have a few hot spots on my feet that, if I'm not careful, could become painful blisters. Overall, not bad for a first day of heavy packing through often-uneven terrain.

Because there are no trees here, I stuff food and toiletries into a heavy, white plastic bag, then cache the bag a hundred feet from my tent, on a small sedge island surrounded by tundra pools. I then place my two cooking pots atop the plastic bag, my attempt at an alarm system in case anything should try to get into the food. None of my foods are strongly odorous, and I've double- or triple-bagged most foods to cut down on smells. I do have some chemicals in my tent, but nothing that should attract a bear: bug dope, bear repellent, and stove fuel, all in cans or bottles. What about the baby powder I'm using to ease the stench of my feet and the deodorant for my armpits? Perhaps with no tentmate to offend, it's better to get stinky.

One final precaution: having heard from a few normally reliable sources that bears are put off by human urine, I pee around both cache and tent. I have no idea if this really works, but can't imagine it doing more harm than good.

I'll later ask some bear experts about this, both to satisfy my curiosity and get a more definitive answer. No such luck on the latter. But the variety of responses is nonetheless illuminating.

Tom Smith, who spent many years studying Alaska's brown bears—the coastal cousins of grizzlies—strongly advises against urinating anywhere near camp: "I actually tested the attractiveness of urine and indeed bears were attracted to it; once onto it they would exhibit classic scent rub/rolling behavior. How far they might detect and be drawn to it I do not know; all I do know is that you don't want anything like that around camps."

Tom adds that his policy has been to urinate at least one hundred yards from camp. He also uses specially marked quart bottles for in-tent peeing during the night. As he explains, "This circumvents a lot of problems including running into bears in the dark."

I am in fact employing the pee bottle strategy—not as a guard against bears, but to keep from having to exit the tent at night when the weather is either cold or stormy. But you can't get careless about it. A spilled pee bottle would be nasty indeed.

In contrast with Tom, bear biologists Larry Aumiller and Sterling Miller say that a bear's response is likely to be determined by its past experiences with people. A bear that's wary of people—which probably applies to most of the grizzlies in Gates—is likely to be spooked by human pee, while a human-habituated bear would pay little or no attention. And one that has learned to associate people with food might very well be attracted by the smell, because of the human-food connection.

Larry, it turns out, has "purposely peed around various camps through the years" to learn how bears would respond. In doing so, he's seen every imaginable possibility, from aversion to disinterest to heightened curiosity.

Another bear-researcher friend, Derek Stonorov, has his own take on these matters: "It's not important whether bears are attracted to human urine or not, it's important that when they come to an area where humans have urinated/defecated that they find nothing further that will reward their investigations."

Derek, like Tom, is a strong advocate of bear-resistant food containers and portable electric fences to keep bears out of camp. Significantly, their work has been concentrated along Alaska's Southwest Coast, where bears are far more numerous than the Arctic and also more habituated to people. Still, they would urge such precautions whenever traveling in bear country. Most important is the experts' bottom-line message: do whatever you can to minimize or eliminate ursine attractants, especially easy access to food.

FIVE

Approaching God's— and Robert Marshall—Country

I NOTICE LITTLE WILDLIFE MY FIRST TWO DAYS, EXCEPT FOR BIRDS. Songbirds are concentrated in streamside willow thickets: white-crowned and savannah sparrows, common and hoary redpolls, even a robin. The robin is a big surprise, because of past associations. Robins were common in my boyhood home, southwestern Connecticut, a much tamer, milder place than this valley. Anchorage, my home now, also has plenty of robins in summer. A surprise at first, their Anchorage presence has only strengthened my tendency to consider them birds of urban or suburban yards and forests and nearby woodlands. Until now, I never would have suspected they might inhabit remote arctic mountain ranges.

The robin reminds me of the dangers inherent in stereotyping. They also remind me that the Arctic is being changed in both large and small ways by global warming. Though bird books list robins as an arctic rarity, they're becoming ever more common in Alaska's northern reaches, just as the boreal forest is expanding, tundra is becoming more brushy, ponds are drying up, and permafrost and sea ice are diminishing. While the changes are barely noticeable from one year to the next, or perhaps even across a span of five to ten years, they're large enough that both scientists and Native residents of the region have detected large shifts over the past quarter century.

Researchers tell us that climate change is not only happening, but it's accelerating at an alarming rate, especially in the world's arctic regions. Milder winters and warmer summers are changing both the nature of tundra and the ground below it—and, almost certainly, the lifestyles of animals that depend on tundra to survive, humans included.

The tundra landscape that I'm passing through appears uniform from a distance, but it is in fact a remarkably complex blend of grasses, sedges, mosses, lichens, berry plants, wildflowers, heather, and dwarf shrubs, most notably willow and birch. But a large and growing body of research is showing that these ground-hugging plants are being replaced by taller, thicker stands of shrubs, particularly willow and alder.

Shrubby ecosystems are much more susceptible to fires, and some scientists are predicting that ever-larger wildfires are likely to sweep across the Arctic as the tundra's makeup changes. Case in point: several years after my passage here, the lower Anaktuvuk River valley will be scorched by the largest wildfire ever recorded on Alaska's North Slope. Started by a midsummer lightning strike, the fire burned more than a quarter-million acres. Though the village of Anaktuvuk Pass wasn't threatened, thick, choking smoke settled upon the community. More directly affected were members of the Western Arctic Caribou Herd, which forage on the area's plants in summer.

Not only do large tundra wildfires increase the release of carbon into the atmosphere, they may further accelerate the takeover of shrubby plants. Some researchers predict that such "feedback processes" may lead to the disappearance of tundra from most of northern Alaska by the end of the century. Such a massive ecosystem shift would mean sweeping changes for the plants, wildlife, and humans who inhabit the Central Brooks Range and other arctic regions and the likely extinction of some—perhaps many—species.

Contributing to this massive habitat shift is the loss of permafrost, the ice and permanently frozen ground that underlies most of the Arctic. Substantial melting of permafrost has already been documented in parts of the Brooks Range and North Slope; in some places huge swaths of tundra have slumped and opened up. That melting leads to the decay of organic material (both plant and animal) that's been frozen for years, decades, even centuries. The decay, in turn, releases huge amounts of methane, a potent greenhouse gas that contributes to the atmosphere's warming.

The presence of permafrost restricts the escape of surface water, which is why this arctic desert can be so doggoned wet. Besides contributing to global warming, its melting allows water to more easily drain through the soils below, leaving less on the tundra's surface. Scientists predict that those drier conditions will accelerate the brushy takeover of tundra, increase the frequency and size of wildfires, and speed the transformation of arctic landscapes.

Eskimos and Athabascans who live in and around the Brooks Range have also observed worrisome changes that are already affecting their subsistence lifestyles. Orville Huntington, a widely respected Athabascan member of the Alaska Native

Science Commission, reports that residents have noticed changes in the number, behavior, or health of many animals, from white-fronted geese to bears, beavers, and salmon. Furthermore, elders say, "winter isn't really winter anymore. It's much warmer than it used to be." Instead of extended periods of extreme cold, with temperatures to sixty or even seventy degrees below zero, winter rains are becoming more common. At the same time, lakes are shrinking, rivers are warming, and the timing of caribou migrations has changed.

I can't help but wonder what changes Robert Marshall might notice if he were to return to the Brooks Range today, more than sixty years after his final expedition. He might be shocked.

MORE BIRDS: ravens, gulls, long-tailed jaegers, and American golden plovers. The latter winter in South America and breed on tundra throughout much of Alaska. The Nunamiut's ATV trail must pass through some prime plover nesting grounds, because several scurry about and whistle alarms at my approach. Breeding males are strikingly handsome, with mottled golden brown back, black undersides and face, and a narrow stripe of white that curls from the head down the side of the neck to the breast, forming a question mark, minus the dot.

While birds have been plentiful, I've seen only signs of mammals, most notably caribou; mostly bleached antlers, sometimes still attached to skulls. Also fur, assorted bones, and one nearly complete skeleton. The abundance of caribou parts reflects the valley's importance as a migration route and its frequent use by Nunamiut hunters.

Other, less pleasing human signs are also scattered along the trail: aluminum soda cans, rusting steel containers, candy bar wrappers, batteries, snowmachine parts, fire rings, bullet casings. Naturally most abundant near the village, the debris has rapidly diminished, mile by mile. I recognize that humans of every sort have traditionally left unnecessary stuff behind when they've returned home from expeditions. I also understand that old habits die hard. But the Nunamiut must understand that plastics and metals don't return to the earth nearly as quickly or completely as their traditional leftovers, and I find it hard not to judge the locals for the amount of trash they've left in this river valley.

I also see evidence of the Arctic's two other large predators: wolf tracks and grizzly scat, plus some diggings that could only have been made by bears. I'm likely sharing the valley with other animals, but my heavy load and the swampy, uneven terrain force me to concentrate on where to step. I spend most of my time peering at the ground before me, only pausing now and then to scan the valley bottom and hillsides for wildlife.

I finally spot mammals after setting up my second camp. First, a loudly chattering ground squirrel protests my temporary intrusion into its neighborhood. Then, in late evening, a lone bull caribou weaves across the tundra. In his prime or close to it, the bull carries gigantic antlers and wears patchy, shedding summer hair. I envy the caribou's easy, high-stepping movement across the tundra, his effortless grace. Unlike me, he seems to have no particular destination and meanders to and fro, stopping occasionally to graze on grasses, sedges, lichens, or willow leaves.

One thing I don't envy: caribou, more than humans or any other large northern mammal, are beleaguered by mosquitoes and parasitic flies that burrow into their nose or hide. Caribou running erratically for no apparent reason are likely trying to escape such pests. This bull doesn't seem especially harried. He makes only one short burst across the tundra and into a shallow braid of the Anaktuvuk River. Is he seeking relief in the stream's cooling waters?

There's another caribou advantage: no worries about wet feet. I watch the bull a half hour or more, then duck into the tent. After setting it up and tossing in my gear, I earlier squashed 131 mosquitoes that had zoomed inside during the door's brief opening. At least four times that many perched on the tent's outer fabric. Now, with both the sun and air temperature falling, far fewer follow me inside.

Mosquitoes have been the most aggravating part of a very tough and tiring slog. I've stayed on the ATV trails as much as possible to ease my passage these first two days. Across dry terrain, I've kept a good pace, maybe two miles an hour. But the route often crosses wetlands, slowing me down and keeping my feet soaked.

Given his legendary hiking pace, Bob Marshall could probably average three miles per hour along this trailed section. For me it's a struggle and I've averaged just over one mile per hour, including rest stops. But I'm a natural plodder. I tend to walk slowly even without a pack, so I can take in my surroundings. Paying attention to the landscape is much harder to do when lugging a big, heavy pack, at least for me. Much of the time I'm simply focused on putting one foot in front of the other, over and over. A long-distance backpacker I'm not; never have been. I could never make it as an explorer. Not enough tolerance for discomfort and pain.

At least I've gotten into the habit of stopping occasionally not only to rest but to reconnoiter this valley. Topping one rise my second afternoon, I looked behind and was greeted by a beautiful sight: the Anaktuvuk meandered through a broad and lushly green tundra valley bounded by massive, gray limestone buttresses. Even though I'm surrounded by mountains, the feeling here, as in much of the Brooks Range, is one of wide-open spaces. I was encouraged by the expansive view down valley, which gave a sense of progress. For all my painful plodding, I've come about fifteen miles after two days. I'll put in a long day tomorrow, then slow my pace. The area near Ernie Pass is supposed to be gorgeous. Raymond

Paneak called it "God's country"—high praise from a local who has seen much incredible country.

With some thirty-five miles still to go, I worry about my body and how it will hold up. I am exhausted and aching from shoulders to toes. Still I'm dry, warm, safe, and, for now, buffered by tent walls from the mosquito hordes.

Shortly before midnight, I exit the tent for a late-night pee. Then, shielded from the ever-present mosquitoes by boots, rain gear, and head net, I sit surrounded by pink plumes, lemon-yellow arctic poppies, and white-petaled mountain avens, and watch the late-night sun reshape the landscape with warm colors and lengthening, shifting shadows. Hills and side valleys I ignored while trudging across the tundra are transformed into mysterious places that demand my attention. Has that pyramidal mountain ever been climbed by humans? Will it ever be? Have grizzlies or wolves walked there? Sitting in shadow, I imagine myself high on a limestone ridge, awash in golden light.

From off in the distance comes the faint chirp of a bird. It calls three times, then falls silent. For the moment, the landscape is serene and ancient, with the Anaktuvuk River below this tundra bench a low, rushing murmur. The air is calm, the sky patchy with blue heavens and white drifting clouds. No human noises; no other sense of human presence, even the ATV trail hidden from this spot. Mosquitoes hum about me, dancing wildly. Part of an immense, unfathomable biomass, they are enlivened by my body's heat and carbon dioxide exhalations in the cooling night air. Immersed in humming, I find myself part of the landscape, not merely passing through. Tonight gives reward, perhaps even meaning, to the drudgery of today's packing. I soak it in, realizing I will likely never pass here again.

JULY 21, my sister Karen's fifty-third birthday. During breakfast—my usual two granola bars and decaffeinated coffee made from steeping a coffee bag in boiled water—I send her "best wishes," from the Arctic to Chicago. We live in such different worlds and don't talk much about my passion for wilderness or hers for big-city life, mid-America style. Memories and photos are proof that we were once best buddies. In one of the most vivid images from my early childhood, I am roaming our house, calling out for "Honey" and searching beneath beds for my sister, who had recently started school. Somehow, in a way I can't recall, we lost that early connection. And while my middle-aged years have brought me closer to my younger brother, Dave, it seems some unbridgeable gulf still separates my sister and me. It's true that Dave and I share a passion for nature, while my sister hardly seems to notice the larger, more-than-human world. Yet it must be more than that. Most times, I feel no inclination to reach across the gap; but occasionally, like this morning, I wonder what happened to separate us so. And I mourn that lost connection.

It's a beautiful midsummer day, with bright sun, warm temperatures, an invigorating breeze, and bright cumulus clouds riding across the sky. Last night was clear and cold, temperatures falling into the thirties. Unfortunately, not cold enough for a mosquito die-off. They're still a constant, swarming presence. I have a theory that the mosquitoes are sent into a frenzy by the heat, perspiration, and carbon dioxide my body gives off when working hard. Around camp, they don't seem nearly as aggressive. I also wonder: do mosquitoes have territories or ranges? If not, why don't their numbers continue to build as a person (or other animal) crosses the tundra? It seems I'm constantly wearing a halo of several dozen to several hundred mosquitoes, but during my daily walks I must flush legions of them from the tundra. Do they follow awhile, then drop behind to be replaced by others?

For all their harassment, I've gotten few bites. Maybe that's because I'm nearly covered from top to bottom. Or because of the DEET, which confuses mosquitoes' heat- and CO_2-seeking sensors. I've used the repellent sparingly, not so much because of its chemicals (which in high concentrations may cause headaches, convulsions, unconsciousness, and even infant deaths) but because I fear running out.

Many explorers have suggested that a person would be hard-pressed to survive the Alaska wilderness in summer without some sort of mosquito defense. I agree, though the primary challenge, it seems, would be staying sane. Marshall too had no doubts about the dangers they pose: "I could see that anyone caught in this country for several days at the height of the mosquito season without special protection would surely be killed." His solution was to clothe his entire body. In describing one trip into the Brooks Range, he commented,

We wore our mosquito nets and gloves practically all the time. As we plodded along, the mosquitoes gathered thicker and thicker on the outside of the nets. After perhaps two hours they would become so dense that vision would be blurred. Then we would stop, build a big fire, get as close as we could to stand the heat, and "burn the mosquitoes off," as the people in the Arctic say.

Today I get a break: after two days of a tailwind, the breeze is now in my face, which pushes the mosquitoes behind me as I walk. I am able, at times, to even go without the head net or ball cap and only a light, synthetic capilene shirt to cover my upper body. Sweet relief! A brief pause, though, and they're right back in my face, so my afternoon snack stops (a mix of cheese, beef jerky, honey-roasted peanuts, and garlic-flavored bagel bits) are short ones.

Now approaching the headwaters of the Anaktuvuk River, my route requires that I recross the stream in order to reach the Arctic Divide and Ernie Pass. This crossing goes easily, partly because I'm much farther upriver, but also because the heavy rains have temporarily ceased. The Anaktuvuk's flow has accordingly diminished and its water has cleared, making it possible to see the bottom.

Dry skies and drier terrain have also helped my sodden boots begin to dry, something I wouldn't have imagined possible a day ago. So I switch to neoprene booties for the crossing. As I'm making the switch, mosquitoes cover my warm, damp, smelly socks. Performing an experimental slap test, I kill thirty-three with one swat. This, I vow, is my last expedition through the Brooks Range in July, the peak of northern Alaska's mosquito season.

Once across the Anaktuvuk, I leave the last vestiges of the Nunamiut's ATV trails and follow a rushing clearwater tributary called Graylime Creek. The name alerts me that I'm about to enter both God's and Robert Marshall's country. Graylime is fed by gullies and brooks that flow off the Arctic Divide, and it's the first landscape feature I have encountered on this trip to be labeled by Marshall. He named the creek in August 1938, on the third of his four expeditions into the Brooks Range. As he later wrote, "It was a large side creek, emerging from a canyon world exclusively made of gray limestone, with a thousand-foot sheer precipice of gray lime rising above it—so we called it Graylime Creek."

Several hundred yards up the creek, I attract the attention of two mew gulls. It's such a strange thing, to find gulls so far from the coast. And in high alpine tundra, no less. They seem as out of place here as the robins. Or wood frogs, which remarkably also inhabit the Arctic.

At first only curious, the gulls soon become aggressive and begin to dive-bomb me. Circling and screeching loudly, they come in low, toward my head, and veer upward at the last moment. At times the mating pair teams up and attacks from different directions. If the goal is to intimidate me, they're successful. I've been dive-bombed before by gulls and terns, but never for such a prolonged spell. I must be close to their nest. I recall stories of people injured by such attacks; how seriously, I don't know. Grizzlies and stream crossings I'd come prepared to meet. But maniacal birds? I imagine a headline: *Adventure writer found in Brooks Range with fatal head wound inflicted by kamikaze gulls.*

My head net and cap don't offer much protection, so I raise a trekking pole above my head whenever the gulls approach and swing it in circles like some medieval swordsman. My intent is not to injure the birds but to defend my body. After several hundred feet of dodging their attacks I leave the gulls' nesting territory and the fiercely parental birds end their assaults.

I set up camp on a tundra bench above one of Graylime's wide gravel bars, within two miles of Ernie Pass. Already I've backpacked farther than ever before, about twenty-one miles by map (longer, I'm certain, by real distance traveled). My shoulder and back muscles are gradually adapting to the load, but now my feet are hurting: my left heel and right middle toe have been rubbed raw. Frequent dunkings have made Band-Aid and mole-foam repairs futile, but my feet will now get a break. I'm staying put for the next couple of days while exploring the area on day hikes.

SIX

Memories from a Geology Past

RAIN POUNDS THE TENT, A LOUD, HYPNOTIC THRUMMING. NO WIND accompanies this latest shower, so the hard and steady splatter of water against nylon is all I can hear until a soft droning approaches from the south, barely audible above the rain. A bush pilot is trying to maneuver his way through this July arctic storm. Good luck, I think. The last time I peeked out the tent, even the bases of the surrounding Brooks Range foothills were draped in gray heaviness, as if a giant woolen shroud had been placed over these mountains, oozing wetness.

Before receding into nothingness, the airplane's faint roar triggers memories of other planes. Helicopters, too. A quarter-century flashback delivers me to the 1970s. I'm a twentysomething geologist again, not long out of grad school and working this same range of arctic mountains. Belted into the cramped backseat of a Hughes 500, I peer out its bulbous plastic windows. The helicopter's blades roar and whine, a god-awful white noise. It's the end of a long workday, which means I've walked several miles across untrailed terrain, collecting rocks and stream-sediment samples along the way. I'm tired, maybe a little grumpy. But our pilot, who's been napping or reading books much of the day, feels rambunctious. Like many pilots who work for mineral-exploration crews, John flew choppers in Vietnam. Today, he decides to show off some of his talents. At speeds exceeding one hundred miles per hour, he skims a valley bottom. Turning right, then left, then right again, he traces the bends of a sparkling mountain stream bounded by spruce forest. I swear we're not more than twenty feet off the ground and silently pray we don't nose into the river or clip a tree and die a horrible, fiery death. John finally lifts the helicopter to more reasonable heights. He's laughing. The geologist beside him is grinning his approval. I'm shaking.

Another memory, a different pilot. Again it's the end of a workday. We're flying high over the mountains, headed for camp, when somebody spots a grizzly. The bear is large, almost certainly an adult male. He has been grazing on wildflowers and other greens in a boggy alpine meadow, but now he sits on his haunches and looks in our direction. "You want a closer look?" the pilot asks. Of course we yell "Sure!" We begin a steep, harrowing dive. This is what a strafing run must be like, I think.

As the chopper closes, the grizzly takes off running. We're amazed at his speed and power, the muscles that ripple along his shoulders and humped back. The bear rumbles uphill across spongy, hummocky tundra of the kind that regularly trips up human hikers, even when walking slowly and with caution. Every now and then the bear looks backward. Tongue hanging out, he sprays shit across the tundra, but he doesn't break stride until reaching the top of a knoll. There he stands and opens his mouth wide. It appears he's growling, but his snarls are lost in the helicopter's roar. Sitting back down, the bear swats at us as we circle two or three times, a couple hundred feet above him. "Seen enough?" the pilot asks. "OK, let's go home."

It's not the first time we've zoomed in for closer looks at wildlife, but this chase, and the bear's certain distress, unnerves me. My stomach is roiling. Beyond the fact that it's illegal, being a form of wildlife harassment, our terrorizing of the bear is simply wrong. I see no hint of disapproval from any of the others. Unsure of myself, I don't protest.

AS AN EXPLORATION GEOLOGIST in the mid- to late seventies, I saw large swaths of the Brooks Range (and other parts of the state) from a helicopter. That was just a few years before Congress designated large sections of Alaska's northernmost mountain chain as park and wildlife-refuge wilderness, off-limits to development. Flown by chopper from base camp to work area, I would traverse a ridge or stream drainage, then get picked up and taken to another area, or returned to camp.

Our crew followed the same routine throughout the summer: a series of helicopter flights and day hikes, looking for mineral deposits rich in gold, silver, lead, zinc, or copper. I don't regret those times. But over the years, as my relationship with wildlands has shifted and deepened, I've come to abhor the idea of helicopter flights and landings in wild areas, whether or not the government has designated them wilderness. Not only are helicopters obnoxiously noisy and air-fouling machines, they are maneuverable enough to reach places inaccessible to fixed-wing aircraft. Crews can set up camps or cache fuel drums almost anywhere and it becomes easier to trash remote landscapes. Plus there's that temptation to zoom in on wildlife for a closer look.

After several years away, I came back to Alaska in 1982, reincarnated as a journalist. I stayed this second time, built a life around writing and my love for wild nature. Since my return, I've explored the state's roadless areas in gentler, quieter ways: by river raft, kayak, foot. Of course many of those trips have still involved the use of aircraft (single-engine planes on either wheels or floats) in order to reach remote wilderness, so my quiet recreation comes with a catch. And as already admitted, a bit of hypocrisy. Such is the nature of late-twentieth and early-twenty-first-century adventure travel.

For all of my desire to explore wild terrain, I've never been a gung-ho backpacker and have become even less enthusiastic as a forty- and now fiftysomething traveler—another difference from Bob Marshall, a legendary hiker and packer who gained a reputation for prodigious thirty- and forty-mile day hikes in the 1920s, while living in the Rocky Mountains. His pace and stamina were equally amazing while backpacking through the arctic tundra. Returning from one foray into Koyukuk country, he and partner Al Retzlaf covered ninety-one miles in thirteen days while lugging sixty-five-pound packs across rugged terrain. Despite the difficulties, Marshall wrote, "there was genuine exhilaration in triumphing over the toughest conceivable travel. Tired we would be, but never worn out; difficult as the going was, we always had plenty of reserve." Even more amazing, perhaps, is that Marshall found the time and energy to climb peaks and explore side valleys on "pleasant interludes." In one case, he took a thirty-mile round-trip solo jaunt, returning to camp "at a four-mile-an-hour clip." That's almost a jog.

Rather than go point-to-point, my preference is to set up base camps and do day hikes in a variety of directions. Such base camping eliminates heavily burdened packing. And though I may not cover as much ground, I become more intimate with a smaller piece of the landscape. Less focused on the miles I must travel or a schedule to keep, I pay more attention to my surroundings.

This trip through the Brooks Range is a backpacking/base camping hybrid. With nearly two weeks to travel fifty miles, I have the flexibility to stay in one place for two or three days. I can more easily remain tentbound when the weather gets nasty or take an extra day when tempted by side trips. Curiously, my increased options sometimes unnecessarily complicate things. Marginal weather provokes internal debates: should I go or should I stay?

So it goes with a worrier. This expedition has shown me how much time I waste in worry. And it leads me to ask: how much does fear, in general, drive my decision making, the way I live my life? It seems that fear is a big motivator. I've also noticed my strong tendency to structure days "by the clock." Five days into the wilderness,

I'm still largely aware of clock time, when I could be operating on "tundra time." There's no daily need for a watch out here, yet to a surprising—and sometimes annoying—degree, I'm still run by my timepiece. It's a difficult habit to break. I see a need for letting go: of worry, excessive structure, my need to figure things out and have everything pat. Wilderness travel is inherently unpredictable. It's an opportunity to become more spontaneous, less tightly bound to schedules and structure.

After some debate, I decide to stay put an extra day and further explore this beautiful area. This is what I've hoped and desired to do. Tomorrow, as the saying goes, will take care of itself. I also decide to put my watch away for at least one day.

Those decisions made, I glance outside the tent. The rainsquall that recently hammered my tent has moved down valley, leaving a patchy blue sky in its wake. Though this part of Graylime is still in shadow, to the south streaks of molten light pierce the clouds and fall on distant peaks across the divide.

There's barely a breeze, which of course means the mosquitoes again are stirring. Swarms or not, I decide it's time to go fishing. I've brought along spin-fishing gear in the hope that I might catch grayling for a meal or two. I don't expect to live off the land except in a token sense: catch an occasional fish, pick some berries. It's also a way to pay homage to the pioneering explorers who truly depended on hunting and fishing for survival. In some small fashion, it's another way I might follow in the footsteps of Bob Marshall and his Brooks Range companions. They regularly hunted wildlife while tramping through the backcountry and supplemented their packed-in supplies with meals of grayling, Dall sheep, moose, and even grizzly steaks.

As it turns out, I would have been better off bringing an extra pasta meal or two. I didn't fish at all while hiking along the Anaktuvuk River, which ran high and muddy for much of my passage. Tonight, I throw gold- and silver-plated spinners into Graylime Creek, which near camp is running fast and shallow. I get only a couple of bites, and no fish, in a half hour's effort. The one grayling I see measures only six inches, barely pan size. It's probably just as well I didn't catch anything, because I didn't plan to eat fish tonight. But it leaves me wondering how I'd do, if I really needed wild foods.

My day ends with yet another rain shower, just before midnight, though it's not as furious as the earlier one. I drift asleep serenaded by gently tapping rain and Graylime Creek's soft murmur.

THE NEXT MORNING I awaken to overcast but dry skies. A light rain resumes after breakfast, but I head out with my daypack, bound for Graylime Creek's upper reaches, bordered on the south by Limestack Mountain, which Marshall named and climbed in 1930. "The view from the summit," he wrote, showed a myriad of wildly thrown together mountains rising from deep valleys, cut up by great clefts and chasms, their bases resting in green vegetation, then rising into rocks—stratified at times and chaotically tumbled at others—culminating in unbroken snow, and framed always by the pure blue of the sky. The number of mountains was bewildering....

I spent more than three bright hours up there on top of the continent, looking in every direction over miles of wilderness in which, aside from [backpacking partners] Lew and Al, I knew there was not another human being. This knowledge, this sense of independence which it gave, was second only to the sense of perfect beauty instilled by the scenery on all sides. My time on the summit was spent by first giving myself to an enjoyment such as another person might experience listening to Beethoven's Fifth Symphony played by some dreamed-of super-Philadelphia Orchestra; I then took pictures and made sketch maps of the topography in every direction.

I'm glad to have Marshall's description of Limestack, because the weather washes away my plans to approach the mountain and explore its flanks. Morning's light rain becomes a monsoonlike downpour. Hard, wind-driven rain soon saturates my rain gear and begins to seep through to my inner layers, driving me back to the tent. An ash-gray ceiling now mostly hides the valley and hills I'd hoped to visit. Instead I remove my sopping rain gear and pile it in a far corner of the tent, then prop my head against the still-dry fleece jacket and curl up with journal, maps, and books.

This is one of the reasons I'm carrying a tent that is roomy even for two people (while its space-age nylon fabric makes it light enough for backpacking). In this tube-shaped shelter, I can fully stretch out in my down-filled sleeping bag and still have plenty of space to spread out my backpack, notebooks and maps, and extra layers of clothing—and keep all that stuff separate from my soggy boots and rain shells. Even if the tent leaks some water during heavy rains, I can plop my sleeping pad and bag in the middle of the nylon floor, a foot or two from the edges where water usually pools, and use my backpacking towels to soak up any wetness along those edges. In fact this custom-made Stephenson's Warmlite tent, handcrafted in New Hampshire, has so far proved marvelously rain- and wind-resistant. Thank goodness for that, because the wind once more pushes and pulls at the tent and the rain beats harder, approximating last night's storm. But this tempest shows no sign of quickly moving through.

While cocooned in the tent, I read passages from *Alaska Wilderness* that describe Marshall's first trip to the Arctic Divide in 1930. Wow, did he and partner Al Retzlaf get hammered by days and days of rainstorms! They traveled later in summer than me, but not much. His descriptions demonstrate how sustained rains can turn Ernie Creek and the Koyukuk's North Fork into unfordable "raging torrents," playing perfectly into my river-crossing fears.

When the rain shows signs of easing, I exit the tent to make dinner. Although I don't consume nearly as much food as in my day-to-day urban life—or perhaps because of that—meals are an important part of the day's routine, a treasured ritual, really, when backpacking. That seems especially true when traveling alone. Back home, I too often rush through meals or am distracted when eating: by the newspaper, by TV, by conversations, by to-do lists. Out in the wilderness, I move more deliberately and attentively through the entire process, especially for breakfast and dinner, the day's main meals. Usually I begin by collecting water from a nearby source. Then I gather together the other necessary items (stove, matches, pots, mug, hard plastic spoon and fork, plastic bags with food); light the stove and adjust the flame; boil the water; pour out water for coffee; then, for dinner, pour pasta fixings into remaining water and stir occasionally while it cooks; and finally I move slowly through the meal, bite by bite and sip by sip.

Tonight's menu: coffee, a broccoli-cheese pasta, and a chunk of chocolate. The sky remains an ominous pewter color, so before starting the stove I set up the ParaWing tarp that I've lugged into these mountains. A gadget-obsessed gearhead friend introduced me to this high-tech shelter years ago. Besides being lightweight and easy to set up, the ParaWing is designed to be stable in high winds, with minimal flapping. It also can be adjusted if the wind changes direction, which isn't so unusual in the mountains. Naturally the tarp is expensive, but I decided it was worth the cost to have a reliable, easy-to-set-up cooking and eating tarp that's made for tundra camping (no trees needed). So I got the smallest, lightest version, which is great for one person, okay for two, and a tight squeeze for three.

Maybe because I'm a tech-challenged sort, it takes me a while to set up the tarp so that it capably blocks the wind and gives me sufficient room to cook and eat. It's unlikely I'll ever be as enamored of the ParaWing as my friend Glenn.

A soft staccato begins to play on the tarp's beige nylon as I heat the water for coffee and pasta. Within fifteen minutes, the noodles and sauce are ready for eating and I scoop the glop directly from the pot. I rarely eat such prepackaged pastas at home, but out here they taste exquisite and I savor each bite. It's absolutely true that everything tastes better on campouts, especially when the weather is raw and a hard-worked body is craving calories. When the pasta is finished, I break off two squares of dark chocolate and slowly nibble it away, allowing each piece to melt in my mouth. I sip the coffee between bites, relish the mingling of flavors. I want this chocolate delight to last as long as possible.

Dinner finished, I head over to the creek. I've brought a plastic scraper and scouring brush, but there's hardly anything left to scour, sauce included. I scoop some sand and rub it around, then rinse the pot clean. Next I refill my two pint-size water bottles, another part of my daily routine. I've brought a water filter to ensure against giardia, a microorganism carried in the feces of many mammals; known to cause severe intestinal problems, it's a legendary scourge among backcountry travelers. I drank directly from streams during my geology days and likely could do so now; cases of giardia from deep in these mountains are rare. But nowadays I'd rather be safe than sorry. Other options are iodine pills or boiling water, but each has its own shortcomings (bad taste and fuel consumption, respectively) and a filter has always worked for me, even if it adds several more ounces to my already-heavy load.

While I'm filling the bottles, the light shower becomes another heavy downpour, so I quickly finish up and once more retreat to the tent and warm, dry sleeping bag: my comforter here in the stormy wilderness.

Again I wonder about this "arctic desert." The weather so far has reminded me more of southeast Alaska and its notoriously soggy rainforest. I go back through my journal and confirm that it's rained every day since I arrived in Anaktuvuk Pass.

This abundant wetness gets me thinking about my first years in the Brooks Range, working on a geology crew. Is my memory that faulty, or have weather patterns shifted dramatically? I remember the Central Brooks Range of the 1970s as a dry, sunny place—so dry that I routinely left my rain gear in camp. Not a good idea, certainly, when traveling through any mountain range, but by day's end our packs usually overflowed with rocks and dozens of stream-sediment samples. Some of us looked for ways to cut down the weight. I often skimped on clothing and, thankfully, got away with it. Was it the season? Much of my Brooks Range geology work occurred in early summer, but I also remember being here in August and September. And are parts of this mountain chain considerably drier than others? In three trips to Bob Marshall country since the mid-eighties—two August visits and this one beginning in mid-July—I've encountered mostly overcast, wet weather. I've also twice explored parts of the eastern Brooks Range, within the Arctic National Wildlife Refuge: once in June, once in August. The weather on both those trips was much drier, warmer, sunnier.

Stirred up by aircraft overflights, climatic conundrums, and too much tent time, memories of my geology past seem to be flooding my internal landscape. That's not such a bad thing. Geology, after all, is what introduced me to the Brooks Range, a place that changed my life and, paradoxically, helped to steer me away from geology. Yet another conundrum. As the rain softens to a gently pleasing patter, my mind drifts through time and I reflect on other aspects of my former life as exploration geologist. I recall a place, far to the west in this same chain of mountains, and a summer now twenty-five years past. Half my life ago; amazing. It was a time—and place—that sparked great changes in my life.

* * *

FOR ALL OF the Brooks Range's allure, by the end of my first summer in Alaska it had become apparent that my attitude toward geology—and mineral exploration in particular—was considerably different than that of my friends and coworkers. For one thing, I clearly lacked their passion for the job. I worked hard and did the best I could and occasionally I exulted over discoveries of sulfide crystals, orange- and green-stained rocks, or other evidence of the metals we sought. But I didn't love what I did. The ridges and valleys I traversed were often stunning in their beauty and wildlife sometimes spiced up my days, but the fieldwork itself generally bored me.

Inwardly I cringed when a crew leader named Joe talked about our work. "You know," he said with gusto, "geology isn't just a job to me. It's my hobby, too." For me it was more chore than challenge. I think of Will Rogers's joke about golf: A nice walk ruined. That's pretty much how I felt about stream-sediment sampling and pounding on rocks while hiking through one of North America's wildest landscapes.

But something else, something vaguely troubling, gnawed at me. Before, during, and after the field season (when a few of us seasonal workers stayed on to help with data compilation), I had the opportunity to work with many of the company's veteran employees. Over time, it became clear that upper management and most, if not all, of the crew leaders—including some of my best friends—had absolutely nothing good to say about environmental groups.

"God-damned Sierra Clubbers," one might grumble. "They don't have anything better to do than come to Alaska and lock up the whole damned state with their parks. What the hell do they know?"

"Yeah," another would chime in, "they should take all their environmentalist bullshit back to California. But no, those assholes have got to meddle in stuff that has nothing to do with them. They're just bloodsuckers."

And then the conversation would really get nasty.

It's as if the Sierra Club were kin to the Antichrist, worthy only of distrust and loathing. The depth of my coworkers' anger shocked me. I didn't consider myself an environmentalist and knew little about the emotionally charged battle over Alaska's wildlands, a battle that many of my peers considered a direct threat to their livelihoods. But I couldn't see what was so awful about the Sierra Club or The Wilderness Society. It seemed to me that they were trying to do some good. I was naive and uninformed enough that I didn't realize many environmentalists would feel the same sort of disgust toward me, simply because I worked on a field crew seeking metal deposits in the arctic wilderness.

At twenty-four, my green ethic was still largely unformed, a vaporous thing still years away from taking solid shape. But I did know this: Sierra Clubbers were not my enemies. Still, it wasn't a perspective I could openly share with my coworkers, even those I considered good friends. I didn't know enough about conservation groups to defend their actions. And I didn't wish to be ridiculed by my peers as an environmentalist sympathizer. So I hid my misgivings and questions. Yet little by little, my discomfort built.

Perhaps my uneasiness was nudged along by Marshall's spirit, or at least his book. *Alaska Wilderness* had somehow made its way into our field crew's library, along with an assortment of novels and other Alaska-adventure books. On one hand, its presence in camp made good sense; Marshall's was a popular book about the very mountains we were exploring. Caught up in the wild allure of the place, several of us—especially those new to Alaska—yearned to know more about the Brooks Range. And here was a story by the guy who'd "discovered" and named many of the rivers and valleys and peaks we worked among. In a way, Marshall could be imagined as a kindred soul, someone who loved the mountains and paid close attention to their form and makeup, to their geology.

Marshall's insight that "only a small minority of the human race will ever consider primeval nature a basic source of happiness" may help to explain why exploration geologists could identify with his writing. Though their work might ultimately lead to mines and roads and toxic waste, my coworkers loved being in the field. And the farther afield the better. That, in large measure, is why many had come to Alaska. They, like Marshall, delighted in long rambling hikes through the Brooks Range wilds. But the jaws of some must have dropped, their tempers flared, when reading Marshall's call to preserve arctic Alaska: "In the name of a balanced use of American resources, let's keep northern Alaska largely a wilderness!"

Marshall made no attempt to hide his biases. If you gave *Alaska Wilderness* (or even the book's jacket) anything more than a cursory read, it quickly became clear that he sought—and found—far different riches than what we pursued. He reveled in the landscape's primeval nature even as he relished the solitude, the sense of well-being, and the spiritual refreshment to be found in this arctic wilderness. In its advocacy of wilderness protection, Marshall's book was a subversive presence in camp.

It's a crazy thing, when you think about it. Here was a pro-wilderness treatise (wrapped inside an adventure tale) by a founding member of The Wilderness Society, being passed among people who, by and large, abhorred anti-mining, tree-hugging environmentalists. Yet no one seemed to notice the irony. I didn't, certainly.

I can't recall how I got introduced to *Alaska Wilderness*. Another crew member may have recommended it to me as a good read, or maybe the title caught my eye while I sifted through the pile of books and magazines stacked in our cook tent. But once I gave him a try, Marshall quickly pulled me into his tales of adventure and discovery. Sitting in the cook tent before breakfast or wrapped in my sleeping bag late at night, I eagerly followed him and his buddies up the North Fork of the Koyukuk and Ernie Creek to the Arctic Divide; past Boreal Mountain and Frigid Crags, his literal—and now legendary—Gates of the Arctic; and to the flanks of darkly ominous Mount Doonerak. Marshall's excitement became my own as he arrived "at the very headwaters of one of the mightiest rivers of the north, with dozens of never-visited valleys and hundreds of unscaled summits still as virgin as during their Paleozoic creation."

The book didn't make me question what I was doing, at least not consciously. But looking back I'm sure that Marshall's passion for wilderness, as presented in those pages, touched mine. In doing so, his writings must have reignited some long-dormant embers by reconfirming the importance of wildness in my own life. Here was a man who loved the mountain landscape and its wild inhabitants for what they are, not for what they might become when utilized by humans. Instead of seeing the Brooks Range as a warehouse of raw materials, Marshall understood its inherent value in a wild, natural state. And he joyously celebrated that wildness in ecstatic prose:

> Three miles up the plunging creek we suddenly came upon a gorgeous lake, a mile and a half long and fresh as creation. Great mountains rose directly from its shores and disappeared about 3,000 feet above the water into low-lying clouds. . . . Seeing the sweep of mountains end in oblivion gave an impression of infinite heights above the experience of man. Nothing I had ever seen, Yosemite or the Grand Canyon or Mount McKinley rising from the Susitna, had given me such a sense of immensity as this virgin lake lying in a great cleft in the surface of the earth with mountain slopes and waterfalls tumbling from beyond the limits of visibility. . . . No sight or sound or smell or feeling even remotely hinted of men or their creations. It seemed as if time had dropped away a million years and we were back in a primordial world.

Marshall's wild desires, combined with his lushly dramatic descriptions of the arctic landscape and the ecstasy he felt there, have prompted some critics to label him a romantic, an escapist. But I sensed the importance of what he sought, found, and then shared through his writings. More than any geologist, he would become a role model and inspiration.

SEVEN

A Life-Changing Discovery

I RETURNED TO THE BROOKS RANGE IN 1975, FARTHER TO THE
west, with a different crew and field boss. We spent much of the summer in the Schwatka Mountains looking for mineral signs, sometimes teaming up with other crews sent there by our Anchorage-based employer. The western Brooks Range was a hot prospect. A few promising deposits had already been found, including a major copper lode called Bornite. Discovered in low foothills just south of the Schwatkas, the Bornite claim had an airstrip, test-drilling pads, and a network of roads carved out by heavy machinery. Though it held high-grade ore, Bornite wasn't (and still isn't) large or rich enough to be a producing mine in the remote Arctic. But along with some other discoveries, none of them economically viable, it hinted of larger treasures.

Geologists had projected a large mineralized belt along the range's southern edge and there had been talk of building an access road into the area from the recently completed Dalton Highway, some two hundred miles to the east. With hopes growing for a major strike—and maybe even a rich new mining district—companies poured money into the region. Adding to the excitement was a sense of urgency. Large chunks of the Brooks Range had been proposed as national parklands and closed to development. Geologists and other mining interests hurried to stake their claims before any additional lands were "locked up" by the feds. The rush was on.

Helicopters and planes buzzed across the sky, and large tent camps peppered the range's major valleys. Mere hints of mineralized rocks propelled us into great staking wars as our bosses tried to outguess and outmaneuver competing businesses. Loaded into helicopters, we flew across the landscape on stealth missions. Sometimes we took long, roundabout detours to our destinations and other evasive actions to be certain no competitors were tracking us, even as we looked for signs of unusual activity.

Dropped at target areas we rushed across rolling hills and hummocky tundra benches, loaded down with maps, compasses, aluminum poles, tape measures, and rock hammers, determined to claim large swaths of land for our clients. Nearly all the staked areas would eventually prove worthless, from an economic geologist's point of view. But back then everyone was caught up in a frenzied war-game atmosphere. Commanders stayed up late at night, plotting strategies. Out in the field, they rallied the troops, barked instructions. We, the foot soldiers, scattered in teams of two and three to "take that hill," claim it for our leaders.

The stream drainages and foothills we searched for minerals were not far from "d-2" lands that the federal government had set aside for possible inclusion in national parklands. Still new to Alaska and disinterested in politics, I knew almost nothing about the efforts to preserve this place, only that these hills and river valleys were gorgeously, ruggedly wild—and vast enough to swallow entire armies of geologists.

AMONG THE MOST beautiful valleys was one through which the Ambler River runs. Born among alpine meadows and boulder fields at Nakmaktuak Pass, beneath gray limestone walls, the Ambler rushes eighty miles to its junction with the Kobuk River in lowlands south of the Brooks Range. Though it begins its life in open tundra, the small, clear-water stream flows through boreal forest for nearly all of its winding path. Steep, jagged-topped peaks to sixty-one hundred feet enclose the Ambler's headwaters, but most hills bordering the river on its run through the Schwatka Mountains are three thousand to four thousand feet high and eroded to softer, more rounded shapes.

A government expedition had traveled up the Ambler in December 1885 while surveying the Kobuk River basin and some small number of gold prospectors and trappers followed. But few people besides the region's Eskimo and Athabascan residents had explored the valley when, in 1972, National Park Service planners debated whether to include the Ambler River and neighboring drainages on its d-2 lands list. They decided against it, concluding that other lands were more important. Two decades later, chief planner John Kauffman would lament their exclusion: "We made a terrible mistake in trimming out the Ambler, Shungnak, and Kogoluktuk valleys.... When at last I got on the ground, I realized how wrong we had been, and I tried desperately to get those valleys back into the park proposal." Kauffman did get the upper Ambler protected, but that was all.

Taking advantage of the Park Service's "terrible mistake," my company in 1975 established a camp along the Ambler River, not far from its junction with Ulaneak

Creek, about twenty-five miles below the river's source. From there we flew by helicopter to targeted areas in each of the three valleys and adjacent highlands that were omitted by park planners. Their loss would become our gain, or so my bosses hoped in our spirited quest for the next great Alaska bonanza.

We set up our tents in open spruce forest on the river's western bank. It was a beautiful spot, the wooded valley bottom bounded by dark, gray-walled mountains that rose to four thousand feet. But especially alluring was the river itself.

The Ambler is braided and shallow where it passes out of the Schwatkas. But near our camp, as in much of its passage through the mountains, it was a single channel with stretches of bubbling rapids and quiet pools of crystalline, aquamarine-tinted water that was surrealistically clear. Since that summer, whenever I've heard the expression "pure mountain water," the Ambler is what comes to mind. It remains the purest, clearest, most sparkling stream of water I have ever seen, or can imagine.

The river was so transparent it created optical illusions. As I stood on a rocky bench above one still pool and stared at the iridescent bodies and spectacularly large dorsal fins of arctic grayling below, my mind was tricked into believing that those northern fish were floating in air. Pools of water that appeared to be waist-deep or shallower might in fact submerge my five-foot-seven frame.

The Ambler's deepest pools were inviting, especially after sweating through a bug-infested, eighty-degree workday. But I wasn't one to take the plunge. Fed by snowfields that may linger through the brief arctic summer, the Ambler River is ideal for grayling and arctic char, but shockingly cold to humans.

The valley carved by these sparkling waters is an important wildlife corridor, traveled for centuries by migrating caribou and the wolves—and indigenous peoples—who hunt them. We did see a few caribou, probably stragglers belonging to the Western Arctic Caribou Herd, but our stay was made more memorable by sightings of other, more secretive, residents. Once, flying by helicopter to our work area, we spotted a charcoal black wolf standing atop a ridge, watching us intently—and, I like to think, defiantly—as we passed. Another time we saw a wolverine loping through forest, creamy streaks rippling across the flanks of its dark back. But the crew's cook was the luckiest of all. On our return to camp one evening, she told us that two adult wolves had appeared across the river, accompanied by several cavorting pups. For the next several days I spent much of my spare time trying to spot the wolves, fervently wishing they would reappear.

Over the years, homesteaders, trappers, and prospectors had built cabins beside the river's lower reaches, but its middle and upper stretches showed few signs of a human presence, other than our tent camp and occasional overflights by helicopters and planes. The summer's most intense prospecting and staking campaigns were to the south; here we were hidden from the main combat zone. I relished our seclusion and pristine surroundings from the start. Yet at first the Ambler didn't seem much different from other northern valleys we had worked, except for the stunningly clear water. That changed as days and weeks passed. The longer we stayed the more the wild beauty of the Ambler River and its watershed took hold of me. Was it the place alone or something else?

The extraordinary nature of some landscapes is immediately apparent. I think of Denali, or Yosemite, or the Brooks Range's own Arrigetch Peaks, with their sharply angled, monolithic rock walls and soaring spires that thrust sharply into the sky, hinting of unimaginable forces that send human senses reeling. For other places—for instance grassy plains or broad, forested valleys edged by gently rounded hills—it's a subtler thing, not easily noticed or explained. Only with time and a deepening relationship is the magic revealed. The revelation may come as a gradual awakening or a sudden bursting of awareness. For me it happened suddenly and unexpectedly on a sunny but brisk July afternoon, with enough breeze to keep the mosquitoes at bay. The day glowed with brightness.

My assignment was to sample and prospect a portion of the upper Ambler, north of camp. As usual I hiked alone (the main exception to that rule involved our staking escapades, which required teams of two or more people) after being dropped off by helicopter. The work itself was routine—bagging samples of stream silt, breaking rocks, making map notations—until I noticed a large patch of green-stained rocks. It was a bright, familiar green, much different than the green of mosses, grasses, or spruce needles. The rocks were coated with malachite, a copper-carbonate mineral.

At first I was excited, immersed in a "eureka" moment. This was just the sort of thing we sought. I busted open several rocks with my hammer, identified other copper minerals: chalcopyrite and bornite, mixed with pyrite. Next I estimated the extent of surface mineralization, collected samples, took notes, marked the spot on my map.

Only then did it hit me: what if, against all odds, this small malachite-coated outcropping was the tip of a copper-rich iceberg of rock? What if beneath this arctic soil there was a mother lode of metals, enough to develop a mine? What if, what if, what if…. Well, I might gain some small degree of notoriety. My company and its clients would get rich. Alaska's economy would get a boost. More helicopter-supported troops of geologists would invade, followed by mining engineers and huge earth-moving machines. And this beautiful, wild valley would be torn apart.

I tried to imagine the changes that would occur here; by my way of thinking, it was an ugly picture. And I realized, with a clarity that approached the Ambler's streaming water, just how special this river and its valley had become to me. It was a remarkable place, even a holy place, whose purity was held and reflected by those sparkling, rushing waters.

If ever a river deserved "wild and scenic" status, this was it. Could I bear to know the Ambler had been harmed because of work I had done? And what about the other wild places where I had hunted metals? I felt a clash of values, more strongly than ever before.

Still, I wasn't yet ready to go over to "the other side," the side inhabited by Sierra Clubbers and their kind; the side that Robert Marshall chose four decades earlier when he sought to "keep northern Alaska largely a wilderness" and helped to found The Wilderness Society. Actually I wasn't sure I had a side. I was stuck somewhere in between, in limbo. At that moment, only this much seemed sure: I would continue to perform my job earnestly and faithfully—and pray that nothing I did, or found, would eventually ruin these mountains, valleys, waters.

Under a sky growing dark with thick, gray clouds I bagged my samples and finished my traverse, then waited for the helicopter to return. Back in camp, I announced my find to the others. They were clearly pleased. This was good news. The crew leader told me to separate out the samples from that area so they could be rushed to a lab for analysis. In the meantime, we would look harder at the area, likely stake some claims to protect the company's interests. "Good job," he said. I nodded my head, not certain I agreed.

DURING THE THREE DAYS I'm camped along Graylime Creek, there's one extended break in the rain. Blue skies and warming, drying sun lure me out of the tent and into the nearby hills. On my ascent of a ridge north of camp on July 22, I am met by strongly gusting wind. Instant bug relief! Not that all the bugs here are bothersome. Besides mosquitoes the most obvious kinds have been bumblebees and brightly colored butterflies. The butterflies, like robins and certain kinds of flowers, seem somehow out of place here, too delicate for the harsh far north climate. But like the flowers they feed upon and pollinate, some species of butterflies thrive in the short arctic summer. Spiders too are common. A few are orb weavers, but most make their living upon the ground. I see them everywhere, scurrying from my approach.

Mammals continue to remain hidden; but birds, like spiders and insects, are everywhere in this high alpine tundra, though in small numbers. Down in the valley bottom are more American golden plovers. They're joined by semipalmated plovers, which may nest on either sandbars or tundra. During the mating season, semipalmated males show off their small but handsome shorebird bodies by crouching low, puffing their feathers, partly opening their wings, spreading their tails, and calling a whistled *chu-weet*.

This ridge, meanwhile, is home to a family of yellow wagtails, sparrow-sized ground birds with olive-gray backs and heads and yellow undersides. My presence alerts the birds, who *tzweep* among themselves as they fly ahead of me. As their name suggests, wagtails flick their long tails up and down while they walk or keep watch on boulders. Like so many other birds that nest here, wagtails travel thousands of miles to reach their arctic summering grounds, most likely from winter homes in southern Asia and the South Pacific Islands. It seems an enormous expenditure of energy and time for a stay that lasts only two to three months. But the Arctic's abundance of insect life—here the much-cursed mosquitoes play a crucial role—make it worth their while. The long-distance migrations of birds are a marvel, but an even greater mystery is this: how did their seasonal journeys across the world evolve? How did the species learn to travel back and forth across the oceans and continents? And for what reasons?

Sam Wright was another who wondered about the vast migration of birds to the Arctic each year. A biologist, philosopher, and writer, Sam homesteaded in the Brooks Range after first traveling here in 1968 with his wife, Billie. Both ended up writing books about their time in the range. Billie's *Four Seasons North* documents one year of their life in the Arctic, while Sam's *Koviashuvik* is more of a meditation on life at their home, whose Native name translates in English to "time and place of joy in the present moment."

Struck by the seasonal abundance of birds in the far north (many more breed on North Slope wetlands than in the mountains), Sam reflected,

> No one knows why the Arctic has such a call for animals that move with the seasons. Perhaps in a warmer age the animal center of population was here and their descendants have the urge to return. Perhaps it is because the north has been remote, a place apart. Or, perhaps it is a response to the country itself, a place where there is a fresh crispness in the air and the sun shines night and day [in summer] but circles the horizon instead of climbing over the zenith so that light and shadow always have the fresh touch of morning.

Thinking about such things, I'm struck by another curious fact: since leaving geology for the writing life, I've become much more interested in the nature of animals and plants than rocks or glaciers. I'm more enthralled by the natural history of spiders and squirrels—not to mention grizzlies and wolves—than the origins and structures of granite spires and limestone hills.

As I make my way up the ridge, I stop now and then to scan land and sky through binoculars. Once, I spot two dark spots circling far overhead: golden eagles, riding thermals. It's a grand afternoon to ride the wind.

Perched on a bench high above Graylime Creek, I spot its confluence with the Anaktuvuk River and also see miles down the east–west-trending Anaktuvuk

Valley. It is broad, green, and gently U-shaped, almost pastoral in appearance, except that the one sign of people is the double-tracked ATV trail. The flanks of limestone hills dip gently toward the river but their ridgetops are contorted into fantastic shapes. Layers of rock once horizontal have been thrust upward to form steeply dipping walls. At their summits are row after row of sharply edged, triangular fangs, the jagged teeth of some primordial rock beast. In another place the limestone has been deeply eroded into a series of near-vertical gullies; five of them join to form a sharp, clawed lizard's foot that points toward the sky.

In all directions are wave upon wave of ridges. Most have been barely touched by humans, some not at all. Far to the west a narrow, pyramidal peak rises above the rest, while to the southeast is a dark, forbidding tower with a small, pale blue glacier on its upper flanks. I suspect it is Mount Doonerak, Marshall's favorite arctic peak. Even from afar it has a looming, ominous nature.

Above the mountains, rafts of billowing clouds float through a deep blue ocean of sky, alternately yielding sun and shade. The day is a beauty, bright and dry, the nicest so far. The terrain adds to my enjoyment of the hike. Even in the valley bottom, the tundra here is drier, smoother, and firmer. There are few tussocks or pools of water in this alpine tundra, which makes for easy walking. Wildflowers seem even more abundant here than in the marshy lowlands, most of them concentrated in moister swales and along creeks. In my journal, I've begun a list of high-alpine species: tall Jacob's ladder, yellow-spotted saxifrage, frigid shooting star, milk vetch, arctic sandwort, dwarf fireweed (also appropriately known as "river beauty"), purple gentian, Richardson's saxifrage (nicknamed "bear flower," because it's a favorite of grizzlies)....In my listing, I wonder if anyone has studied the different plant assemblages here. The diversity is quite remarkable, given the short growing season and often-harsh conditions.

I leave my perch and climb higher up the knife-edged limestone ridge. At forty-six hundred feet (about fifteen hundred feet above camp) I take shelter from the wind behind a boulder—and am greeted by a handful of mosquitoes. What the heck are they doing up here? Apparently surviving on the nectar of hardy alpine wildflowers: blue mountain harebell, white mountain heather, and valerian.

Looking north, I take in parts of the Anaktuvuk's upper valley. The river's source is hidden from here but my map helps me picture its birth in a glacier-carved amphitheater bounded by steep and jagged limestone walls. The stream then splashes down a series of dark green tundra-covered steps that look, from a distance, like cultivated terraces. Pools of water alternate with cascades and waterfalls, some of them hundreds of feet high. A part of me wishes I had the time and energy to take an extended detour and explore the valley's hidden reaches.

Marshall did, in 1938, with three companions. In Anaktuvuk's uppermost basin they found a dirtied remnant glacier.

"We climbed on top of the glacier," Marshall wrote,

> and stopped for an hour at the center where a pile of rock had fallen from the mountain above. It seemed to be the end of the earth or the heart of another earth as we perched on top of this remnant of a long-vanished age. Everything we looked upon was unknown to human gaze. The nearest humans were a hundred and twenty-five miles away, and the civilization of which they constituted the very fringe—civilization remote from nature, artificial, dominated by the exploitation of man by man—seemed unreal, unbelievable. Our present situation seemed also unreal, but that was the unreality...of a remoteness which made it seem as if we had landed miraculously on another planet which throughout all passage of time had been without life.

To give the Nunamiut and other indigenous peoples their due, it's almost certain their travels brought them to this "end of the earth" place long before Marshall. And members of the Nunamiut tribe were likely far closer than he imagined during his wanderings through the Brooks Range.

Returning my attention to this unnamed spine of tundra-fringed rock, I resume my own unhurried explorations. There are moments on this ridge walk when my heart sings. I don't know how else to put it: I feel bursts of joy that I can't explain. Nothing specific seems to trigger these moments; no special insights or revelations accompany them. It is, I think, the entirety of this day, this trip. My spirit has been stirred and lifted by this glorious landscape, Marshall's presence, and memories that stretch back a quarter century. In a receptive mood, I am touched by wildness—and perhaps my own wildness responds.

The wind picks up in late afternoon and clouds the color of bruises build to the south, so I begin a leisurely descent. On my way down I discover dried wolf scat that is rich with hair and small bone fragments. Near the top of this same limestone rib there were caribou antlers. It's a delight to know I have shared the ridge with wolf and caribou. I imagine wolf traveling here, perhaps stalking prey or gazing across the same vast landscape that I've been relishing. Maybe howling to packmates. Without thinking I face west, where the Ambler River flows, and howl my own pleasure.

PART TWO

Ernie Creek passes though the Valley of Precipices, seen from a tundra bench north of the valley.

EIGHT

Seeking the Roots of a Paradox

MY LAST NIGHT CAMPED NEAR THE ARCTIC DIVIDE, WITH CLOUDS still hanging heavily and darkly over the mountains, I go for a late-evening tundra walk. Following Graylime, I hike south, toward the pass that I'll be crossing tomorrow. Along the way another pair of gulls attack me. Screaming, they come in head-high several times before veering off at the last moment. Pole extended upward, I pick up my pace and exit their territory. I have no desire to pick a fight or cause the birds unnecessary upset. Later I cross paths with a semi-palmated plover. He puts on quite a display, though I'm not sure it's intended for me or a female of his kind. Once the plover lifts both wings above his head; more frequently, though, he bends over and shows off his white-feathered bottom. From what I know about plovers, those are likely breeding displays. But I don't notice any mate to impress. Is this a shorebird mooning?

Angling across the tundra, I next come across an impressive tundra excavation, made earlier this year. But how long ago I can't tell. Days? Weeks? I wonder if a modern Nunamiut hunter, or for that matter a talented urban naturalist, would be able to estimate its age. The grizzly digging is more trench than hole, about ten feet long and up to three feet deep where the bear got serious about pulling out a ground squirrel.

I once watched an adult male grizzly go after a squirrel. Totally focused on the job at hand, the bear hurled clods of dirt and stones bigger than my daypack out of the way, as if made of Styrofoam. Within minutes, little more than the bear's shoulder hump was visible in the hole he'd ripped into the rocky soil. Just when it seemed the squirrel must have escaped into its underground system of runways, up one popped. Bad mistake. Zigzagging across the tundra, the squirrel didn't get more than twenty feet before the grizzly jumped out of the hole and pounced on the rodent. Maybe it was a lucky grab. But as one who's chased a squirrel or two, I was mightily impressed by the bear's quickness and agility. It showed, firsthand, the folly of any person trying to outrun a bear.

On my return to camp I feel a deepening sadness. It has less to do with me than something emanating from the landscape itself. Life is hard here, in marginally productive conditions. Yes, there's an explosion of life (particularly mosquitoes) in summer, but that outburst is short-lived. It lasts perhaps two months, maybe less, in some of these high alpine valleys. It's a spare landscape, reminding me of the Arizona desert in that respect. Here, as there, moisture plays a role, but the larger factors are temperature and light. For nearly two-thirds of the year, and longer at the highest elevations, ice and snow blanket these mountains. And in deepest winter the sun disappears for weeks. Then it would surely qualify as a frozen wasteland, in which life as we know it is all but suspended. Plants and insects have gone dormant and most mammals and birds have either migrated to more temperate locales or gone into hiding within the frozen earth. The Brooks Range would indeed seem a lonely, desolate place then.

I'm still struck by the paucity of mammals, big or small. Even the bird life, though ubiquitous, is not abundant except in spots, for instance creek-side willow patches. Life seems to be concentrated in valley bottoms and occasional lush alpine meadows. I'm still close enough to Anaktuvuk that the Nunamiut community could be a factor; subsistence hunting is permitted throughout this park. But I get the sense that these lands and waters near the divide simply don't produce enough food for many animals, especially larger ones, to survive the harsh conditions. Yes, wolves and caribou and grizzlies pass through here, but they don't stay long.

Many people, even Marshall at times, have called this arctic tundra landscape "barren." I don't see it as that. Spare, yes. But *barren* implies sterile, lifeless, empty, unattractive. In summer, at least, the Central Brooks Range is none of those things.

JULY 24. Time to resume my journey. That means breaking camp, something I hate to do in the rain. And it's pouring again. Few people enjoy wilderness packing when soaked, but my dislike is almost neurotic. I suppose it's connected to my desire for comfort, or being in control of my environment. At least my tiny piece of it. Back home, I am what some folks call a "neat freak." Some might add "control freak." They're likely the same. I need order and structure and routine in my life. That's less true out here, but it's not so easy to let go of old, familiar patterns, as my watch monitoring demonstrates.

There is, in fact, good reason for caution in these mountains: the weather out there—beyond my tent walls—is classic hypothermia weather: wet, windy, cold. An accident or mistake that might seem trivial in warm, dry conditions could become life-threatening here. Yet I'm a sensible guy experienced in backcountry travel. I've survived fierce storms high on Denali's slopes and along the Alaska coast. It's reasonable to assume I can travel in this weather and be OK. Yet I feel a knot in my stomach. I think of Marshall and John Muir, two heroes of mine who relished challenging weather and terrain. And I can't forget the Nunamiut, who live out here.

I'm reminded too of Thor Tingey and his three buddies, on their five-hundred-mile trek. Thor was so matter-of-fact about it: "We're wet almost every day, all day. Staying dry is not a possibility." At least not until evening, when they gather wood to build a roaring fire.

Marshall was another who regularly built campfires to dry out and warm up. Such a strategy worked well when few people traveled these mountains; but nowadays, with a steady (if small) stream of backpackers passing through, wood supplies wouldn't last long if adventurers routinely built campfires. Aware of this, park managers encourage visitors to build wood fires only in emergencies. Wishing to limit my impact, I won't build any during my two-week trek. Instead I do my best to stay dry. A good tent here could mean the difference between life and death. The same is true for good judgment. And traveling alone, my margin for error is much narrower. There's no one nearby to help if I should hurt myself, become chilled, or get into other forms of trouble.

Still I wonder: am I such a softy? Do I judge myself too harshly? Is this part of my personal test, my quest? As John Muir once told a tentmate, "It's only water." But water here can kill. Yet I have a bomber tent, dry sleeping bag, backup clothing. Such agonizing! Should I go or stay?

For now, at least, I can afford to hold back, stay in my cocoon. But for how long? Let's do some math: counting today, I have nine days to reach my rendezvous with friends. Assuming I have thirty miles to go, that means four or five days of traveling, at my present pace. Say five days, conservatively. That means four days of staying put. I'd like to use those for exploring, but they could be stay-put weather days if necessary. Perhaps it's best to travel on marginal days and save the beauties for side trips. Or I could put in more miles on the days I'm packing; another couple of hours could cut my travel days down to three. And so it goes, back and forth, back and forth.

I tell myself to embrace the rain and raw cold: it is part of the wilderness I claim to adore. A short meditation helps to resolve my indecision, if only temporarily. For now I'll embrace this alpine storm from my tent. My goals and aspirations are not the same as Marshall's, Muir's, or Tingey's. To be here for now is enough, snuggled in my sleeping bag, reading Marshall and Loren Eiseley's *The*

Immense Journey, a marvelous book that interweaves science with Eiseley's own brand of mysticism.

To cut down on weight and bulk, I tore a few key sections out of Marshall's *Alaska Wilderness*, though the few ounces I saved there were more than counterbalanced by supplies I didn't really need, the fishing gear being a prime example. Eiseley's book is small and light enough, yet filled with engaging, provocative stories, that I stuffed the entire thing into my pack. An anthropologist by training, and a visionary and storyteller by nature, he's among the handful of authors I return to time and again, for delight and inspiration and guidance. As one who became a bird enthusiast relatively late in life—and also one who is drawn to the mysteries of life—I count two of his essays among my all-time favorites: "The Judgment of the Birds" and "The Bird and the Machine." If Marshall has helped me better understand the importance of wilderness, Eiseley has shown me the value of letting the imagination run free and the possibilities that open up when "in the flow of ordinary events" a person can recognize "the point at which the mundane world gives way to quite another dimension."

So, curled up with my books and journals, I choose patience and caution over ... what? Daring? Reckless abandon? Adventurousness? Maybe I can go easier with myself, recognize my limits and strengths. Maybe I'm closer to Thoreau than Marshall in my desire for wildness. Now there's a thought. But from what I know about the two, I'm more like Marshall on the homebody–backcountry traveler spectrum. For all my small worries, I enjoy journeys into deeper wilderness. In fact I relish such adventuring, while Henry David Thoreau seemed plenty happy staying close to home, even when "alone" at Walden Pond; and he was clearly discomfited when faced by the rigors of exploring Maine's Mount Katahdin, as Roderick Nash points out in his provocative and influential book, *Wilderness and the American Mind*.

Though I'm not a student of Thoreau and have read only bits and pieces of his writing, I recognize his importance to nature writing, our society's rekindled appreciation of wild nature (including our own), and the American wilderness-preservation movement. Later, back in Anchorage, I will look up that passage of Nash's because it illuminates both Thoreau's importance to the wilderness movement and his own ambivalent relationship with wilderness. It reads, in part:

> While Thoreau was unprecedented in his praise of the American wilderness, his enthusiasm was not undiluted; some of the [culture's] old antipathy and fear lingered even in *his* thought. Encountering the Maine woods underscored it. Thoreau left Concord in 1846 for the first of three trips to northern Maine. His expectations were high because he hoped to find genuine, primeval America. But contact with real wilderness in Maine affected him far differently than had

the idea of wilderness in Concord [Massachusetts]. Instead of coming out of the woods with a deepened appreciation of the wilds, Thoreau felt a greater respect for civilization and realized the necessity of balance.

The wilderness of Maine shocked Thoreau. He reported it as "even more grim and wild than you had anticipated, a deep and intricate wilderness." Climbing Mount Katahdin, he was struck by its contrast to the kind of scenery he knew around Concord. The wild landscape was "savage and dreary" and instead of his usual exultation in the presence of nature, he felt "more alone than you can imagine."…To Thoreau, clinging to the bare rocks of Katahdin's summit, wilderness seemed "a place for heathenism and superstitious rites—to be inhabited by men nearer of kin to the rocks and wild animals than we."…Identity itself had vanished. It was a rude awakening for a man who in another mood had wondered "what shall we do with a man who is afraid of the woods, their solitude and darkness? What salvation is there for him?"

It's been pointed out to me that not everyone agrees with Nash's interpretation, but to me Thoreau's uneasiness is clear in his description of Katahdin, which reads in part,

Vast, Titanic, inhuman Nature has got him at a disadvantage, caught him alone, and pilfers him of some of his divine faculty. She does not smile on him as in the plains. She seems to say sternly, why came ye here before your time? This ground is not prepared for you. Is it not enough that I smile in the valleys? I never made this soil for thy feet, this air for thy breathing, these rocks for thy neighbors. I cannot pity nor fondle thee here, but forever relentlessly thee hence to where I am kind. Why seek me where I have not called thee, and then complain because you find me but a stepmother?

I understand why Thoreau, overwhelmed and humbled by his ascent of Katahdin, might associate such wilderness with pagan rites and worship. Yet it has also been a place of revelation for Judaic and Christian prophets, and Christ himself. And I see the vanishing of "identity itself," the dissolving of personal boundaries and a merging with greater creation, as a powerfully hopeful thing. It's something that mystics—including those of the Christian tradition—have celebrated across the centuries.

Two other aspects of Thoreau's nature and philosophy resonate strongly with me. First, his love of and need for solitude. In that respect, I'm much more like him than Marshall, who was clearly more of a people person. Second, Thoreau sought out, and reveled in, "a sort of border life," that edge between wilderness and civilization. And he believed that the best sort of lifestyle was one that permitted regular passages between the two. I absolutely agree. One of the things I love most about my adopted hometown is its abundance of such borders or edges (something I'll return to later).

Whether I'm more like Thoreau or Marshall in my approach to wilderness and life, one thing is certain: I am not, and have never claimed to be, an extreme-adventure wannabe. Perhaps I am the fair-weather trekker. Hmmm. That might fit. Here's something else that might fit. What keeps drawing me back to the Brooks Range is not the thrill of outdoor adventure as much as the opportunity to "lose" myself, so that I may gain something much greater.

Here, then, is the paradox: I am a man who seeks comfort and day-to-day routine, yet I've also chosen the uncertainties and anxieties of a freelance writer's life. And I'm drawn out of my comfort zone by an even greater need: to be immersed in wild nature. I suspect it's a way of letting go, like meditation; a way to escape the ego, become part of something greater. It's a way to heal, to open up to mystery, to touch—or at least approach—the divine. In that, I know I'm not alone. Many of my friends, including some who are Christians, have told me they feel the most spiritual, the closest to God, whatever that concept means to them, when out in wild nature.

By moving into more-than-human nature, I most closely approach that threshold between the mundane world and what Eiseley calls "quite another dimension." Immersion can happen at home, in the back or front yard, with chickadees or spiders. But there are times when I have to go deeper. And there is simply no place that has touched me—or released me—like the Brooks Range.

Given all this, I am drawn to consider the roots of my behaviors and wild desires and the start of the path that led me to Alaska's arctic wilderness. This means traveling across the continent and through decades of time, to my first homeland, Trumbull, Connecticut. There, in my early years, I moved back and forth between two great influences: the Lutheran church and wild nature.

NINE

A Sheltered Childhood

IN RECENT YEARS, WHEN DISCUSSING SPIRITUAL MATTERS OR MY pagan tendencies or the religious baggage I carry around, I've sometimes joked that I'm a "recovering Lutheran." It almost always draws a laugh. Many of the people in the circles I inhabit (tending to be green and liberal) can relate. But as a new acquaintance pointed out not long ago, it would be more accurate to say I'm a recovering fundamentalist Christian. She understood the distinction, having been raised in a righteous Roman Catholic family. I got it, too, as soon as she spoke the words. Like my parents and siblings, all my other relatives, and nearly all my childhood friends, I was raised in the fundamentalist tradition. I was taught to believe that the Bible is the literal Word of God. There is one way to paradise, and it's spelled out in the Scriptures. No matter that Christ died for all of us and our sins, you've got to believe in the Triune God, Father, Son, and Holy Ghost, to earn a ticket to heaven. Only true believers—that is, true Christians—are heaven-bound. Everyone else is headed to hell.

It was a very strict yet very easy to understand black-and-white sort of belief system. No matter how saintly a life you led, I was taught, if you didn't believe that Jesus died for your sins, you were a gonner, damned for eternity. Of course that meant an awful lot of people were damned.

For eighteen years I didn't question any of this, simply because it was all that I knew in my sheltered, insular existence. My family's life revolved around the church and our Lutheran beliefs. Dad served as a deacon and both parents taught Sunday school or Bible classes at one time or another. Along with my older sister, Karen, and younger brother, Dave, I regularly attended both church and Sunday school and sang in the choir. As if that weren't enough, all three of us attended Zion Lutheran School, which had three teachers for the one hundred or so students who attended grades one through eight in the small, red-brick schoolhouse. At home we prayed at all our meals, before bed, and sometimes upon waking up (we often forgot that one in our rush to get ready for the day).

Off and on we also gathered weekly in the family den for Bible lessons. Dad would read from a chapter in the Bible; then we'd turn to a lesson guide and he'd ask us a series of questions, both for discussion and to be sure that we'd been paying attention. I didn't particularly like that ritual, since it usually cut into TV time. And, to be honest, I thought we did plenty with all our churchgoing and schooling.

Of course the most important holidays were religious. And the two biggest celebrations, Christmas and Easter, were preceded by weeks of preparation, during Advent and Lent. That meant additional church services, choir practice, school skits, on and on.

Beyond my immediate family, nearly everyone I knew through the end of grade school was either Lutheran or Catholic. My relatives belonged to Lutheran congregations in either Bridgeport or Trumbull or—on my mother's side of the family—in Waterbury. All my parent's best friends and closest acquaintances were Lutherans, while all but one of mine were Christians. Only Billy Rosenberg, who lived a mile or so up the street, belonged to the Jewish faith. A friendly kid who joined us for sports and occasional romps through the woods, he nevertheless was considered different and maybe a little suspect, simply because of his religion.

Besides being Christian, nearly everyone I knew was white and had European roots. Most were second-, third-, or fourth-generation Americans whose parents, grandparents, or great-grandparents had come to the United States from Germany. In my case, both sets of grandparents had come to America in the early 1900s. So these were my people: white, Germanic, Lutheran. Hard-working, patriotic, and religious, they tended to see things as black or white, right or wrong.

I DON'T WISH to imply that my Lutheran upbringing was oppressive. Not consciously, anyway. It was strict, yes; but once you knew the rules, you had an inside track to heaven. Understanding this, I was a good Lutheran lad. And especially in my early years I was an absolutely devout believer. I was such a believer, I didn't understand how anyone could *not* believe that Jesus was God and had died for our sins. Christianity's Triune God was a simple and obvious fact of life, as real to me as any tree or frog or person. I had a child's faith in Lutheran things unseen because that was all I'd known since my earliest days on earth.

As an adult and fallen Christian, I better understand how fundamentalist notions of right and wrong can breed intolerance, hatred, discrimination, even wars and other atrocities. And looking back I can see the undercurrent of judging and prejudice that colored my clan's perceptions and relationships with non-Lutherans and especially heathens. My parents sometimes made fun of my Catholic friends' beliefs and behaviors. But at least they were Christians. Jews, on the other hand, were both damned to hell and resented for their business practices. "You can't trust them," Dad complained. "They'll take every penny you've got." It didn't help that a Jewish neighbor had taken my father to court and ruined his construction business, when Dad's only crimes were being less talented as a businessman than a carpenter and too naive in his dealings with clients. As for worshipers of Islam or Buddhism or other Eastern faiths: they were so different as to seem alien, otherworldly. Certainly they were far beyond the realm of my small world.

Looking back now, I think ignorance, more than intolerance, defined my boyhood community's relationship with other cultures and ways of being (though of course the two are related). Ignorance, and pity. Imagine all those poor heathen souls, damned to hell.

MY LIFE WAS sheltered in other ways. Well-meaning but overly protective parents, Mom and Dad kept a tight rein on their kids. They had strict rules about where we could go even in our semirural, middle-class neighborhood, where everybody knew everybody else and crimes of any sort were rare. For years—it seemed like ages—we were forbidden to cross Old Town Road without Mom's express permission, while my buddies the Wallace twins, Barry and Brian, and Tommy Seperack had the run of the neighborhood.

Even worse, we were often kept inside the house when friends were playing outside. One memory is especially strong. It is a warm and bright summer evening. I'm standing at my sister's window, which faces the open lot where my friends and I play softball and, beyond that, the house and yard where my closest relatives live. Resting my head against the fine-mesh screen, I look with longing toward Uncle Peach's home, where he is out in his garden and his two boys—both of them younger than me—are squealing and laughing and racing around the yard. I am jealous of my cousins and tortured by their laughter. But more than that, I am heartbroken to be trapped indoors on such a gorgeous night. I'm so angry at my parents and hate their unreasonable rules. How can they keep us inside on such an evening, when all of nature beckons? I wish I could live with my aunt and uncle, if only for a while. I'm sure there were many nights like that, confused by arbitrary rules, wishing for release.

Another memorable summer evening, my parents' concern kept me from going fishing with Uncle Peach. The night was rainy and cool and Mom worried that I might catch a cold. I pleaded and sulked and tried to win Dad's support, but he would only say, "Your mother has spoken." Being forced to stay home was bad enough. But later that night, Peach stopped by on his way home to show us a stringer full of bass and trout. Following him into our kitchen were his two boys, Jim and John, nearly four and six years younger than me, respectively. I was crushed, from both disappointment and embarrassment.

Mom was the household's number-one worrywart, the one who fretted about our safety. I'm sure that one of the reasons she kept me locked inside so often was my fragile health. For most of my childhood and into my early twenties, I suffered from asthma and allergies. They were severe enough that, for many years, doctor visits were a dreaded but routine part of my life.

I was allergic to all sorts of things, from cats and dogs to eggs, penicillin, tomatoes, and chocolate. I also had really bad hay fever. Especially when I was little, Mom would keep me inside for days at a time, for my own good of course. At school she'd instruct the teachers to keep me in the classroom during recess. Now and then, softened by my tearful pleas, she'd relent and let me run outdoors. All too often, I'd go into sneezing fits. Eyes watering and itching, chest wheezing, nose stuffed so much I could barely breathe, I'd stumble back into the house wondering why I'd been so cursed. Didn't God know how much I loved being outdoors? Why wouldn't He heal me? Was this some test, like Job had undergone?

NOT MANY OF my Lutheran friends and relatives were what you'd call enthusiastic nature-loving folks, the most notable exceptions being Uncle Peach and his good friend and fishing buddy, John Trotz. Dad's younger brother loved to hunt and garden and camp. But more than anything, Peach loved to fish. A guy whose moods swung back and forth between gentle sweetness and crotchety meanness, Uncle Peach loved to laugh and joke and tease and touch. Sometimes he'd grab you in a great big bear hug. Or he'd squeeze your leg or pinch your cheek, or affectionately rub your head. Though occasionally he'd drive me to tears or embarrass me with his behavior, Peach was my favorite uncle. He was also my first outdoors mentor.

When I was in sixth grade, Uncle Peach invited me to go trout fishing with him and Johnny Trotz. Talk about excitement. Though I'd done some pan-fish angling with Peach and his kids, this was the first time I'd join the adults for some serious fishing. I could barely sleep the night before the opening of Connecticut's sportfishing season. Waking up in the dark, I quickly dressed and gobbled down a breakfast prepared by Mom. Then I waited anxiously by the den window, until the two old fishermen drove up in Uncle John's sedan. Rushing into the chill, calm predawn air of an April morning, I grabbed a seat in back and we drove to Old Mine Park, where dozens of anglers crowded the edges of a pond-sized pool of water, anticipating the six a.m. start. As we waited, Peach warned me there were bound to be tangles and coached me to be patient. He also shared a few sips from his thermos of coffee, the dark adult drink lightened and sweetened by lots of cream and sugar.

At precisely six, people started tossing their lines into the water. Right away, men to the left and right of me (nearly everyone at the hole was male) started hauling in the hungry, naive, hatchery-reared brownies. My uncle almost exclusively used live bait and on this morning we cast nightcrawlers into the dark waters. A few nights before, I'd gone nightcrawler hunting with Uncle Peach. It was a back-aching but necessary and satisfying part of the ritual.

Despite my jitters and inexperience, I landed a trout or two, to the "attaboy" praise of Peach and John. I couldn't have been prouder. Or happier. In a way, this was one of my few guided initiations into manhood. All of it was grand, from the late-night search for nightcrawlers to the fidgety night before, the early-morning rising, the fish stories and camaraderie, the catch of trout and congratulations from uncle and stranger alike, the coffee and sandwiches, the showing off of the catch back home, even the cleaning, and then, finally, the eating. It was the first time that I'd played the role of provider.

That was the start of a relationship unlike any other I'd had, one that lasted into my late teens. Every summer for six or seven years, Uncle Peach and John Trotz and I would fish streams and lakes and reservoirs, later to be joined by my brother Dave and Peach's two sons in what was an exclusively male fraternity.

For all that he taught me about fishing, Uncle Peach gave me mixed messages about the value of other life forms. To him, fish came in three distinct categories: game fish, bait fish, and trash fish. As with religion, things were pretty much black-and-white, with only occasional shades of gray, like white lies. Trout, bass, pickerel, and even catfish were desirable. Sunnies and goldfish and especially carp were trash. Catch a carp and you tossed it in the grass or on the dirt, to flop around until it suffocated to death. Or, as we kids learned to do, you might instead toss a sunfish or carp as high as you could, then wait for the loud "smack" as the fish hit the water, or the thud of its body pounding the ground.

As I got older, it didn't seem right that some fish were good and others bad, just because we didn't like their taste or they weren't good "fighters." In the same way, it began to bother me that some people were doomed to hell, simply because they'd been born into a different faith or culture. Mom and Dad would tell me they could convert to Christianity and be saved. But what if you never got that chance? Or what if you grew up in a family that fervently believed its religion to be the true one? What about somebody like Billy Rosenberg? How easy would it be for Jesus to reach into Billy's heart, when he lived in a family of devout Jews?

No one else seemed troubled by such things, so I tried not to worry about it. At least those closest to me would be saved. Still, it seemed that life wasn't nearly so simple or clear as those around me tried to make it. Little by little, I began to see the world in fuzzy shades of gray.

TEN

Across the Divide and
into the Valley of Precipices

AFTER ALL MY AGONIZING—DO I LEAVE GRAYLIME CREEK OR DO I stay?—the rain weakens to a light mist by midafternoon on July 24, prompting me to pack my stuff. Once I'm moving, the drizzle inevitably becomes a heavier, soaking rain. Some of the wetness penetrates the rain gear, but I stay warm enough in my synthetic shirt and long johns. Now that I'm moving I feel energized, perhaps an influence of the cool, brisk wind.

After crossing ankle-deep Graylime Creek I head for the divide. A gradual ascent of two hundred feet across easy-walking alpine tundra brings me to thirty-five-hundred-foot Ernie Pass, a well-defined ridge separating Graylime and Ernie Creeks. It's as if a giant mole had tunneled its way across the tundra, lifting the land into an undulating, moundlike wall. On the one side, Graylime's waters flow north and west into the Anaktuvuk River, then the Colville, and finally the Arctic Ocean's Beaufort Sea. Ernie Creek feeds the Koyukuk River, which in turn feeds the Yukon, flowing southwesterly to the North Pacific's Bering Sea. Besides dividing north- and south-draining streams, Ernie Pass roughly marks a political boundary. From here on, I'll be trekking through designated wilderness.

I take one final look to the north, offer a good-bye salute, then descend into the broad, green, soggy bowl of upper Ernie Creek. Bounded by gray and brown hills, the saucer-shaped basin is covered by a tundra quagmire. Boots and feet are once more doomed to sogginess: large expanses of white-tufted cottongrass, a sure sign of wetlands, spread before me.

Resigned to my fate, I plunge ahead. I suffer no complete dunkings into icy puddles as on my first day, but rather a gradual soaking from rain and wet grasses, sedges, knee-high willows, wildflowers, and spongy carpets of mosses that ooze H_2O. I plod in my usual way through tussocky meadows, but speed across occasional mounds of higher, drier tundra. I can almost imagine myself maintaining Marshall's three-mile-per-hour pace on these dry fingers, but in truth I rarely go that fast even on flat, hardened trails with no pack on my back. Still, for the first time, there are stretches when I forget my burden and body aches. Can I really be getting used to this packing? Never!

As advised by ranger Mike Haubert, I stay on Ernie's northeastern flank and well above the creek, which a mile below the divide plunges into a winding, narrow, and steep-walled canyon. Two miles beyond the pass I come to a side creek. It too has cut deeply into the area's sedimentary rocks. To avoid a steep descent followed by a strenuous climb out, I sidehill upstream to a place less severely notched. Crossing the tundra and gravel slope isn't difficult, but a slip on the slickened grasses would send me cascading one hundred feet or more into a boulder-filled creek bottom, to arrive bruised and battered—or worse—so I step gingerly.

I'm out of the side creek, crossing a tundra meadow, when a hole opens in thick clouds to the west. A burst of early-evening sunlight shimmers blindingly on a massive slab of bare, black rock that is hundreds of feet high. The meadow in which I stand is equally breathtaking, a riotous mix of lush green grasses and white, yellow, pink, lavender, blue, and purple wildflowers, including some of my favorites: frigid shooting stars, black-tipped fuchsia flowers that rocket above green leaves, and purple monkshood. For the first time on this trip I also find Alaska's state flower. Thick clusters of alpine forget-me-nots give parts of the meadow a sky-blue cast.

The loveliest tundra "rock gardens" are usually in protected swales and this one is among the most gorgeous I've encountered. So delicately beautiful, yet incredibly hardy, the flowers bring vibrant color to even the grayest, most dismal summer days.

I continue on from "Gorge Creek" (my name) toward Grizzly Creek, where in 1929 Robert Marshall shot a grizzly that wandered into camp. His partner Al Retzlaf had gone to do some gold panning despite a drenching rain, while Marshall stayed put, content, on that soaking morning, to read *Diana of the Crossways*. Shortly before noon, the men's two horses began snorting loudly, so Marshall peeked outside and saw them "dashing hell-bent toward the tent, hardly hampered by their hobbles." Marshall tried to calm them with sugar and gentle strokes, but they remained agitated. Suddenly, he later recounted, "Bronco gave a tremendous leap, tore completely out of my grasp, and started like fury down the valley." He managed to hold onto Brownie, though he was dragged across the slick ground. While clinging to the horse, he looked toward the hill above camp. Busting through the brush, some two hundred yards away, was "an immense, whitish-brown humped mass" followed by a second, smaller grizzly.

Still holding Brownie, Marshall managed to grab a rifle from the tent. With the grizzly continuing its approach and the horse becoming ever more agitated, he decided to fire a warning shot:

> I could not take aim at the bear without dropping the halter and losing Brownie, so I shot from my waist without aiming, still holding the halter tightly. I thought I would scare the bear, but the shot must have echoed, because the grizzly seemed to imagine it came from behind him. Anyway, he proceeded with doubled speed toward the tent. Now I knew there was no choice but to let Brownie go and shoot in earnest. I hit the bear, but not fatally and he turned around and retreated into the hills. The other bear had already disappeared.

Marshall spent the next hour and a half trying to coax the two horses back to camp, finally helped in that task by Retzlaf, returned from his prospecting. The grizzlies never returned and the men made no attempt to track the wounded bear.

MY PATH BRINGS me to a broad, rolling plateau, several hundred feet above the valley floor. The bench tilts slightly upward toward the south, so I can't tell what's beyond it. When I finally reach that southern edge, I am stunningly greeted by Marshall's famed "Valley of Precipices." Seven hundred feet below me, Ernie Creek meanders in braided channels through a steep-walled enclosure that rises more than twenty-five hundred feet to summits shrouded in clouds. The northeast wall of hills is higher, but those on the southwest—the precipices—thrust more abruptly and starkly above the valley bottom. The contrast is deepened by the green valley's pastoral nature and the black, brooding aspect of the cliffs.

Marshall believed the Valley of Precipices surpassed "the grandeur of Yosemite." I'm not sure about that; the precipices, though steep, are not vertical or overhanging like some of Yosemite's granite walls. But they are grandly spectacular in their own right. Instead of sheer, monolithic rock cliffs, their "faces" consist of black, layered sedimentary rocks (Marshall called them slates) that rise, in stair-step fashion, to jagged tops eroded into towers, turrets, and spires. Mosses, lichens, and even some tiny meadows cling to the cliffs, giving their dark visage a green, whiskered look. Clouds and a bend in the hills prevent me from seeing all of the precipices, and the map's tightly squeezed contour lines suggest those farther downstream may be even steeper. Still, I'm not sure that entering this valley along its floor from the south, as Marshall did, could be any more startling than from here, where the view has exceeded my expectations—a rare thing. More distant knife-edge ridges and pyramidal peaks visible from this perch only add to the terrain's rugged aspect.

Two other magnificent watersheds open up from my vantage point and I can't imagine a more sensational seat to take it all in. To the southwest is Kenunga Creek, where a narrow cascade drops several hundred feet in a series of waterfalls. Marshall estimated the falls at fifteen hundred feet high, but the map shows it to be closer to six hundred or seven hundred. This unnamed cascade is a gleaming silver necklace on the mountain's black body. Farther up the valley are immense slab-sided walls to six thousand feet or more, their dark cliff faces now powdered white with fresh snow.

Immediately below me and to my left, Grizzly Creek cuts a gorge through conglomerates and other sedimentary rocks. Canyon walls have dropped huge boulders, some the size of trucks, into its narrow bottom. Flushed with recent rains, the creek tumbles wildly through a narrow slot, a froth of whitewater. Far up the valley, yet another black, brooding tower of a peak juts into the gray sky, its uppermost reaches dusted white.

I'd love to camp here, to wake in the morning to this miracle of a panorama, or stay up late, reveling in its harsh, wild beauty. But a fierce wind howls across the bench and I can't find a nook that would provide sure shelter if another violent storm were to move through. So I'll continue down to the valley bottom. But first I spend some time drinking in this ominously vertiginous landscape, made even more dramatic when golden sunlight breaks through, first lighting up Ernie Creek valley, then some of the eastern hills and the steep-sided cliffs that hem Kenunga Creek. I want to imprint these images, these moments of exquisite beauty, on film as well as brain. I race around with my camera, ignoring the cold that penetrates my clothes and body, even as my fingers and hands go numb and my body shivers in the biting wind.

In my racing, I slip on a wet, lichen-slickened rock, but somehow maintain my balance. I could have easily cracked into one of the many boulders here and turned an ankle, broken a bone, smacked my head. I force myself to slow down. For all my earlier anxieties, I now risk hypothermia in my frenetic state. My shivering body tells me I have in fact entered its earliest stages. Hood drawn, rain parka zipped tight, I still feel the wind's cooling effects. I need my wool cap, fleece gloves, and jacket. Or I need to descend. Because it's already evening and I don't know how long it will take to find a decent campsite, I choose to move on. Reluctantly, I work my way down gullies and scree slopes to Grizzly Creek. There I face a new obstacle.

The frothing stream I saw from above is, up close, a roaring, menacing rush of runoff that bounces wildly among conglomerate boulders. Normally easy to ford, the rain-swollen creek with its boulders and holes now makes for a dangerous crossing, one I hadn't anticipated. A small slip in that torrent and a foot could easily get wedged beneath a boulder. I lay down my pack and seek a way across, first two hundred yards upstream, then several hundred yards downstream, until dense stands of willow halt my progress. After much searching I find a place where the river widens. It is shallow here across most of its width and largely boulder-free. Only at the far side are there larger rocks and deeper water.

I make a test run without pack or radio, which I've been wearing on a separate belt around my waist. To keep the radio protected—again the sky is pelting rain—I place it beneath the pack cover. The creek's shockingly cold water comes up to midcalf and splashes above my knees. Some small rocks roll beneath my feet. But I go slowly and, using my trekker's pole, stay balanced. Along the far bank the creek rises above my knees and pushes harder at my legs. But one more step and I'm across. I retreat, get my pack, plunge in, and repeat my fording, heart thumping in a now-familiar way.

Only when I take off the pack do I notice a loose lump inside its rain cover and recognize my incredible mistake—and amazingly good fortune. Why my loosely tucked radio didn't fall out, I can't explain. Such relief! It would have been a hugely horrible error to lose the radio, especially with others expecting me to have it. I've made a couple of blunders today and survived them without serious consequences.

By now it is after eight p.m. (yes, I'm back to occasionally checking my watch). I still have to find a campsite, set up the tent, put on warmer, drier clothes, and make dinner. I finish eating at ten thirty, one of my latest meals ever. Savoring the last of tonight's chocolate rations, I review the day and feel encouraged. I've survived a couple scares, packed six miles in sometimes heavy rain and high winds, put up my tent in a light shower, and somehow kept things dry.

After dinner I take a short walk, scan the landscape with binoculars, and pick a few blueberries from scraggly bushes that hug the ground; the tundra fruits are just now ripening and more sour than sweet. I retire to the tent shortly before midnight, to end a memorable day that had moments of terror, moments of grace. And the rain keeps falling. Will the sun ever return, except for brief glimpses? It better if I'm going to ford the North Fork…

ELEVEN

A Place of Refuge

MORNING BRINGS MORE MIST, FOG, AND WIND. AND COLD: MY minithermometer reads in the low forties. This will be another rest day, mostly tent-bound.

The landscape voices I've heard off and on throughout the trip are growing stronger. Last night I was sure I heard voices chanting a Celtic song. Mostly female, with a deeper male voice occasionally blending in. The songs were more unnerving than pleasant and I imagined arctic Sirens, calling to lure me into the frigid waters of the creeks below camp. This river-crossing stuff isn't playing on my mind too much, is it?

The songs weren't just a flash and gone. They lingered. What are these conversations, these songs I'm hearing? Creek music, I suppose, emanating from the pulsing, churning stream water. Sam Wright sometimes heard creek voices too, during his homesteading days in the Brooks Range: "The voices of Koviashuvik Creek could be heard like the voices of children on a playground when voices are heard but not the words. Everywhere voices can be heard, but not the words."

A good friend, William, has shared stories with me about his listening to trees. Another, Margot, has communicated with ants and trees and other beings. The experiences of both would be written off as weird or woo-woo or just plain wacky by mainstream society, yet I sense truth in what they share with me even if I don't fully understand them. What might they say about this?

It's the most natural thing, to want to connect with nature. For as much as we ignore or deny the fact, we are of nature. It's our original, most deep-rooted home. And it's a miraculous place, with all sorts of marvelous beings. When we're new to the world, I think we sense, we intuit, the wonder and mystery all around us. But as we grow older, we seem to lose that understanding, and, as Loren Eiseley writes, "tend to take [the world] for granted." This is especially true in modern high-tech cultures like ours, where we keep ourselves busy with daily routines, "all the time imagining our surroundings and ourselves quite ordinary creatures."

In our society, and increasingly around the world, there's a large and growing disconnect between humans and wild nature. This is old news, of course. Visionary Americans have been telling us so since at least the latter half of the nineteenth century. Yet it continues to happen, at what seems to be an accelerating pace: we grow more and more separate from the natural world as our attention increasingly turns toward the technological wonders and distractions of our time: TV and cell phones, movies and videos, computer games and the Internet, snowmobiles and jet skis, cars and trucks and SUVs. We go from home to car to office or shopping center or health club or movie theater, barely noticing the wider, more-than-human world around us. It's not just in the cities. Even a place like Anaktuvuk Pass has satellite dishes, televisions, and computers with Internet links. The Nunamiut regularly travel on ATVs and snowmobiles and jets.

Kids everywhere spend less and less time outdoors. They learn less and less about the nature of the places where they live. As Richard Louv's *Last Child in the Woods* makes clear, today's culture is in many ways pushing children away from direct contact with nature. The result is what he calls "nature-deficit disorder," which in turn can lead to all sorts of associated problems, including childhood obesity, attention disorders, and depression. Perhaps most importantly, he argues,

> as the young spend less and less of their lives in natural surroundings, their senses narrow, physiologically and psychologically, and this reduces the richness of human experience.... Reducing that deficit—healing the broken bond between our young and nature—is in our self-interest, not only because aesthetics or justice demands it, but also because our mental, physical, and spiritual health depends upon it. *The health of the earth is at stake as well* [emphasis mine]. How the young respond to nature, and how they raise their own children, will shape the configurations and conditions of our cities, homes—our daily lives.

THE "NATURAL WORLD" was an essential part of my boyhood in Trumbull, a place of refuge, play, and healing, except my buddies and I didn't call it that. To us it was the outdoors. Or even the outside. "I'm going outside, Ma" had all sorts of meanings. It usually meant that homework or house chores had been done, which in turn meant play. And freedom. Escape from the rules and demands of adults. Escape from the tyranny of judgments.

This, then, was my world, as best as I can reconstruct it more than four decades later. My family and I lived on Old Town Road, a roughly east–west street that was a dividing line of sorts. On the south side of the road was Bridgeport, one of Connecticut's largest urban communities, a large industrial city of nearly 160,000 people in the 1950s. To the north—my side of the street—was Trumbull, a still largely rural-suburban community. I liked to tell people that Old Town Road marked the edge of rural New England; not exactly true then, and not true at all now. But our neighborhood did have a country feel to it, especially in the fifties. Ours was among the first houses put up along Old Town Road, or at least the mile-long stretch that I would come to consider my home turf. Dad and Peach built it with their father, just as they built Peach and Grandpa's houses, a row of three Sherwonit homes separated by large empty lots.

Looking back now, two aspects of that neighborhood stand out. First, all of its families were white and middle-class and nearly all were second- and third-generation Christian Americans of Irish or German descent. Second, the neighborhood had lots of open space in which to play. For starters, there were the empty lots on either side of our own spacious property. Even better, our backyard abutted acres and acres of New England forest. "The Woods," we called it. Or "Sherwonit's Woods," as many of the neighborhood kids called it. In fact much of it *was* "ours." Dad inherited nearly two dozen acres of forested land when his father died from a heart attack in 1954, though he'd eventually lose most of it in business dealings that went bad. By my teens, much of those woodlands beyond our house was gone, cut down and replaced by new roads and neighborhoods.

The Woods was open forest, with stands of oak, maple, and pine intermixed with grassy meadows and thick patches of briars and brush. It was hardly pristine; parts of the forest, if not all of it, were second growth, crosshatched by stone walls and trails that marked past human uses. Bounded by neighborhoods and the Merritt Parkway, our patch of New England woods didn't harbor many large animals. I don't ever recall seeing even a deer or coyote, let alone a bear or bobcat. Still, it was wild and unruly, a place beyond the ordinary, with snakes and skunks and hawks and foxes, a place filled with the possibility of adventure. There, hidden from the oversight of parents, we built forts, played war games, staged battles between cowboys and Indians; we climbed trees and the rocky ledges we called mountains, hunted for snakes and salamanders, searched for crystals in the gray, lichen-covered rocks.

For me, the Woods was something of a scary place, too, at least in its depths. Whether it was a fear instilled in me by my parents' worries or something of my own creation, I was afraid I might get lost in the woods if I strayed too far from the paths and glades we knew. I never admitted my fear to anyone, particularly my friends. That would have set me up for unmerciful teasing, the label of scaredy-cat. For all that I loved the woods, I never ventured far into it alone. I stayed on familiar paths and played at well-known haunts. And when I went with friends, I rarely took the lead if we ventured into unknown territory. Barry and Brian Wallace, especially, seemed to have a knack for cutting through the woods, taking a shortcut through unfamiliar ground, and finding their way back home. I envied that and hoped to God they wouldn't ask me to take a turn up front.

Back then, neither the Wallaces nor I would ever have imagined that Billy Sherwonit, the timid explorer, would eventually travel to our nation's Last Frontier and go deep into the wilderness, on trips that might last days or weeks (or, as geologist, even months), while the Wallace twins would stay put in an increasingly urban East.

By its simple, nearby presence, the Woods added drama and adventure to our lives, often in the form of snakes. I hunted snakes not to kill them, but for the fun of the chase and to keep them a while and admire. The flicking tongue, the piercing eyes, the sleek, slithering, scaled body—all of these gave snakes a sort of ominous beauty. Although serpents were a metaphor for temptation and evil in the Bible—or perhaps partly because of that—I found them fantastically alluring.

WE YOUNG ADVENTURERS were blessed with another nearby wild place to explore. Not much farther than a long stone's throw from our driveway was a small channel that dissected the large empty lot separating our yard from Uncle Peach's. It also drained the Swamp, a boggy place of mud, trees, reeds, frogs, snakes, catfish, crawfish, ducks, and snapping turtles.

The Swamp wasn't very large; just a few hundred feet long and maybe a hundred wide. (I suspect that much of it had already been filled in by the road construction and land clearing that opened up our neighborhood.) But it was so different from anything else in my small world, it held a special allure. It held mystery. That was especially so in summer, when the bog's waters and muck were rich in strange critters. It also presented some danger, I suspect. My mom certainly believed so. Time and again she warned her boys to "Stay away!" But the call was too great and we prowled the Swamp's edges, hunting for animals.

Now and then I would push inside its boundaries, but never very far. The small islands of dry ground were too few and too far apart to use as stepping-stones; and while much of the water was shallow, the pond's muddy bottom was too soft and deep for easy walking, even in rubber boots. Our parents warned us there were places where the mud could suck us right in, like quicksand. Plus, the Swamp held snapping turtles. Uncle Peach caught a huge one in his net and hauled it onto his lawn while a crowd gathered round. He held a broom handle in front of the turtle, bigger than a watermelon, to show us its strength. The snapper didn't break the handle, but once he grasped it he wouldn't let go, even when shot with a .22. Peach had to shoot the snapper several times before it would die.

In winter, when the Swamp froze over, its inner parts were easy to explore. We skated there, among the trees and tiny islands, stood around bonfires that our parents sometimes built, played hockey and other games like steal the flag. But the Swamp itself was dormant then; it didn't really come alive until spring and summer. That's when it was the greatest fun to me.

Mostly I just wanted to catch things, and plenty of life forms inhabited the Swamp's edges, so I really didn't mind staying on the fringes. The cider-colored water was a marvel in itself, with its assemblage of strange aquatic insects. Long-legged pond skaters—also known as water striders—streaked lightly and swiftly across the surface as they hunted other insects or escaped my approach. Shiny black whirligig beetles danced in wildly gyrating groups, their circular paths turning the sun's reflection into dozens of swirling and sparkling explosions of light.

In any scoop of water I might find several sorts of aquatic beetles, water bugs, and other insects, including one type named water boatmen for their long, oarlike back legs. As a boy, I simply knew them as "diving bugs." When they're not actively swimming, boatmen naturally sink to pond and swamp bottoms, where they feed almost exclusively on plants. Another type of divers are called backswimmers. Buoyant insects, they float rather than sink when still. And unlike the vegetarian boatmen they're voracious predators that feed on everything from moths to fish and tadpoles. Insect books warn readers to handle backswimmers cautiously, if at all, or risk a painful sting. I learned that lesson the hard way: playing in our swamp, I reached down and grabbed a diving bug—and felt the sharp prick of its bite. That was the last diver I handled so carelessly.

Besides the myriad bugs, the Swamp was summer home to legions of tadpoles, or pollywogs as we usually called them. They hugged the mucky bottom, attached themselves to aquatic plants, and moved, in tail-wiggling fashion, through the dark water. The coolest tadpoles were the ones becoming frogs, their bodies transformed as tiny appendages became legs, the tail was lost, and gills gave way to lungs. Several types of frogs inhabited the Swamp, from tiny peepers to leopard frogs, pickerel frogs, green frogs, wood frogs, and huge bullfrogs. I grew to love the songs of frogs; they're among the summer sounds I've missed the most since moving north, along with the chirps of crickets and buzz of cicadas.

Some of my most vivid early memories echo with frog songs. In one, I'm standing at my sister's window; the glass pane is raised and I push my head against the screen. Peering into the darkness, I feel the warm, humid breath of a midsummer night, and I listen to a two-part orchestra. The deep bass croaking of bullfrogs mixes with high-pitched peeps of spring peepers. The calls draw me out of ordinary time, deep into the night, and I feel a soothing calmness. Another time I'm sitting on the back porch with my dad after an extended-family barbecue. There is laughter and conversation inside the house, as Sherwonits and Schmollingers crowd the kitchen, but my attention goes to the frogs and their sweet summer serenade.

One of my strongest and most delicious childhood memories is this: the echoing of frog songs, the brilliant flashes of fireflies in the darkening night, and the feel of grass against head and back as I study a star-studded sky. Frogs, lightning bugs, and shooting stars are night mysteries and I have no desire to understand, only to marvel.

Curiously, Mom tells me I was initially terrified by the eerie noises coming from the Swamp when my family moved to Old Town Road in 1953. Only three years old, I would awake and cry in fright. My parents had to assure me over and over that "it's only frogs, nothing that will hurt you" before I let go of my fear and welcomed the strange sounds.

I regularly hunted frogs for years, sometimes with friends but more often alone. They were more abundant than snakes or turtles, easier to find and catch—and they didn't bite or snap. Most often we caught them with our hands. Nets seemed like cheating, somehow. Occasionally we'd find frogs on shore, but usually we hunted them as they floated in the Swamp, only their heads above water, with front legs pushed forward and long back legs stretched out below, as if suspended in a jump. Sometimes we'd let the frogs go right away. Other times we'd put them in a bucket of water, haul them to the house, and keep them a few hours or even overnight. The chase and catch were the main things when hunting. And making that brief connection with the mysterious other.

Sadly the Swamp, like the Woods, was diminished during my teens. In a sense, it was tamed, by being cleaned out and made into a pond. Most of my neighbors liked the change, including several friends, who began calling it "Sherwonit's Pond." Many, if not all, of the same critters occupied its waters and margins. And after Peach stocked it with bass and pickerel and bluegills, it became a neighborhood fishing hole. But something was lost in the process. Much of the place's natural allure, its sense of otherness, had been removed with the trees and muck and other swamp life. Now it was more people friendly. But to me that wasn't necessarily a good thing.

* * *

AS OUR FORAYS into the Woods made clear, I wasn't especially adventurous when measured against my friends—and certainly not compared to the young Bob Marshall. Though he grew up in New York City, Marshall spent his boyhood summers in the Adirondacks. There he would explore the woods for hours, often alone, and over the years he came to know every ridge and creek and game trail, while demonstrating his penchant for naming things, for instance Found Knife Pass and Squashed Berry Valley. After climbing his first mountain while in his early teens, Marshall moved ever higher and deeper into the Adirondacks. I, meanwhile, was content to stay in the known and nearby wild, never venturing far from the familiar.

Though a rather timid outdoorsman, I loved the outdoors. The Woods and Swamp and even the yard were my refuge, places where I could escape family feuds and tensions and the roles I'd learned to play: the good and obedient son, the good student, the choir boy. Expectations and judgments dropped away. I could be more myself. Curiously, given my fears of getting lost in the woods, I could easily lose myself in nature, at least the judgmental self. In the community of humans, it seemed that people were always judging each other. And of course God was omnipresent, watching, watching. Being good Christians, my family, friends, and I had to set a good example to the rest of the world. The standard was impossibly high: perfection.

Complicating things was this fact: using the Bible as their evidence, my parents, pastor, and teachers hammered home the fact that, by nature, humans were sinful. Bad. We had to guard against our sinful tendencies and the influence of Satan. Being a sensitive sort, I took these lessons to heart. For all my talents and good behavior, I came to believe I wasn't good enough. I sure tried, though.

Outdoors, especially by myself, I didn't have to try. I could simply be me, while doing what I loved. As if by a miracle, the judgments vanished—if only for a while—as I hunted frogs and snakes, fished for rainbows, explored the Woods, or skated across the frozen Swamp. Nature drew me out of myself into something bigger. I still can't define that something bigger, but it had nothing to do with religion; and unlike my Lutheran God, it wasn't judgmental. Nor did it seem indifferent. It's often said that wilderness—or, more generally, wild nature or the universe—is indifferent to the fate of humans: the wilderness doesn't care if a person drowns while crossing a stream or is killed by an avalanche or hypothermia or a bear. Yet I sensed something different. I don't know if it was nature itself or something even bigger than nature, some creative force or energy. But I felt accepted by the natural world. As a young boy I sensed a beneficence that was "out there" but somehow included me. Sometimes I sense it even now. I suppose it may simply be my projection, but I don't think so.

This isn't so different from some Native Alaskan beliefs. As Richard Nelson writes in *Make Prayers to the Raven: A Koyukon View of the Northern Forest*,

> Traditional Koyukon [Athabascan] people live in a world that watches, in a forest of eyes. A person moving through nature—however wild, remote, even desolate the place may be—is never truly alone. The surroundings are aware, sensate, personified. They feel. They can be offended. And they must, at every moment, be treated with proper respect. All things in nature have a special kind of life, something unknown to contemporary Euro-Americans, something powerful....The world is ever aware.

One significant difference between the Koyukons and me, it seems, is that I didn't fear offending that greater, wild otherness in nature. Perhaps it was simply a child's naiveté, but at some level I must have experienced the natural world as an embracing and forgiving presence, tolerant of a youngster's mistakes and occasional meanness. Though I didn't always treat small critters respectfully or mercifully—in fact, I did some awful things to frogs and fish and insects—I think I always had a reverential attitude toward larger nature or what you might call creation. Maybe that made the difference.

My experience is perhaps more closely tied to what Robert Bly describes in *Iron John: A Book About Men* and his discussion of the "Wild Man" (or Wild Woman) who exists within us modern Westerners, whether we recognize him or not. In one passage, Bly describes the Wild Man as a sort of mentor, who guides us into larger nature and reveals the nonhuman intelligence or awareness to be found there. Bly suggests there may even be a sense of eyes looking back (not so different from the watchful world, the "forest of eyes" that Nelson describes) from a pool or water, a forest, or a mountain. For some people, this sense of eyes, of wild nature's own consciousness, "arrived early in childhood, when we were amazed by woods and gardens [or swamps], and knew they were 'alive.' "

Gary Snyder, too, touches upon this notion of wild intelligence, in *The Practice of the Wild*: "The world is watching: one cannot walk through a meadow or forest without a ripple of reports spreading out from one's passage. The thrush darts back, the jay squalls, a beetle scuttles under the grasses, and the signal is passed along. Every creature knows when a hawk is cruising or a human strolling. The information passed through the system is intelligence."

* * *

ANOTHER MEMORY, perhaps distilled from many childhood nights. Again I'm standing at a window, this time in my own bedroom, facing west. It's late at night and Dave is breathing softly. His face, turned toward me, looks so peaceful. I'm restless, unable to sleep. Maybe I've been having nightmares or I've heard my parents quarreling. I place my hands against the knotty pine wall, lean my head against the glass, and look out into the night. Deep inside, a longing wells up. I need hope. I need to know I fit in, somehow, somewhere.

I gaze toward a familiar form, an old oak tree that's perched upon a knob above the house next door. It used to be Grandpa's place, but the Seperacks live there now. The season must be fall or winter, because the great tree's limbs are bare. It's a huge skeleton, standing black against the sky and dominating the horizon. I wonder what secrets such an old, grandfather tree might hold. After a while, my attention is drawn from oak to sky. It's a clear night, a starry night, and as my thoughts move among the stars, I try to imagine infinity, endless space. Of course it's impossible to grasp, so I settle for something else: wonder. I shrink in size, humbled by the immense grandeur of the universe, the untold numbers of suns, many of them dwarfing our own. My life, in this context is so tiny, so insignificant. Yet, paradoxically, my life takes on greater meaning: to be part of such a mystery is a true blessing. In my own boyish way, I come to sense a sort of holiness that I don't get from religion. And a voice, or something like it, whispers out of the night. *You are safe. You are cared for.*

TWELVE

Passing Through Grizzly Country

MY SECOND MORNING AT GRIZZLY CREEK I AWAKEN TO A FOGGY, overcast, and windy day. And snow! A light flurry of snow "balls," more rounded than flaky, falls from dark skies. Temperatures hover in the low to mid-thirties, so I add an extra layer before exiting the tent. I'm bummed by the cold, dreary weather, but the chill does have one pleasing side effect: mosquitoes have all but vanished. I didn't see any yesterday and I'll see few today.

I also wake to neighbors: three tents, a quarter-mile away or less, are parked down valley among willows, closer to Ernie Creek. These packers must have arrived late; I took one final look around the valley last night at eleven or so and saw no tents or people. I wonder if they noticed my campsite. Two of the tents are large, blue-and-gold domes, the third a smaller tube-style tent. There's no sign of activity and my route doesn't require me to pass nearby, so I'll detour around the camp, not wishing to disturb its members—and not really in a mood, this morning, for human company or conversation.

Figuring on a long, cold day, I supplement my usual granola-bar breakfast with a serving of instant-mashed-potatoes-and-gravy mix. Pretty tasty, actually, at least in this raw, blustery weather. And it helps warm my innards. I also warm, and hydrate, myself with decaf coffee, followed by Sleepy Time herbal tea. Is this any way to charge my batteries? All I've brought are decaffeinated drinks. I'm now wondering if high-test coffee might be a helpful boost to begin heavy packing days.

Out of my sleeping bag at eight, I leave camp just before eleven, my second-earliest start, and initially stay high on the tundra hillside, above the heavy brush that borders the river. I can't entirely avoid the "green hell," however; side gullies and swales are lined by dense thickets of willow, soon mixed with alder. The alder is something new, its presence an indicator of some subtle shift in climate and soils. Some thickets rise above my head and are so dense I can't see more than a couple feet in any direction. The poor visibility, loud creek rumbling, and head-wind all increase the possibility that I'll stumble upon a grizzly. So for the first time on this trip I go into my bear chant. Its frequency and volume are directly proportional to the height and thickness of the brush.

"YO, BEAR!...YO, BEAR!..."

Or, "HELLO, HELLLLL-OHH."

Sometimes I add, "Human coming through," or "I mean no harm, only passing through." Not that the bears can understand the words, but perhaps they can sense my humility and harmless motives.

I feel a bit silly, chanting so. Yet any embarrassment fades in the face of this fact: a high percentage of grizzly maulings occur in just this sort of thick brush (or dense forest), where humans and bears surprise each other at close quarters. Such an incident happened in Gates of the Arctic not so many years ago. Two backpackers ran into a grizzly in dense brush and the bear attacked, killing one of the men.

I had my own frighteningly close encounter in 1987, while exploring the northern end of the Kodiak Archipelago, in the Gulf of Alaska. Knowing that a female brown bear with cubs inhabited the small island we were exploring, a backcountry guide and I had gone where we shouldn't have: into a dense stand of spindly spruce trees. Sam opted for the trees as a shortcut; I followed, despite some misgivings. After all, I figured, he was the guide and must know what he's doing. Bad mistake.

The spruce were twenty to thirty feet high, spindly, and densely packed, so we couldn't easily see more than ten to fifteen feet ahead, sometimes less. We were walking slowly, talking loudly, when suddenly a huge bear charged out of the forest's shadows. The brown bear mom must have tried to hide her family in this stand, but we'd stumbled into her sanctuary and threatened, however innocently, her offspring. Retreat hadn't worked, so her only option was to defend her cubs by force.

Things began to speed up and, simultaneously, move in slow motion around me. Less than twenty feet away, the bear was a blur of terrible speed, size, and power—a dark image of unstoppable rage. Her face was indistinct, and I sensed, more than saw, her teeth and claws. Two giant bounds were all it took for the bear to reach Sam, five feet in front of me. Somewhere, amid the roaring that filled my head, I heard a cry: "OH NO." I was certain that Sam was about to die, or be seriously mauled, and feared that I might also.

The last thing I saw was the bear engulfing Sam. Then, despite everything I'd learned about bears, I turned and ran, breaking one of the cardinal rules of bear encounters. But my instincts were strong, and they told me to get out of sight, out of the woods. Climbing one of the slender trees wasn't an option, and without any weapon, there was nothing I could do to help Sam. The only question was whether the bear would come after me when finished with him. I ran out of the forest onto a narrow stretch of beach; I knew I had to find the other three members of our party, get Sam's rifle from his kayak, and try to rescue him.

Back in the forest Sam was doing what he had to, to survive. As the bear charged he ducked his head and fell backward. Falling, he saw the bear's open mouth, its teeth and claws. Hitting the ground, he curled into a fetal position, to protect his head and vital organs, and he offered the bear a shoulder to chew on instead. Then, with the bear breathing in his face, he played dead.

The bear grabbed Sam in a "hug," woofed at him, and batted him a few times like a kitten playing with a mouse. But she struck him with her paws, not her claws. There was no sound of tearing flesh. And when, after several moments—or was it minutes?—she sensed no response from her victim, the bear ended her attack just as suddenly as she began it. The threat removed, she left with her cubs.

I was still standing on the beach, listening and looking for any sign of the bear, when, incredibly, I heard Sam shout: "The bear's gone....I'm all right." Miraculously, he hadn't been injured, except for a small scratch on the back of his hand, which he got when falling backward into a small spruce.

Hours later, as we rehashed the attack, Sam told us, "I felt no sense of aggression or panic. I believe animals can sense a person's energy. If you're projecting aggression, or if the adrenaline is flowing, they know it. I was very calculating as to what I should do." It turns out he did everything right—once the bear attacked. Listening to Sam's story, still pumped with adrenaline, I could only shake my head and marvel at our escape.

MEMORIES OF THAT attack flash through my head as I bushwhack my way down valley. A few places in particular get me spooked. Once I find bear scat: fresh, but fortunately not steaming. I also see grizzly tracks and bear diggings. There's a grizzly (or two) somewhere in this valley. Am I being watched?

An especially thick and ominous patch of near-impenetrable willows forces me to the river after a couple miles of bushwhacking. There, both to my chagrin and glee, I discover long, open stretches of gravel bars along the meandering creek. Even where there's willow, the bushes are more dispersed. I go into Bob Marshall–like cruising speed for one and a half miles, until a river meander and cutbank force me back up onto the tundra. I now return to the river bars whenever possible, because the walking is so much easier.

I'm not the only one to follow the river: the bars are tracked by caribou, wolves, bears—and people. I make out six sets of boot prints in the sand and gravel, all fresh and pointed upstream. They must have been made by the packers now camped near the Ernie and Grizzly Creeks confluence. I'm both surprised and impressed that the first two groups I've met have been trekking *up* Ernie Creek. I'd been told that the standard route nowadays is east and then south, from Anaktuvuk Pass to Ernie Creek and then down to the North Fork.

The boot prints raise my spirits: more evidence that the braided North Fork is still fordable, even with continued heavy rains. Ernie Creek, on the other hand, looks impossible to cross, its floodwaters squeezed into a single channel. In fact it looks challenging for a river runner. Let's put it this way: I wouldn't want to float it today without an expert at the paddles. Standing waves reach three to four feet high and in flatter stretches the water careens wildly downstream.

I exit the Valley of Precipices in early afternoon, snow now transformed to drizzle. Both the bushwhacking and anxieties about bears have kept my attention focused more on the immediate surroundings than the high peaks that surround me. Besides, the weather hasn't been the sort for mountain gazing. The upper reaches of Blackface Mountain—whose eastern flanks form the principle precipices—remain hidden by clouds as they've been throughout my sojourn, so I haven't seen them at their grandest. But even with blue skies I'm not sure this valley would outdo Yosemite. I also remain convinced my high tundra bench is among the best places—if not the best—to look upon the valley and its bordering cliffs.

Just south of Blackface Mountain, I begin to see tree-size willow and alders. Some are twelve, fifteen, maybe even twenty feet high. Yet this is well north of the "official" tree line, as marked on maps. Don't these species count? A few miles south of the first willow "trees" I see a large stand of cottonwood in the valley bottom. Several trees are at least twenty to thirty feet high. Yet these too are north of the tree line, at least as shown on maps. Marshall concerned himself with spruce when he mapped out the central Arctic's tree line in the 1920s and '30s. What about today's botanists? I meet the first scraggly spruce about a mile below the cottonwoods; on the map, it's very close to where cartographers have marked green to indicate the start of forest. From here on, I move between tundra and open spruce forest.

I wonder if any contemporary researchers are studying the Central Brooks Range's boreal forest. Marshall postulated that the northern tree line is tied more closely to the region's most recent glacial retreat than to conditions unfavorable for tree growth. "According to my theory," he wrote, "the spruce stands eventually will extend to the Arctic Divide and cross over into the sheltered valleys north of the divide."

To test his theory, Marshall extracted seeds from local spruce cones and planted them along Grizzly Creek, about twelve miles north of the tree line. "If successful," he figured, "this experiment constituted an advancement of the timber line of about 3,000 years according to my estimate of spruce-migration rates."

When Marshall returned to Grizzly Creek eight years later, he was disappointed to learn

the seeds had not developed. My experiment was a complete, dismal failure on both plots. There was not even the sign of a dead seedling, just two patches of bare ground, marked with willow stakes in the ground. Whether the failure was due to infertility of the seeds or faulty sowing technique or an unusually rainy autumn after sowing, which rotted them, or just unfavorable climate according to the usual theory I could not tell.

While wondering about trees and their northern movement, I've also been keeping an occasional lookout for signs of a cabin. My USGS topographic maps show three cabins within a few miles of Ernie Creek's confluence with the North Fork. It's likely that one of them was built by Marshall's good friend Ernie Johnson. A Swedish immigrant drawn to Alaska by gold fever in 1904, Johnson eventually settled along the creek later named in his honor. By the time Marshall came north in 1929, Johnson had earned a reputation as the "most illustrious hunter and trapper of the Far North, a sort of Daniel Boone among the pioneers of this arctic frontier." For both that reason and the fact that the two men "hit it off fine from the start," Johnson accompanied Marshall on three long expeditions into Koyukuk country.

Johnson continued to work his arctic claims into his seventies. In 1957, he informed Bob Marshall's brother, George, "I intend to stay in the Hills until the end." That came four years later, when Johnson died of a heart attack.

Is his cabin still standing, nearly forty years later? Or has it begun a slow decay back into the arctic soil? Whether the three mapped cabins are simply hidden among the trees or fallen down, I see no signs of any structure during my passage down Ernie Creek. But I don't go out of my way to look for them, either.

BESIDES THE LONG, open river bars, I am blessed by two saving graces on today's long march. One is the abundant blueberries. Scattered here and there are lush patches of berry plants, anywhere from ankle- to knee-high. The berries themselves are plump and juicy among the dark green, ovoid leaves and in places hang from branches like miniature clusters of grapes. They are so thick, so abundant, that I can sometimes pull off a dozen or more while swiping my hand along the bushes' tiny limbs. I stop several times to graze in this berry heaven and by day's end consume scores of the tart, purplish-blue fruits. I'm always careful to leave plenty of berries at each of my stops, as a courtesy to bears and other berry-grazing critters. I may not catch any fish, but at least I'm sampling the land's fruits.

David Cooper did more than nibble berries during his epic solo arctic journey in the late 1970s, described in *Brooks Range Passage*. He depended on them for necessary calories. A college student from Colorado, Cooper, like Marshall a half century earlier, wished to immerse himself in "true wilderness... the kind that comprised North America before man built his trails and roads." Also like Marshall, Cooper supplemented his own grub with wild foods, though he relied on plants instead of meat (except for the occasional fish he would catch in creeks or lakes along the way). This meant he had to learn the region's edible roots, flowers, and berries, and regularly harvest and cook the plants as part of his meal plan.

Cooper entered the Brooks Range at Anaktuvuk Pass. But unlike most who begin their treks at the Nunamiut village, he turned his sights west, toward the Arrigetch Peaks. He left the community determined to be "totally free to move as I pleased without any concept of time, except how many more weeks my food supply would last." Without any food drops or other support, he carried enough basic foods—flour, rice, lentils, granola, and the like—for six weeks, plus fishing gear and bow-and-arrow. Loaded down with a hundred-pound pack (something I can't even imagine) he hiked one hundred and twenty miles through valleys and over passes, then built a raft and floated one hundred and sixty miles down the Alatna River. He finished his trip, more than five weeks later, in the Athabascan village of Allakaket.

Even with a great knowledge of plants, Cooper was pushing his luck. The abundance of wild berries, for example, may vary greatly from year to year, depending on the weather. And fishing may prove impossibly difficult, if heavy rains roil the range's streams. Some experienced arctic travelers have criticized Cooper's approach, among them John Kauffman, who in *Alaska's Brooks Range* writes,

> I am puzzled, however, by Cooper's rationale for how he conducted his journey.... He planned to live largely off the land, and in some degree he did so, but his approach to that was somewhat atavistic and contradictory....
>
> It seems unfortunate that Cooper saw fit to write words of encouragement to those who would live off the country, or even supplement their carried food sup-

ply to any large extent. Arctic Alaska is a rather bare cupboard; wild foods do not grow just anywhere for an ever-increasing number of visitors to gather. Even the Native people have to know the country intimately to subsist.

I understand Kauffman's concern that too many Cooper (or Marshall) wannabes would harm the Arctic's finite resources. But I didn't interpret Cooper's account as advocacy for such an approach, but something of a personal experiment. In fact, up front he cautions the reader, "I did not intend the journey as one that just anyone should undertake. It demands a great deal of preparation and knowledge of the area, not the least of which is a thorough understanding of the plants if one intends to eat them."

More important, I would argue, is Cooper's call for increased connections with the larger, wilder world:

Most human experiences will not occur in remote areas such as the Brooks Range. But it is very important for us to seek out undisturbed quiet segments of our environment in order to feel the incredible simplicity and wonderment of earth as well as the difficulties and suffering that such encounters inevitably bring. We need to allow our minds and senses to be open and attuned to the natural world around us, for it is as real and provides as much meaning as our man-made world.

Five hundred years ago on this continent, man lived in wilderness.... We must have room to experience wild lands on this planet, for they are a vital tie to our ancestry and heritage besides being a vital need of our minds and bodies.

Amen to that. But to Cooper's essentially egocentric argument, I must again add that we need to preserve wildlands and wildlife for themselves, regardless of how they benefit us humans.

On at least a couple points, both Kauffman and I agree. For one, Cooper's journal describes "the texture, the tactile qualities of Brooks Range tundra vegetation with such care that even a blind person could see its beauty...in a story sensitively and gracefully told." And his writings affirm the need to slow down in order to attain a greater understanding of what's around and within us.

Besides berries, my other saving grace is game trails. Used by wolves, caribou, bears, moose, and smaller critters, the trails come and go, distinct in places then fading out and later reappearing. Where present, they make travel across tundra so much easier, especially through shrub birch and swampy sedge tussock mazes, of which there are many the farther south I go. I might have floundered several hours more if not for these pain- and time-saving paths, traced by locals familiar with the landscape.

Speaking of pain, here's a scary notion: my pack is almost beginning to feel comfortable on my back, like it belongs there. This is particularly true early in the day and when cruising gravel bars. My body is strengthening even as the pack is slowly but steadily getting lighter. I'm starting to feel like a real packer.

NOT LONG BEFORE the end of my day's workout, I'm busting through yet another green hell of willow, birch, and alder, when I stumble upon a bleached, well-preserved skull. About the length of my hand, it's a predator's skull, with large canine teeth. From its shape and memories of other skulls, I guess it to be that of a grizzly cub (later confirmed). I also find the lower jaw, in two pieces.

Bear cub or not, it's an exciting find, the finest skull I've ever discovered. Given its excellent condition, my natural instinct is to collect the skull and take it to my rendezvous with friends at the Gates. Maybe even take the skull back to Anchorage and show it to a bear biologist friend, then send it back east to my brother Dave, who like me is a wildlife enthusiast. Those ideas are quickly tempered by another thought: park rules prohibit such bone collecting. The only objects that people can legally remove are rocks or the meat from fish or wildlife they've killed. In the end I take it, figuring there's no harm in hauling the skull to the Gates and leaving it there. Putting the skull and jawbones into a plastic bag, I'm reminded of Loren Eiseley's reference to "bone collectors"—he himself was one—in *The Immense Journey*.

Still, I have mixed feelings. Maybe it's wrong to take these bones, for reasons beyond park regulations. Alaska's Native peoples have long-standing rules that govern the treatment of animal parts, particularly those of bears, animals believed to possess both great physical and spiritual power. Humans who violate taboos risk bad luck, sickness, even death. The Koyukon people, who live in villages south of the Brooks Range and sometimes hunt in the chain's southern foothills, traditionally spoke of the grizzly in hushed tones, if at all, because of its great power.

Among all the animals that share their world, the Koyukons have an "unparalleled feeling of awe toward the brown bear," Richard Nelson writes in *Make Prayers to the Raven*. In the old, traditional ways, the taboos were strictest for women. They were not allowed to hunt bears, generally avoided all direct references to the animal, and had to look away if one came within sight. A woman who ate or handled grizzly meat, even unintentionally, risked illness or insanity. The men, too, had to carefully follow prescribed rituals. Never should a hunter brag about killing or even hunting a grizzly; one who did would risk harm to himself, maybe even death. When a bear was killed, the meat was left outside the village for days or even weeks, because otherwise "it is too fresh and potent with easily affronted spiritual energy." Even in death, all of the grizzly's body parts—bones, hide, skull—had to be treated with respect.

Though I come from a much different culture, one in which animals are more often treated as hard-wired things rather than sentient, spiritual beings, I appreciate the Koyukon perspective and believe their attitude of deep respect is worth emulating.

Minutes after I resume my packing, I take a frightening fall while descending a rain-slickened slope of willow, birch, and grasses. It happens so fast: feet slip and I flip head over pack, then slide out of control for several feet before stopped by a clump of willow bushes. My body, amazingly, is unharmed. No sharp pains, no evidence of bruised muscles or broken bones. No apparent damage to my gear, either, until I notice my trekking pole is sharply bent. I must have landed on it when falling. This could be bad news; I need that pole for my river crossings.

I test the pole by pushing on it with all my weight. It still seems sturdy enough, though it no longer telescopes. And its structural integrity has been compromised. I'm immediately reminded of the many newspaper and magazine articles I've read—and even a few I've written—over the years that analyze wilderness mishaps. Often, backcountry deaths or serious injuries result from a series of seemingly minor mistakes. Added up, they may lead to disaster. Is this such a blunder? Did it begin with taking that skull? And did I add to my errors by attempting a shortcut through this brush? Will my bent pole come back to haunt me when I cross the North Fork?

Because the fall comes so quickly after my heist of the skull, I connect them in my thoughts. It can't possibly be a cause-and-effect thing…can it? The two events also add to my uneasiness in this dense brush, with its abundant grizzly sign. It seems that every few feet I find diggings, or scat, or tracks. There's an eerie, forbidding presence here. Have I broken some greater taboo by taking the skull? I begin to feel like a grave robber. It seems silly, I know, but I also wonder about curses. Silly or not, photos of the skull will have to do. Upon reaching my campsite for the night, I place the skull and jawbones on the gravel bar, take several pictures, then find an out-of-the-way place, deep in a willow thicket, and place the remains so they're looking to the north. Then I whisper a short prayer to honor the animal's memory. This feels better. It feels right.

My brief ceremony ended, I pitch the tent, eat dinner, and crawl into my sleeping bag. A light rain falls, as it has almost all day. I've seen blue sky and fiery sun maybe a half hour over the past four days. Today the sun appeared now and then as a milky orb behind thin clouds, but mostly it was hidden behind thick veils. My face feels burned, but it must be from the incessant headwinds.

THIRTEEN

Days of Rocks and Minerals

BY THE TIME I FINISH RECORDING MY THOUGHTS AND OBSERVATIONS for July 26, I've filled seven pages with notes. Three pages record my start-up of the bear chant and the later discovery of the skull and subsequent tumble. Others are filled with notes on blueberries, game trails, the weather, tree line, and meals. Only one short paragraph is devoted to a description of the Valley of Precipices during my passage. If I were to go back through my journal, I'd find few discussions of the range's geology, its structure and rocks. I'm much more interested in the natural history and behaviors of grizzlies and wolves, or even wagtails and mosquitoes, than I am in the origin of the range's landforms. This may seem strange for a guy who earned an MS in geosciences. But it's been that way, more and more, since I left geology.

Certainly there are times when I'm overwhelmed by the grandeur of a mountain landscape or dazzled by the beauty of a crystal. And I know that a contorted, upthrust bed of limestone holds as much mystery as a wood frog hopping through arctic tundra. But nowadays—and for many years now—my attention is mostly drawn to critters, just as it was decades ago when I hunted frogs and snakes in the Swamp. I can't explain why, exactly, though I have some ideas. Here's one. While I was considered a competent, even talented, geologist with great potential, I never felt comfortable with my so-called expertise. I worried that some day my bosses and peers would discover what I already understood: I didn't know nearly as much as people believed I did. Not that I was trying to trick anyone. But how do you tell people, "Look, I'm not as good as you think," when you're trying to build a career? Even now, I sometimes get embarrassed when friends or acquaintances ask me to identify rocks or glacial landforms on trips into the hills. It's as if my past training still makes me an expert. I've gotten better at simply saying "I don't know" or "I'm not sure" when in doubt, but I tend to steer away from discussions of geology. Or, with people who don't know my history, I might avoid any mention of my geosciences training. So besides being a recovering Lutheran, I'm something of a failed geologist.

As a nature writer I have none of those anxieties. Being a writer allows me to play the role of student, not the expert. I can be the one who asks the questions rather than he who has the answers. (At the same time I recognize that the best scientists are those who are lifelong students of their fields, constantly questioning and probing.) And these days what most piques my interest, ignites my passion, raises the most questions, is wildness in its many and varied guises: animal, plant, bug, weather, sky…and yes, land and seascapes. More than that, I'm intrigued by the natural history of life forms with which we humans share the planet, especially the ones that inhabit this place we've named Alaska; by different ways of knowing, from science to indigenous traditions to mysticism; by questions of spirit and worlds beyond this world. Geology fits in there but it's nowhere near the top of the list.

Still, there was a long period in my life when rocks and minerals grabbed my attention and gave me hours of delight. Along with basketball (another whole story) and my neighborhood's wild places, rockhounding helped get me through my darkest, most troubling years. I suppose you could say it grounded me, even as it lifted my spirits.

Miss Anderson, a science teacher at Trumbull High School, was the one who set me on the path to becoming a rock hound and eventually a geologist. I got transferred into her earth science class during my freshman year at Trumbull High School, after first being misplaced in sophomore-level biology. It turned out to be lucky break, or maybe divine intervention of some sort.

Among her gifts to me, Miss Anderson showed kindness to a shy, timid kid who felt lost and scared among the throngs of strangers. By the time I graduated from Zion Lutheran School I'd become something of a shining star: a top student, star forward on the soccer team, basketball hotshot, and popular with the other kids. After all, I was in my element, my comfort zone: I had grown up at Zion, knew just about all of the one hundred students, and had been given lots of attention by the teachers. It was, at the same time, both a nurturing and sheltered environment. All of that vanished when I entered THS, where I became an instant nobody.

Being a freshman is tough enough. But to be a small, introverted, self-conscious ninth-grader who knew almost no one, tossed into the cultural chaos of high school amid fifteen hundred other teens seeking their position in the high school pecking order—well, it was my kind of hell. Miss Anderson sensed that I was a lost soul. Right from the start she welcomed me into her class and showed me warmth and brightness amid the chilling harshness of my new world. A few scattered beacons of light enabled me to navigate the dark landscape of my teens. She was one of the brightest. (Another was Mr. Ritchie, my algebra teacher. He so inspired me that I went to college believing I might become a math major, but the abstract thinking required by higher mathematics quickly changed that notion.)

My memory of Miss Anderson is blurred by time. Or perhaps it's that even the happiest moments of those years are edged in shadows. But what I recall is a smallish woman with short dark brown hair, high-pitched voice, and first name of Donna. She could be stern or warm, as the situation dictated, but what I remember most is her firm but gentle nature, her encouraging manner. She wasn't the type to bubble with enthusiasm, yet I sensed her passion for earth science. Miss Anderson made the class come alive. She, in turn, noticed my natural affinity for the subject.

The course, like the teacher, is something of a blur. But I know I was fascinated by studies of dinosaurs, the fossil record, the different kinds of rocks that make up the earth's surface, and, most of all, minerals. The school had a rather minimalist collection, but I loved the forms and colors of the common minerals we studied: quartz, feldspar, calcite, talc, pyrite, galena, gypsum. And the crystals! Such fantastic shapes. A whole new world had opened up. Both Miss Anderson and I were delighted to discover that I was something of a natural; I quickly learned to identify the rocks and minerals she brought into class. I wanted to learn more.

Though exciting, this new world also could be troubling. Many of earth science's most basic tenets challenged my deep-seated Lutheran beliefs. I'd always been taught that the Earth had been formed in six days and our planet plus all of its creatures were five thousand to six thousand years old. This was my truth. I'd never doubted the Bible's creation story. Why would I? It was all I knew. Now I was being told that our planet was billions of years old. And humans had not been created in God's image, but had evolved from the apes. How could this be? I don't recall discussing this dilemma with my parents, but ultimately my religious beliefs and faith in God held strong. I would accept science's version for the class, but the Bible's explanation remained my truth for several more years.

Through my earth science class, I learned that some people actually made a living studying rocks, even collecting minerals. Even better, there were stores that catered to rock hounds. And there were places in Trumbull and nearby towns where you could find crystals. One was at Old Mine Park, where Uncle Peach had first taken me trout fishing.

It didn't take too much pleading to convince my parents I simply had to get some essential rockhounding gear, things like hammer and chisel, magnifying glass and guidebook. At first I was content to hunt for treasures in my own neighborhood. But Old Town Road's empty lots and acres of woods held few interesting rocks and nothing that compared to the minerals I'd studied at school. I began building a collection, but the samples were drab, ordinary pieces of rock. Eventually I got my parents to take me to Old Mine Park, where we followed trails into the forest and the remains of mine dumps. At one time the site had produced tungsten, but a fire destroyed the ore-processing plant and ended the open-pit operation in 1916. Now all that remained were mounds of dirt and rock. But those humble mounds held great riches for a beginning mineral collector.

Using the pick end of my hammer, I dug into the rubbly dirt, looking carefully through my hand lens at the bits of minerals I unearthed. Few, if any, of the pieces I found were of museum quality. But now and then I'd find clusters of crystals or the familiar metallic luster of common sulfides: pyrite (iron sulfide), chalcopyrite (copper-iron), or galena (lead sulfide). Once I found a tabular, gray-green crystal no longer than one of the bright green inchworms that hung from trees and sometimes found their way onto my head or arms. All the ID tests I performed pointed to topaz, a mineral that in its most perfect form is a highly valued gemstone. This small specimen was hardly gemlike, but to me it was a prize. I wrapped the topaz crystal and other delicate samples in tissues and then newspaper. Other, larger, and less fragile pieces I simply piled into my pack.

The hours passed quickly and my often-worried mind grew calm as I lost myself in the hunt. I never would have guessed the woods and ground of my hometown held such magic. Back home, I unbagged my samples, washed off the dirt, found boxes to hold them, and set aside the unknowns to identify. Then I took my most precious finds up to the bedroom to admire and safely store away.

Over time I would expand my high school rockhounding to abandoned mines and pits throughout Connecticut. None of my friends caught my rockhounding fever, though Uncle Peach's youngest son, John, eventually became a fellow mineral collector and joined many of my expeditions. Some of my sport-loving buddies considered the new hobby rather odd. You're collecting *what?* But I didn't mind. This was something I could do—and enjoyed doing—in solitude.

MY COLLEGE YEARS were a time of great revelation, as my world opened up in ways both marvelous and agonizing. For the first time in my life, I'd be on my own. I looked forward to my approaching freedom with great anticipation, mixed, of course, with considerable anxiety. After being swallowed up by Trumbull High, I wanted a college that was small; a thousand students or less seemed ideal. Guided by that criteria I also aimed for one that was liberal-arts oriented, with both math and geology programs, and close to home—but not too close. In the end, I chose Bates College in Lewiston, Maine, a six-hour drive from Trumbull.

In the four years I attended Bates (1967–1971), the school and I went through enormous changes, in part reflecting tectonic cultural shifts. My freshman year, men and women were segregated into their own dorms. Women had a curfew and men had to sign in and out when visiting a woman's dorm. On the drug scene, those who smoked pot were, if not exactly outlaws, certainly on the fringes of society. (Bates may have been slightly behind the national curve in that regard, but probably not by much.) Politically, only radicals protested against the war in Vietnam.

By my senior year, students lived in coed dorms, there was no such thing as curfews, and nearly everyone I knew smoked grass, or had at least tried marijuana. Still not entirely freed from the clutches of my conservative upbringing, I was among the last in my dormitory to do pot. I finally gave in my senior year, to the laughter and applause of the guys on my floor. "Hey Trums, welcome to the club," crowed Phil, one of my neighbors from down the hall.

My politics, too, were transformed. Both my parents—and all my relatives, that I could tell—were staunch Republicans. In 1960, we rooted for Richard Nixon to beat John Kennedy. Not only was JFK a Democrat, he was—*shudder*—a Roman Catholic. Would he have to answer to the Pope, as some political analysts suggested? Even the possibility seemed scary. Once in office, though, Kennedy proved a better leader than any of his critics had predicted. I only vaguely remember the Cuban missile crisis, but clearly it was a frightening time; and it seemed a turning point in how people regarded the president. And like most Americans, we were horrified by JFK's assassination.

By the time I entered college, I had begun to veer ever so slightly from my parents' political views. But I was hardly a political animal. My disinterest, and that of some other friends, infuriated my roommate, John Millar. "Don't you guys care what happens to this country? You're so apathetic it's disgusting." He was right, until my senior year. Among the first of our generation to be entered into the draft lottery, my college buddies and I began paying more attention to Vietnam and the atrocities happening there. Though I was hardly a firebrand, my final year at Bates I joined my first protest march, even carried a sign. The same man I'd vicariously supported in 1960, I now rallied against as president. Slowly, almost imperceptibly, I was moving across the political spectrum, from far right to left.

Even more dramatic were the changes in my religious attitudes. For the first time my beliefs were seriously challenged by non-Christians. My sophomore year, I got into some serious arguments with a friend who was as devout an atheist as I was a Christian. I must have known such people existed, but I'd never met one before. Over and over, we challenged each other's beliefs. "How can you be sure there's a God?" he would ask. "What proof do you have?" At first I pointed to the Bible, but he'd have none of it. The Bible was written by men, not God. And how could we know for certain it had been "inspired" by God? Finally it came to this: believing in God was a matter of faith, not proof. Fine, he said. But he was equally sure that God didn't exist. And, by the way, he asked, what about all those wars and other atrocities that Christians had perpetrated on "nonbelievers" over the centuries? Was God responsible for all of that?

I refused to give in or show any sign of doubt, but secretly I began to wonder about my Christian convictions. The impenetrable fortress of faith in which I'd been raised was starting to show some cracks. I decided to have a conversation with God and ask for a sign that Jesus Christ was my savior. So I prayed and waited. And I prayed again. And again. I looked for a sign. But I received no answer, that I could tell. Was this a test of my faith? Seeing this as my own failure, I chose not to share my desperate questioning with anyone. At age nineteen I was having my first real spiritual crisis.

Academically, I was doing great. Still shy, especially around women, I hardly socialized beyond my small circle of friends in the dorm. I devoted my energies to sports and studies, simultaneously a gym rat and bookworm. For some reason I still can't explain, I never got involved in the college's outdoors club. With no car of my own, and none of my closest friends drawn to outdoor adventures, I seldom traveled far from campus. During my four years at Bates, I hardly got to know the Maine landscape, one of the few regrets from my undergraduate days.

I had officially entered college as a mathematics major, but I switched fields before the end of my first semester. I enjoyed college algebra, but I loved geology, with its study of rocks and minerals, fossils and landforms, and occasional field trips (the one thing that pulled me off campus). An understanding of the science came to me easily and my instructors—Drs. Farnsworth and Morrison—encouraged my work. My junior and senior years, I got summer jobs with the U.S. Geological Survey, helping to map areas of Massachusetts. Now and then, on visits back home, I returned to familiar rockhounding haunts and continued adding to my collection, which now numbered hundreds of specimens and included some museum-quality crystals.

Geology, in its own way, added to my spiritual worries. No longer was it so easy to ignore the differences between biblical and geological time scales. Everywhere I turned, I faced challenges to my faith. Less than a decade after leaving the protective cocoon of home and church, I would turn my back on the Christian church, though not what Christ stood for. What ultimately settled the question for me was this: I could no longer believe in an almighty God who would damn people to hell for eternity, simply because they were born into other cultures or other religions. I wasn't exactly sure what I did believe in; but the God of my youth and young adulthood had become too unjust for me. That's not to say I had entirely escaped my earliest influences. Even into my thirties, I would occasionally have nightmares in which I was damned to hell.

From Bates I headed west, at Dr. Morrison's urging. My Bates advisor said that's where the best geology was displayed so I should continue my studies there. Among the schools that accepted me for graduate school, I chose the University of Arizona. My path to the far north would go through the desert Southwest.

FOURTEEN

Meeting Bear,
Crossing the North Fork

JULY 27. I WAKE, AS USUAL, TO THE TAPPING OF RAIN ON MY TENT.
It's been misting or drizzling for the past twelve hours. And there's no wind, which suggests another low-pressure system has settled on this part of the Arctic. Everything is oozing water.

I'm now within three miles of the North Fork of the Koyukuk and the building anxieties of recent days have reached a crescendo. I want to get this river crossing behind me, yet dread having to do it. I fear that I'll be stranded by floodwaters and require rescue. Or worse, I'll attempt to cross despite high water and lose my balance, my gear, maybe even my life. Searchers will find my broken and swollen body weeks from now, wrapped around a snag.

An account of Marshall's 1929 expedition hasn't helped matters. On their return trip to Wiseman after three weeks of exploring Koyukuk country with two packhorses, Marshall and Al Retzlaf found themselves trapped between two raging rivers. Heavy rainfall had turned the previously "easily fordable" North Fork into "a wild river, uncrossable except by boat or raft.... We wondered how we could get across. Our old ford had become impossible." A North Fork tributary, the Clear River, had risen three feet or more and was now a raging torrent. The men and their horses eventually crossed the Clear, but just barely: "By walking with the current, bracing ourselves for all we were worth, and using the horses for support, we barely managed to get across. Several times we were swept off our feet, but by clinging to the halters were able to regain our footing.

Within five minutes we stood on the far shore, miraculously escaped from our flood-lined trap."

Talk about feeding my fears. It's amazing how much energy I give to these worries. I'm reminded of performance anxieties from many years ago, times that I faced an important exam, a big game, a job interview, or a first-date phone call. No matter how hard I prepared, I worried about the test, the possibility of failure. College dating was the worst. I would prepare my "lines" for days. Then, when I'd worked up enough courage, I would pick up the phone, put it down, pick it up again, put it down. Finally I'd stumble through my invitation. It was agony. And while I usually ended up doing pretty well on exams and in sporting events, my batting average in dating was awful. I was oh-for-my-first-two-years-in-college. Not that I tried very often. Through my childhood and teens and into my twenties, I was painfully shy around girls and later women.

In this case, I'm not even sure how prepared I am for the test ahead. The consequences of a screwup while traveling deep in the wilderness are considerably more serious than rejection by a cute coed whom I barely knew, but while in college it sure seemed like life and death.

Not long after breaking camp, my river-fording fears are temporarily pushed aside by more pressing matters. I'm headed across a gravel bar when a blond, fur-wettened grizzly steps out of the forest and starts to dig in the stream bank less than two hundred feet away. For reasons I can't fully explain, I guess the bear to be a young adult female. Her body shape, as much as anything, suggests maturity: though weighing perhaps only two hundred to two hundred fifty pounds, she's fuller bodied, less gangly, than "teenage" bears. And northern grizzlies are on average much smaller than the coastal brown bears I'm more used to seeing.

The stream is raucous and the wind blows toward me, so the bear can't hear or smell my approach, and so far she hasn't looked in my direction. After digging furiously a minute or two, the grizzly hops the bank and disappears back into the woods. Because she's in my general path, I want to track her whereabouts. I too leave the gravel bar and head uphill to a clearing near the edge of forest and tundra. Soon I see her, headed toward me but attention drawn elsewhere. It's time to act. I shout: "HELLO BEAR, HELLO."

From that moment on, our meeting becomes a textbook encounter.

The bear stops short, half stands, pauses, then lopes forward a few paces. She's not charging, but I guess that her adrenaline is now pumping fiercely through that powerfully muscled body, just as it is through my much frailer one, pushing her forward. More softly, I speak again, a now-familiar line: "Hello bear. It's just me, a human passing through." The bear stops and stands up fully on her hind legs. She's trying to get a better idea of who, or what, is "talking" to her in such a way. A few moments later, back on all fours, the bear retreats twenty or thirty feet, moving at a lope. Then she begins to circle toward the tundra bench above us. "That's it," I encourage her, "no need to come closer."

I've remained calm through this entire encounter, except for my initial start when the bear first stepped out of the woods. Many years spent in the company of bears have taught me composure and to trust my instincts—and those of bears. The grizzly, too, has stayed calm despite the surprise of our meeting. I've sensed no agitation, no aggression. Her initial confusion may have been joined by curiosity, some desire to get a closer look at, and whiff of, this strange, hairless biped standing before her. Then caution, perhaps tinged with fear, pushed her into retreat. I wonder if she's ever seen or smelled a human before. For all the horrific bear-attack stories I've heard and read, it's been my experience that northern grizzlies are inherently shy around people, especially deep in the wilderness where they've had few, if any, encounters with our kind. I've met many arctic grizzlies over the years—from a distance, I should add—and they've always retreated, usually in great haste. Close, surprise encounters are an entirely different matter, as I've already recounted. None of this is to say that grizzlies should be taken lightly. They are powerful beasts, with the teeth and claws of a predator. If treated disdainfully or maliciously, they can become an explorer's nightmare. But the evidence is overwhelming: bears have much more to fear from humans, than vice versa.

The grizzly glances my way now and then while loping uphill in an arc that gradually takes her farther from me. I'm impressed, as always, by how easily and swiftly bears move through terrain that's so rugged and difficult for us humans. She passes over a rise and disappears, ending an encounter that lasted no more than five minutes. I too head upslope, to more open ground, though I angle away from the bear. Thank goodness she chose to go north.

As always, I feel privileged to share the landscape with a bear. With so much sign, I figured it was only a matter of time. But you never know. Now I must be careful not to let my guard down. Just because this one has skedaddled, it doesn't mean there won't be other grizzlies ahead.

On the bench above the forest, I stumble and lurch through more sedge tussock tundra, then meet another game trail. It's generally headed where I want to go so I follow the path for a mile or more. This one has been heavily used by wolves. Along the path are abundant doglike turds, rich in fur and fragments of bone. In places, scat of varying freshness has been piled. Are these marking spots? I love the idea of following wolves across the tundra.

Eventually the trail bends away from my route. Leaving it, I angle across tundra and then through open spruce forest toward the North Fork–Ernie Creek confluence. Out of the woods, I come to sandbars imprinted by numerous wolf tracks, of many different sizes. Among them are the largest wolf prints I've ever seen, several inches across. Some are fresh, made within the past few days. Is this a rendezvous site? Is there a den nearby? What brings so many wolves here?

I splash across some side channels and step onto a gravel bar that borders the North Fork. The river here is flowing in a single channel, fast and deep; there's no chance of crossing without going for a swim. I've got to go northeast, upstream from the confluence, where the North Fork becomes braided. Now that I'm here, I don't want to delay. I need to find out: can I make it across? After several minutes of searching, I find a place where several braids pour into one channel. They all look doable—except, perhaps, for the one that flows along the near shore. Its roiling waters pile against a cut bank, eroding away the forest floor. I skirt this channel several hundred feet, to a place where it widens. If I follow the riffles and maybe do some zigzagging....

This is good, in a way: the crux is right at the beginning.

As at the Anaktuvuk River and Grizzly Creek, I set aside pack and radio, grab my now-bent walking pole, and plunge in. The water is a murky bluish green, but where shallow I can see the bottom. This is a great relief, because I can more easily pick a path across. Once I'm in the water, fear gives way to total focus. I'm engaged in the act of fording, making constant choices, moving ahead. Diagonaling upstream, I stay in ankle-high water for about fifty feet. Then it deepens. Still, along one line I can make out the bottom. It looks even, gravelly. No apparent holes. The water is now midcalf, now at my knees, splashing higher. And COLD. The water pushes at me but the footing is good and my pole adds balance. A few more feet and I'm across. What a relief! Not nearly as bad as I feared. I whisper a short prayer of thanks, then retrieve my pack, wrap the radio belt around my waist, and retrace my path. I go slowly, cautiously, no missteps.

The rest of the channels are easy to negotiate, never reaching my knees. I reach the far side and find a place to sit down. I've made it! The group of four had it right: knee deep, not a problem. (Thor's party, it turns out, had a much hairier time along the North Fork than I, including some dunkings in Class III rapids while rafting much of the river between its headwaters and Ernie Creek. "Nearly everybody fell out of the rafts and took a swim somewhere on the trip," he'll tell me weeks later back in town. "That part wasn't so much fun, getting dumped in icy water, but no one got seriously hurt. Hypothermia was the scariest part and we had to build some big fires to warm ourselves and dry out." I'm grateful he didn't share those episodes with me when we crossed paths in the Arctic.)

I pull off my pack, remove my waterlogged boots, and sprawl happily on the ground. My body is spent, more from anxiety than exertion, and for several minutes I'm content to close my eyes and lie upon the damp ground beneath a gray but dry sky. Only when my body rumbles its hunger do I rise, dig into my pack, and pull out a slab of cheese, a few pieces of jerky, and a water bottle. I nibble slowly and contentedly at my snack. There's no longer any reason to rush and I need to unwind before setting up camp. I'm past my biggest obstacle. I'm going to be OK.

PART THREE

Mount Doonerak.

FIFTEEN

Gates of the Arctic

NOW ONLY TEN MILES OR SO FROM MY RENDEZVOUS POINT, I'LL BE staying at the North Fork–Ernie Creek confluence at least three nights, so I want a good campsite. I find one at the edge of spruce-birch-cottonwood forest, in a mossy clearing that is nice and flat, and out of the wind.

Next I explore the sand and gravel bar that borders my temporary home. This must be a major wildlife corridor, because the ground is filled with tracks: wolf, caribou, bear, moose, hare, squirrel, bird, human. Other tracks were most likely made by weasel. Yesterday, not far from the bear skull, I found the carcass of a short-tailed weasel. Little remained, except for fur and bones. It must have been a winter kill; the fur was white, except for the tail's black tip. Here on the sandbar I also find a bleached, rodent-nibbled moose antler plus piles of moose nuggets, the first signs of moose I've come across. The first red squirrel chatter, too, from out of the forest.

My initial explorations done, I haul my food onto the gravel bar a hundred yards or so from the tent, then set up the ParaWing and start the stove. I brought three bottles of white gas and still have more than one remaining, so I have plenty of fuel and sufficient food for the remainder of my solo trek.

After dinner I spend considerable time glassing the landscape with my binoculars, a favorite camp activity. Across the North Fork, miles away on an unnamed mountain, nine Dall sheep graze in a high alpine meadow. I'm at about seventeen hundred feet elevation; they're at forty-five hundred feet, according to my map. Even with magnified eyesight, the sheep aren't much larger than white dots. Two appear to be this year's lambs, so the others must be ewes, with perhaps some adolescents in the mix. At this time of year, mature males keep to their own company. After a week with almost no mammal sightings, I've entered a place with abundant sign and even some of the animals themselves. I know it's an exaggeration to call this a "Northern Serengeti," but the landscape here certainly appears lush, particularly at lower elevations, with "pastures" of tundra and bushes dotting the hillsides and forests along the valley bottom. Life must be considerably easier here than at the divide, little more than ten miles away as the raven flies.

The evening is mostly calm, after a blustery day, but steady mist is again drifting down from the darkly gray sky. The stillness seems to reflect my own inner peacefulness, now that my biggest hurdle is passed. I've moved into a state of relaxed contentment, my reward for a task well performed today. It took some courage to push through my river-crossing fears. Adding to my serenity is the continued absence of mosquitoes. For the second straight day I've needed neither head net nor bug dope.

The weather changes again after I've moved indoors for the night. A sudden upriver breeze alerts me, and a quick peek outside the tent reveals a wall of gray approaching from the south. The last sounds I hear before sleep are the blended rush of river and wind, the hard tapping of rain against tent. Another desert storm.

JULY 28. The first of three days of R&R. With no schedule to keep or destination to reach, I allow myself the luxury of sleeping in, but by midmorning the tent is too warm to remain comfortably inside. Now there's a strange circumstance.

Drawn outside, I bask a while in sweet sunshine, then tend to aching feet. My left heel and right middle toe are badly blistered and they hurt with every step. A few other toes have less serious blisters. I try the neoprene booties, but they only aggravate the raw heel wound. I've survived grizzlies and stream crossings, but blisters may be my undoing, and only because of my own carelessness. First, for not sufficiently dealing with the blisters when they were mere hot spots; second, for not bringing enough mole foam and bandages. Now I'm trying to figure how to best patch my feet for the remaining ten miles of packing. The blistering has been aggravated by wet terrain and stream crossings, which have kept my feet soaked and wrecked my first-aid attempts. But I could have anticipated that. The fact that my boots have gone through several soak-dry cycles has worsened things too. At least I have a few days to rest my battered feet. Today's sun helps, because my boots—and socks and feet—quickly dry and the boots, surprisingly, are easier on my feet than the booties. I'll get to the rendezvous site OK, but maybe with a severe limp. There's also the question of how much day hiking I can do while here, given my worsening feet.

After a leisurely breakfast, I grab binoculars, journal, and sleeping pad, and nestle beside the North Fork under an expansive blue sky. The river serenades me with an orchestra of sounds. Putting my head close to its galloping current, I hear liquid rattling, perhaps from a nearby channel that flows fast and shallow over a gravel bottom, moving stones around, bouncing them into one another. More sounds: rushing, gurgling, tinkling, and a deep bass throbbing. At night, from a distance, the river murmurs.

Looking north from my streamside perch, I can still see the entrance to the Valley of Precipices, now nearly ten miles by foot upstream. Some eight miles to the south is the northern end of the range's famed Gates of the Arctic, "a precipitous pair of mountains, one on each side of the North Fork," named by Marshall during his first trip into the Brooks Range in 1929. Easiest to see from this gravel bar is the Gates' western portal, Frigid Crags. A dark, massive mountain, its lower third is bearded in tundra, thick brush, and, near the base, spruce forest. Above this green growth Frigid Crags soars skyward in a towering succession of black spires, needles, and buttresses. Or as Marshall put it, "a whole series of bristling crags."

Across the North Fork from Frigid Crags, much of Boreal Mountain is hidden by nearer hills. But I can see the peak's jagged summit ridge, sharp rocky spines like those of a platy-backed dinosaur. The desolate upper reaches of both mountains evoke images of the Himalayas, especially when covered in snow, as they are now. Later in the day, swirling clouds will stream off Boreal Mountain's dark summit, giving stronger definition to knife-edged ridges, rocky steeples, and sheer walls cut by couloirs. There are sharp angles everywhere, accentuated by the recent snow. Rays of low-angled evening sunlight briefly break through the clouds, adding to the dramatic effect. It seems an ominous place of rock, ice, and snow, a world drawn in black and white.

BESIDES DAZZLING BOB MARSHALL, the Gates, with its huge, soaring portals enclosing the North Fork's broad, forested valley, got him thinking. "Fortunately," he wrote, "this gorge was not in the continental United States, where its wild sublimity would almost certainly have been commercially exploited [much like Yosemite, which Marshall sometimes compared to parts of the Brooks Range]. We camped in the very center of the Gates, seventy-four miles from the closest human being and more than a thousand miles from the nearest automobile."

Writing decades later, John Kauffman would call Marshall's naming of the Gates "his greatest descriptive coup." Kauffman, the chief planner for Gates of the Arctic National Park and Preserve and author of *Alaska's Brooks Range: The Ultimate Mountains*, explained why: "There are a number of formations in the Brooks Range that resemble in shape, size, and significance the Koyukuk Gates, but so evocative has been the name that it has captured the imagination of all who have heard it. It did much to bring about national park status for the area."

Marshall didn't imagine the Gates as the centerpiece for a Brooks Range parkland. His vision spread far beyond the mountains both north and south, encompassing most of arctic Alaska. Inspired by his expeditions into the arctic wilderness, and recognizing that Alaska presented the nation's last, best chance to preserve the "emotional values of the frontier," he proposed an immense wilderness zone north of the Yukon River, free from roads and industrial-scale development: "Alaska is unique among all recreational areas belonging to the United States because Alaska is yet largely a wilderness. In the name of a balanced use of American resources, let's keep northern Alaska largely a wilderness."

Because no imminent development threatened the arctic wilderness—and because few others shared such a grandiose preservationist vision for Alaska—Marshall's pleas were largely unheeded until the 1950s. Even then, the first place targeted for protection lay east of Marshall's beloved Koyukuk country, in a region explored and popularized by two other renowned wilderness advocates, Olaus and Mardy Murie.

Though the Muries' passionate embrace of northern Alaska—and their decades-long work to protect it—would ultimately be centered in the eastern Brooks Range, their arctic love affair actually began in the Koyukuk region. As documented in Mardy's celebrated book, *Two in the Far North*, she and Olaus were married in late summer 1924; that same year, they embarked on their "honeymoon journey," a 550-mile mushing expedition from Interior Alaska to the Middle Fork of the Koyukuk River. Olaus's caribou research inspired the trip, but Mardy's account makes it clear that both were enchanted by the landscape and its people. Upon entering the range's foothills in late October, Mardy observed, "they rose all around us, on both sides of the river, and they seemed friendly and welcoming," despite the subzero cold and tough trail conditions.

Later she would describe "the glory of another short arctic day ending. It seems that to compensate for its fleeting hours, the winter day begins and ends in a riotous prodigality of color—red to rose, to vermilion streaked and fringed with ocher, saffron, lemon—but all so brief, fading as you try to imprint it in memory, now pale green, now the stars; the mountains draw away into darkness, close black ranks of spruce draw near."

Given the timing of the Muries' expedition, a person might wonder if word of their 1924 journey reached Marshall and perhaps influenced his own decision to explore the Koyukuk region. In *History of the Central Brooks Range*, William Brown reports that's just what happened: "Preservationist Bob Marshall read Olaus

Murie's writings [about his Koyukuk encounters with arctic caribou] and later consulted with him and Margaret. This association helped to lure Marshall to the central Brooks Range." But I've found nothing in either *Alaska Wilderness* or James Glover's definitive biography (*A Wilderness Original: The Life of Bob Marshall*) to suggest that's the case. In fact, Glover plainly states that Marshall only learned about Mardy and Olaus during his own arctic sojourn. In a 1933 letter to Mardy, Marshall wrote in part, "Of course I've heard of you often and your fame still lingers in the Koyukuk as the most beautiful woman who ever came to that region.... Mr. Murie's fame also lingers in the Koyukuk."

What is certain is that Marshall and the Muries eventually became good friends and strong allies in the movement to protect America's remaining wilderness areas, including those in Alaska.

FOR ALL OF the Muries' considerable influence, it fell to a senior Park Service planner named George Collins to instigate the process that would establish the Arctic National Wildlife Range, eventually to become the nineteen-million-acre Arctic National Wildlife Refuge (ANWR). Assigned to Alaska in the early 1950s, Collins eventually discovered for himself the eastern Brooks Range. Together with adjacent lowlands, it offered "an ideal chance to preserve an undisturbed natural area large enough to be biologically self-sufficient...[also valuable] for scientific study and public enjoyment."

Then director of the Wilderness Society, Olaus Murie made it his mission to build public backing for Collins's proposed wildlife range. Though not Alaskans at the time, both Olaus and Mardy had resided in the territory for several years (Mardy, in fact, spent much of her first three decades in Alaska). They understood Alaskans' resistance to government "lockups" of public land. To gain local support, the Muries took a low-key approach. In a letter to Collins, Olaus explained,

An old-timer up north once said to me, "Easy does it." I met with many people from Fort Yukon to Juneau, and I can't remember a time when I came right out and said, "Support this wilderness proposal." I told them what our experience was, and I sincerely wanted them to make up their own minds. Without the sincere backing of people who have thought things through, I feel we can get nowhere.

Joining the growing wave of ANWR boosters were the Alaska Federation of Women's Clubs, the Fairbanks Garden Club, the Anchorage chapter of the Izaak Walton League, and the Tanana Valley Sportsmen's Association. Even the *Fairbanks Daily News-Miner*, Fairbanks Chamber of Commerce, and territorial governor welcomed the idea. It no doubt helped that Interior Secretary Fred Seaton also announced plans to open twenty million acres of North Slope land to mineral leasing.

Alaska's political leaders reversed course in 1959, after the territory became a state. They didn't want any portion of the Arctic closed to mining, as the range would do. But by then the national groundswell was too strong. The 8.9-million-acre Arctic National Wildlife Range was established in 1960.

The effort to protect the Central Brooks Range was a more drawn-out affair. After Marshall's death in 1939, no one championed its protection until Roger Allin in the fifties and sixties. During his Alaska travels (first with the U.S. Fish and Wildlife Service, later with the National Park Service), Allin noted twenty areas with outstanding wilderness values, including three that "just had to be saved for posterity." One would later become Wood-Tikchik State Park; another, Lake Clark National Park and Preserve. The third was the Central Brooks Range's Arrigetch Peaks–John River region.

In a 1966 report that urged more northern parklands, Allin wrote of the Brooks Range: "This is raw, uninhabited, undeveloped nature at its best. Here is a place to prove one's worth. With the exception of a cabin or two it is a true wilderness, used only by sportsmen or wilderness seekers. [Like Marshall before him, Allin largely ignored the presence of Native Alaskans.] While in this part of Alaska nature is a tough and unforgiving adversary, here also she is beautiful beyond all description—remote, pristine, undiscovered and unspoiled."

Four years later, a park planning team led by Merrill Mattes intensively explored the Alatna River–Arrigetch Peaks area, at the far western edge of Marshall's Koyukuk country. Upon his return, Mattes raved about the region, describing it as a landscape that "has been waiting, like Cinderella, for something to happen." He went on to add, "What could and should happen, is the creation of a national park in this Arctic wilderness."

The notion that wilderness might be "waiting" for some human action shows just how deeply anthropocentric even forward-thinking preservationists can be. Perhaps we twenty-first-century wilderness advocates are more open to the notion that wild nature has value in and of itself. But all too often, even today human utility trumps everything.

Mattes's team proposed a two-unit park, split by the John River valley, then assumed to become a transportation corridor; only two years had passed since Governor Walter Hickel sent heavy equipment up the John River to punch a winter road through the Brooks Range to Prudhoe Bay's oil fields. The eastern park would include Marshall's beloved North Fork–Ernie Creek region, with its Valley of Precipices, the Gates, and Mount Doonerak. The western side would encompass the Alatna River, 8,540-foot Mount Igikpak, and two National Natural

Landmarks, Walker Lake and the Arrigetch Peaks. The park's proposed name: Gates of the Arctic.

Mattes's recommendation didn't lead to any direct action, but ultimately that proved to be a fortuitous thing because it allowed an even greater wilderness vision to take hold.

First imagined in the early 1900s by people like Robert Marshall, Charles Sheldon, and the Muries, that preservationist vision was moved along in 1971 by the Alaska Native Claims Settlement Act. Among other things, ANCSA gave Alaska's first peoples nearly $1 billion, plus the right to select forty-four million acres of federally owned land. Section 17(d)(2) of the act also directed the secretary of the interior to withdraw eighty million acres for study as possible parks, wildlife refuges, national forests, and wild and scenic rivers. Based on those "d-2 land" studies, Congress would then officially establish the new national-interest lands by December 18, 1978.

Among the areas to be studied: a huge portion of the Brooks Range, stretching from the Canadian border west to the Chukchi Sea. One block of land encompassed the earlier proposed two-unit park plus the John River Valley, saved from development when the Trans-Alaska Pipeline route was shifted sixty miles to the east for political and economic reasons.

I WAS COMPLETING my first year of grad school at the University of Arizona when the d-2 planners arrived in Alaska in May 1972. Still largely apolitical, I had no idea of the forces reshaping Alaska's landscape. Neither the last frontier nor the push for wilderness preservation was of special interest to me, though my world continued to expand. Until flying to Tucson in the fall of 1971, I'd never been in a jet, nor had I been farther west than Minnesota, or ascended high into mountains and sat on rocky perches, broad basins spread fantastically below me.

I quickly grew to love the desert, with its spare beauty and unusual life forms. The landscape was so much grander than anything I'd known in the East. It seemed to stretch on forever. With its expansive flats and rugged mountains jutting from the lowlands, this was big country like I'd never known and the possibilities it held tugged at my imagination. At the same time, smaller life forms gained my attention in a way that they hadn't since preadolescence, perhaps because they seemed so exotic. The ground literally crawled and buzzed with creatures I'd only read about or seen in books, on TV, and in museums: tarantulas, scorpions, rattlesnakes, horned toads, fleet-footed lizards, road runners, and more. The knowledge that some could injure or even kill with their poisonous bites added the allure of physical danger, something that had been missing since my early days of exploring the Woods and the Swamp back in Trumbull.

For the first time in my life, plants were nearly as alluring as animals, especially the cacti: saguaro, ocotillo, cholla, barrel, prickly pear. How wondrous that their strange, spiny forms could produce such gorgeously soft and bright flowers. The abundance of new shapes and rich colors helped turn this point-and-shoot picture-taker into a serious amateur photographer, an important if surprising step in my evolution from geologist to writer. The fact that my box camera produced impressive images said more about the landscape than either my equipment or my capabilities as a photographer. But I was encouraged enough to get myself some advanced gear: a 35mm camera with two or three different lenses. My small successes as a fledgling photographer drew me even deeper into the desert's wonders and I paid ever more attention to form, texture, and color. The search for images and new forms of life slowed me down and drew me out of myself in a way that I hadn't been for years.

I loved the hot, dry climate, too, though not the searing summers, when even late-night temperatures might reach above one hundred degrees. Stepping out of the air-conditioned jet in early September was like stepping into a furnace. Both the thunderstorms and sunsets were the most spectacular I had ever witnessed. As the sun dropped from view and twilight set in, the western sky would sometimes flare into a golden glow and then slowly deepen to orange, rose, purple, and finally indigo. When darkness set in, the desert's night sky held other forms of magic: on moonless nights deep in the desert, immense numbers of stars sparkled in the equally unfathomable blackness, and the Milky Way formed a pale band across the heavens.

From its plants and animals to the landscape and the weather, Arizona was wilder and more exotic than anything I'd known. There, unlike Maine, I felt pulled away from campus. Part of that was by necessity: my classes required that I do substantial fieldwork. But I also explored the landscape for recreation and solace. Beside the classroom challenges, my grad school years were tough ones emotionally, as I continued to struggle with human relationships—especially those involving women and romance—and some long-buried demons from my boyhood began to haunt me. Once more, I found refuge and hope in wild nature.

The more I came to know it, the more I cherished the desert country outside the city. And for the first time in my life, I began to spend substantial time in the mountains. My favorites were the volcanically formed Tucson Mountains. More hills than mountains, they were easy to reach and explore. I would go there when I needed time away from school or people, to watch the evening sky, walk among cacti, photograph desert plants, or search the ground for unusual creatures. More than anywhere, that's where I found solitude and peace.

Like most of my classmates, I took three years to complete a master's degree. I planned to specialize in mineralogy until learning that line of study involved more time in the lab than the field, more analyzing than collecting. So I switched to petrology: the study of rocks. Though it too required hours in the lab, often staring through a microscope to puzzle out the textures and mineral makeup of rocks, it also demanded plenty of fieldwork in the desert and mountains.

Always the good student, I did well in graduate school. Yet the academic study of rocks and minerals and landforms didn't excite me the way my earlier rockhounding had. Arizona's copper deposits produced spectacular crystalline masses of deep green malachite, sky blue azurite, and other sparkling minerals, and I still did some collecting when possible. My studies, ironically, kept me from doing much of that. I most enjoyed the area's volcanic landscape, but at the suggestion of my advisor I chose the Catalinas' granitic gneisses to study for my thesis. The rocks didn't inspire me, I'm sorry to say, and I think my thesis, though accepted, reflected that fact. And the most vivid memory from my forays into the Catalinas has nothing at all to do with my thesis.

What I recall is this. At the end of a long, hot day of pounding rocks, I am walking the trail back to my truck, eager to get a cold drink and remove my pack, heavy with the gneiss samples that I'll cut and grind and study beneath a scope back at school. My mind wandering, I round a bend in the trail and nearly step on a rattlesnake that's sprawled across the dirt path. Somehow I seem to change direction in midair and leap off the trail, even as the snake—apparently as shocked as I—streaks to the other side, then coils and rattles its warning, a little too late for both of us.

After two and a half years of hoping to see a rattlesnake in the wild, my wish has finally come true. Even more stunning than the rattler's presence, however, is the fact that I didn't get bitten. Now beyond the snake's striking range, I stand motionless while the pounding inside my chest subsides and my fear gives way to delight and gratitude. The snake and I watch each other a minute or two and I wonder what it's experiencing. Then I pull out my camera and snap a picture of the coiled rattler. Guessing that the snake is still in a state of alarm, I move on, not wishing to cause it any additional distress. Heavy load forgotten, I head down the trail with spirits lifted in a way that my geology studies simply couldn't manage.

As the end of my thesis and graduate schooling neared, I had no idea what I would do with my degree. Maybe try to get a full-time job with the U.S. Geological Survey? Then, in spring 1974, Tom Andrews popped the question that would bring me to Alaska.

WHILE I WORKED toward my degree, John Kauffman and his NPS planning team studied Marshall's Koyukuk country and the lands surrounding the Noatak River, which is born on the flanks of Mount Igikpak and then flows nearly four hundred miles west to Kotzebue Sound. To meet the deadline imposed by its

Washington, D.C. bosses, the team had less than six weeks to look at the Central and Western Brooks Range and make its initial recommendations. As Kauffman recalls in *Alaska's Brooks Range*, "Nearly all of our work had to be done by air, of course. We did take a couple of probing hikes to learn how the country 'felt,' and we used a helicopter on occasion to check out some of Bob Marshall's special wonders." The team's grandest expedition was a float trip down the Noatak River: "To my knowledge, there had not been such a voyage down almost the full length of the river, at least not an official one, since Philip Smith's Geological Survey trip of 1911. We felt not far behind S. B. McLenegan's first exploration of [the Noatak basin in] 1885."

Steven Young, a biologist with the Vermont-based Center for Northern Studies, also surveyed the Noatak River and surrounding lands. Amazed by the variety of arctic flora, Young worried that the area's rare and fragile habitats could be easily harmed. "Even recreational use," he warned, "could result in the extinction of many species in the course of a single summer." As evidence of human disturbance, he pointed to the impacts of an ancient Native settlement, still visible two thousand years later. Young also argued eloquently for wilderness preservation because of its importance to humans:

> The whole human race evolved in wilderness, and it is part of the human psyche to be involved with and concerned with wild areas and the idea of what is over the next hill....I hate the thought of my grandchildren not having a chance to do what I'm doing here. We can't preserve the unknown but we can preserve the wonder and vastness and scope, so that future generations will have some feeling of what the world in general was like and, particularly, what the far north was like, and hopefully continues to be like.

Though based on his experiences in the Noatak valley, Young's comments applied equally well to Koyukuk country and, arguably, the entire arctic region. As their explorations took them across the Brooks Range, Kauffman and his coworkers realized that

> the most critical resource was size, spaciousness itself....Where animals must forage so far, where all life is stretched so thin, protections must come broadly.
>
> And it was important to preserve as much as possible for people themselves. With awe and dread, we realized that this was America's last big chunk of raw wilderness, the last land of solitude. There would never be any more. For more than 300 years, Americans had always been able to count on a frontier, and a wilderness hinterland....Somehow, the nation would have to make this last

remnant do, forever, what the whole American wilderness had done to challenge and mold and temper and inspire us as a people and nation.

When figuring how the new park should be developed, the planners believed it best to follow Marshall's advice: do nothing. Construct no roads, trails, campgrounds, interpretive displays, or other visitor amenities usually associated with parklands. Gates, in Kauffman's vision, would be a "black-belt park. Not for neophytes, it would be at the ascetic end of a spectrum of national parks in Alaska that would range from the comforts of hotels and cruise ships to the most basic of wilderness survival."

The park would also be a "great land trust," to be handed down to future generations "when the great-great-grandchildren of present-day Americans would need a wilderness dimension of life."

An aside here. While exploring the Brooks Range during the 1970s, Kauffman occasionally hauled along a writer or two. Among them—on separate trips, as you'd imagine—were John McPhee and Joe McGinniss. Both McPhee's *Coming into the Country* (published in 1976) and McGinniss's *Going to Extremes* (1980) include long passages about their arctic expeditions. I have long believed it a tribute to the Brooks Range's wild grandeur that two robust best-sellers, written by high-profile authors who take very different approaches in their books about America's "Last Frontier," would devote significant and beautifully written sections of their books to this landscape. Of course it also says much about Kauffman's efforts to spread the word about this "ultimate wilderness" and get as much of it protected as possible. McPhee wrote about a trip down the Salmon River, which would eventually earn "wild and scenic status" within Kobuk Valley National Park, just west of Gates, while McGinnis documented a trip into a remote area just north of Bob Marshall's beloved Koyukuk country, within what is now Gates of the Arctic.

While Alaskans have largely embraced McPhee's book, most have decried McGinnis's portrait of their homeland. Indeed, parts of the book paint a dismal, even ugly portrait of Alaska and its residents. Yet the Brooks Range section is written in a glowing way, by someone who's been bedazzled by the place. As Kauffman himself writes in *Alaska's Books Range,*

A chapter of special beauty forms the final part of Joe McGinniss's *Going to Extremes* (1980). In his superb telling of a journey into an unexplored cranny of the Brooks Range, McGinniss relates with quiet intensity the awe and the rapture to which Marshall alludes. It is of mystical experience that McGinniss writes. I know whereof I speak, as I was with him when, reverently, we entered the cathedral that we found. I remember instinctively doffing my hat.

* * *

IN EVALUATING THE importance of this far north wilderness, Kauffman knew he had to consider its value to humans, as well as its preservation of arctic landscapes and ecosystems. In that respect, too, his philosophy mirrored Marshall's.

In 1928, while Marshall was working for the Forest Service, a colleague named Manly Thompson wrote an article for the *Service Bulletin* that protested wilderness preservation. He argued that since less than 1 percent of the U.S. population were wilderness goers, protecting large areas from development was bad public policy. Marshall immediately began work on a rebuttal. Titled "Wilderness as a Minority Right," it disputed Thompson's statistics. But more than that, he wrote, "The real question is whether this minority, whatever its numerical strength, is entitled to enjoy the life which it craves." Though democracy is based on the idea of majority rule, many of its greatest champions, from Voltaire to Thomas Jefferson, had recognized its sometimes dangerous tendency to ignore minority rights. In America, not only were minorities protected, they were sometimes given special treatment, for instance through publicly funded museums and art galleries.

Marshall also emphasized that many of America's greatest thinkers and "men of action" felt a longing "to retire periodically from the encompassing clutch of a mechanistic civilization. To them the enjoyment of solitude, complete independence, and the beauty of undefiled panoramas is absolutely essential to happiness." Such disparate figures as Thomas Jefferson, Henry David Thoreau, Herman Melville, Henry Adams, William James, George Washington, Andrew Jackson, Robert E. Lee, Ulysses S. Grant, and Theodore Roosevelt all considered wilderness crucial to their lives; for several it was a source of inspiration. In concluding his argument, Marshall noted that a wilderness lover had written that people are endowed by their creator with certain inalienable rights, such as life, liberty, and the pursuit of happiness. And for some, at least, "the full enjoyment of those rights is possible only in the wilderness."

In their planning for Gates, Kauffman and his team recognized, like Marshall, that wilderness's value to people can't be measured by statistics: "A single person's awareness, understanding, and concern deepened through wilderness involvement may be of more help and benefit to us in our Earth care than the machine-derived pleasure of thousands."

It will come as no surprise that I wholeheartedly agree with Marshall and Kauffman's arguments about the need for governments to provide activities, programs, and places that serve "the minority," whether that minority needs increased educational opportunities, medical benefits, or spiritual enrichment through wildness. I also see myself and many of my friends in their words. Alone or in small groups, we return again and again into wilderness for solitude, rejuvenation, inspiration, challenge, and revelation. The farther I go—whether measured in miles or time—the easier it becomes to shed the pressures, anxieties, "shoulds," and spinning-out-of-control busyness of day-to-day urban or suburban life. It becomes easier to *feel* the oneness with creation that I have intuitively understood to be true, first early and then again decades later in my life—a "knowing" that I largely denied or suppressed for years, because of the influences of family, religion, and our larger culture.

Three of Western society's greatest influences—mainstream religion, science/technology, and capitalist philosophies—each tend to put humans outside, and usually above, the rest of nature. Instead of being a part of the natural world, we study it, manage it, control it, have dominion over it. Everything becomes a natural resource, even to those who wish to steward and protect wildlands and wildlife.

Even now, this intuitive "being part of" is something I too easily forget when immersed in urban routines, though in my middle-aged years I have done a better job of regularly bringing wild nature into my daily life. And myself into nature. I have managed this through year-round walks, natural history studies of the plants and animals with whom I share the Anchorage landscape, journal writing, and the midlife discovery of the joys inherent in bird feeding and wild berry harvesting. Still, I don't know that I would have been able to (re)establish a deeper relationship with both the wild "other" and wild inner self without the awareness I've gained through deeper trips into wilderness, where society's influences are stripped away to reveal what's essential.

The shifts of consciousness that occur seem nonlinear, almost quantum jumps, as my time in the wilds increases from an hour or two to a day, a week, a month. The more deeply I move, both into wilderness and out of regular time and busyness, the more cultural layers I shed and the more easily I become part of the larger nature that's always there.

ANOTHER ESSENTIAL to becoming intimate with wildness, and discovering—or rediscovering—our place in creation (both individually and as a species), is solitude. It's no coincidence that saints, prophets, messiahs, creative geniuses, and other visionaries across the centuries have found illumination while alone, whether on vision quests deep into the wilderness, or in monasteries, or while locked up in prison cells. I think of the prophets and spiritual leaders Elijah, Moses, John the Baptist, Jesus, Mohammed, and the Buddha, and, more recently the likes of John Muir, Robert Marshall, Thomas Merton, and Nelson Mandela, just to name a few.

Several of my favorite writers and philosophers have addressed the ancient and powerful tradition of solitary journeys into the wilderness, from scientist Loren

Eiseley to mythologist Joseph Campbell, human ecologist Paul Shepard, wilderness advocate/environmental historian Roderick Nash, and Christian theologian Matthew Fox. I owe them many thanks for their reflections on the importance that the world's great religious and cultural traditions have placed on the role of wilderness solitude in seeking—and often gaining—wisdom and new ways of understanding our place in the universe.

Eiseley's take on the matter is characteristically playful and provocative. He begins one of my favorite essays, "The Judgment of the Birds," with these observations:

It is a commonplace of all religious thought, even the most primitive, that the man seeking visions and insight must go apart from his fellows and live for a time in the wilderness. If he is of the proper sort, he will return with a message. It may not be the message from god that he sought out to seek, but even if he has failed in that particular, he will have had a vision or seen a marvel, and these are always worth listening to and thinking about.

The world, I have come to believe, is a very queer place, but we have been part of this queerness for so long that we tend to take it for granted. We rush to and fro like Mad Hatters upon our particular errands, all the time imagining our surroundings to be dull and ourselves quite ordinary creatures. Actually, there is nothing in the world to encourage this idea, but such is the mind of man, and this is why he finds it necessary from time to time to send emissaries into the wilderness in the hope of learning great events, or plans in store for him, that will resuscitate his waning taste for life. His great news services, his world-wide radio network, [and, we might add now, the Internet] he knows with a last remnant of healthy distrust will be of no use to him in this matter. No miracle can withstand a radio broadcast, and it is certain that it would be no miracle if it could. One must seek, then, what only the solitary approach can give—a natural revelation.

Eiseley goes on to reveal a few personal revelations, which form the heart of his essay, then closes with a section that includes this observation: "It was better, I decided, for the emissaries returning from the wilderness, even if they were merely descending from a stepladder, to record their marvel, not to define its meaning. In that way it would go echoing on through the minds of men, each grasping at that beyond out of which miracles emerge, and which, once defined, ceases to satisfy the human need for symbols."

I love that idea. It prompts me to wonder whether I spend too much time trying to understand and explain—to myself and to others—the wonders and mysteries I encounter in the wider, wilder world. (There I go again, trying to understand.) Maybe recording them, whether internally or in images or words, is enough. Happily there are times, however rare, when I move beyond my inherent push to explain or try to figure things out and simply embrace the miracles that come my way.

In a more scholarly approach, Nash devotes an early chapter of *Wilderness and the American Mind* to the ancient traditions that laid the groundwork for our nation's schizophrenic attitudes toward wilderness. In that chapter, he notes that the Bible's Old Testament treats wilderness as both a cursed land and "a place in which to find and draw close to God." A testing ground for the Israelites,

> Wilderness never lost its harsh and forbidding character. Indeed, precisely *because* of them it was unoccupied and could be a refuge as well as a disciplinary force....
>
> When a society became complacent and ungodly, religious leaders looked to the wilderness as a place for rededication and refuge.... When Elijah sought inspiration and guidance from God, he went into the wilderness a symbolic forty days and received it, like Moses, on a deserted mountain.

Christianity, like Judaism, found wilderness to be both a place of evil and pagan rites *and* a place of refuge and spiritual purity. Nash points out that "A succession of Christian hermits and monks (literally, one who lives alone) found the solitude of the wilderness conducive to meditation, spiritual insight, and moral perfection."

Here I should note that both Nash and Joseph Campbell, among others, point out the dramatic difference between traditional Eastern and Western attitudes toward wild nature. Since getting a primer in Eastern beliefs through Campbell's dialogue with Bill Moyers in *The Power of Myth*, I've been struck by the fact that my own core beliefs—and those of many who embrace wildness—more closely parallel those of Eastern religions.

"In the Far East," Nash writes,

> the man-nature relationship was [and is] marked by respect, bordering on love, absent in the West. India's early religions, especially Jainism, Buddhism, and Hinduism, emphasized compassion for all living things. Man was understood to be a part of nature.... As early as the fifth century, BC, Chinese Taoists postulated an infinite and benign force in the natural world. Wilderness was not excluded. Far from avoiding wild places, the ancient Chinese sought them out in the hope of sensing more clearly something of the unity and rhythm that they believed pervaded the universe. In Japan the first religion, Shinto, was a form of nature worship that deified mountains, forests, storms, and

torrents…In linking God and the wilderness, instead of contrasting them as did the Western faiths, Shinto and Taoism fostered love of wilderness rather than hatred.

In *Original Blessing*, Matthew Fox emphasizes that Christianity's earlier mystical traditions, largely overlooked in recent centuries, also saw larger nature—or creation, if you will—as a wondrous good, not a curse. While the harmful notion of original sin has become a Christian creed, it was preceded, centuries earlier, by the notion of original blessing.

"What I call 'original blessing'," Fox explains,

can also be named "original goodness" or "original grace" or "original wisdom." It is not just about the goodness of our species but about the goodness and blessing that fifteen billion years of the universe's grace has revealed and shared with us.…This goodness is inherent in the beauty, wisdom, and wonder of creation. Goodness and creation go together as do goodness and God.…Original blessing is a commitment to putting biophilia first. Biophilia, or love of life, is a synonym for eros, which in turn is a synonym for wisdom.

Talk about blessings! Though I have evolved into something of a pagan panentheist (someone who believes, as Fox puts it, that "God is in everything, and everything is in God"), what a gift it has been to learn that my original faith also has traditions that respect, celebrate, and even glorify wild nature. And that Jesus Christ both espoused and personified such a way of being in the world. Here, as Fox says, is immense reason for hope.

OF COURSE YOU don't have to be a mystic or prophet or artistic genius to gain insights, whether big or small, from what Anthony Storr calls "the peace of solitude." In *Solitude: A Return to the Self*, he writes, "Removing oneself voluntarily from one's habitual environment promotes understanding and contact with those inner depths of being which elude one in the hurly-burly of day-to-day life." I suspect that Loren Eiseley would vigorously agree.

This removal of self is not without its dangers: "Any form of new organization or integration within the mind has to be preceded by some degree of disorganization," Storr cautions. "No one can tell, until he has experienced it, whether or not this necessary disruption of former patterns will be succeeded by something better."

In my experience, the rewards far outweigh the risks.

It's possible to find such "peace of solitude" in many ways: meditation, prayer, research done in libraries, or work done at home in an otherwise empty house. But for many of us modern Westerners, who mostly live in urban or suburban areas, there's almost no escape from the noises and other distractions that offend the senses without getting out into the wilds. Even cafes, which I dearly love, have a bustle about them, and, too frequently, loud conversations and background music. Whenever I need to clear my head or think things through, release stress, or be more playful, it's usually time to get outdoors. Alone.

Only in recent years have I begun to fully appreciate how the quality of my own connection to nature depends on whether I'm with others or by myself. That might seem obvious to some. But what has struck me is the depth of the difference. Even the presence of one good friend dramatically changes the dynamic. I've seen this phenomenon most clearly in Anchorage, while hiking local woodland trails. With friends, I predictably become engaged in conversations that diminish my awareness of the surroundings. I simply don't pay the same attention, and the forest and its inhabitants become the backdrop for our own ideas and dramas. Even when we're listening to birds, identifying plants, or noticing some other aspect of our homeland's natural history, our relationship with the landscape tends to be superficial. There's nothing wrong with this. I greatly enjoy sharing wildlands and wildlife with others; and there are times when the presence of a friend or lover can deepen my appreciation of an encounter with wildlife, the grandeur of a sunset, the beauty of an alpine meadow. But to go deeper into the experience, I normally must go alone. So I do.

I regularly hike alone, mostly in local woodlands, but also in Anchorage's coastal flats and in the Chugach Mountains east of town. And I make it a point to annually go on solo retreats, sometimes camped in the backcountry, other times at a public-use cabin. Alone in the wilds, I can go at my own pace, be serious or silly, engage in conversations with chickadees or squirrels if I choose. I can also reflect, free associate, make connections, allow memories to bubble up. Now and then, I can also move into the still, quiet state in which ego washes away and, for a short while, I experience myself as truly part of a grander, more mysterious whole. Such moments are difficult to share, without seeming "woo-woo" or sentimental or overly romantic. But they happen, with chickadees and pine siskins as well as with bears and wolves. Sometimes they occur when noticing the wind moving through trees; or when sitting upon the base of an old, deeply furrowed cottonwood; or standing alone on a ridge, immersed in a landscape that glows with the setting sun; or waking in the middle of the night and looking out the tent and seeing millions of stars blinking wildly in an otherwise pitch-black sky.

More and more frequently, such moments also occur in my yard. Once it happened on take-out-the-garbage night. A great horned owl hooted in the darkness and I spent a half hour or more listening and imagining, drawn out of routine, the house, and ideas of what I should instead be doing. It's also happened while watching an acorn-sized mass of newborn spiders, each no bigger than a pinhead, wriggling their first steps.

These moments of grace also happen now and then in the ritual spaces of meditation, music, prayer, and writing. This is the other, more cultural, way I've found of opening up and entering a larger reality, as the ego shrinks or simply gives way. Of course there's no firm divide between the two. One of my middle-aged lessons has been the understanding that the many parts of my life—again, like larger nature—are inextricably intertwined. Family, prayer, meditation, mountain scrambles, writing, spirituality, sports, politics, friendships, daily walks, sexuality, intimacy, social justice, environmental health, wildness in its many forms: they're all interconnected, in complex ways we can only begin to imagine.

Looking back across my life, I see I've always had this need for solitude from humans, which paradoxically often leads to deeper communion with the larger world. But early on, I also became a good friend with solitude's unhealthy twin, isolation. For many years, I couldn't see the difference between solitude and isolation; now I understand solitude to be spirit lifting, isolation to be spirit damaging, even deadening. But for me, at least, there's often a fine line between the two.

When family, friends, or life became too overwhelming, I learned to remove myself entirely. Isolation is a deep, dark place of disconnection and despair; but early in life, it was a way of escaping other, greater emotional wounds. And it was a place, a way of being, that I embraced more and more frequently as I entered adolescence. Internally, I lived in my own world. At the same time I secluded myself emotionally, I longed for romantic love, which, I believed, might save me. But I didn't seem to be worthy of it, or know how to get it.

Though I spent lots of time alone during my later teenage years and early adulthood, I didn't frequently venture in nature—with the notable exception of my rockhounding forays, later followed by my college field trips and geology thesis studies, and then my mineral explorations in Alaska. Thinking about it now, those earth science interests were, like my earlier boyhood romps in woods and swamp, another sort of saving grace. They kept me going until I could find my true calling.

During those confused and lonely years, when fortunate to have some out-in-nature epiphany or be overwhelmed by the beauty of a place or moment, I would be saddened, even despairing, that I had no one to share it—a reflection of my deeper longing to be part of a loving, shared relationship. Perhaps because I've been blessed with an abundance of human love and friendships in my middle age, I no longer suffer such feelings of loss when "alone" in a miraculous moment. Being part of the moment—and perhaps knowing there are others to share it with later—is reward in itself.

THERE'S A MESSIER SIDE to this desire for wilderness solitude that needs to be addressed. The longing may be so great that it leads to a kind of selfishness. I've sometimes seen this greediness arise in myself and friends when "our" remote valley, or mountain, or fjord has been invaded by other adventurers, themselves also likely seeking the joy and peace of a secluded place. Instead of welcoming the other wilderness lovers, we—I—have been aggravated by the intrusion.

In the account of her Koyukuk mushing adventure with husband Olaus, Mardy Murie describes an entirely different sensibility: "It creates a special kind of feeling to meet another soul unexpectedly in a very large wilderness. It must be the same feeling our forebears had when, slipping through the primeval forest, they glimpsed the smoke of another campfire wafting over the treetops."

The writings of both Murie and Marshall reflect a welcoming attitude and generosity of spirit toward other backcountry travelers (and residents). Nowadays we more often try to avoid each other. This likely is tied to the stresses of contemporary urban life and the hope to escape such stresses in the wilds. The arrival of other people in what had seemed to be an uninhabited place, even if the others are miles away, can create a false—but still very real—sense of crowdedness. One of the reasons we have gone deep into the mountains or to some remote island is to leave people behind.

The Wilderness Act, which so greatly influences our contemporary image of wild landscapes, makes it clear that these are places "where the earth and its community of life are untrammeled by man, where man himself is a visitor who does not remain." The farther we go into wilderness, the more we expect to be left alone. The presence of even a few other people may, sadly, diminish our experience.

That's likely less true in Gates of the Arctic, a place distinguished from other parklands because it's an *inhabited* wilderness. If you've done your homework, you know going in that people live in and around Gates. They're an integral part of the landscape.

I also suspect a welcoming attitude grows the longer a person remains in the wilds, when the need for solitude has largely been satisfied or even exceeded. This must be especially true after months, or years, of being alone and it helps to explain the joyous, talkative way that many Koyukuk residents greeted the

Muries in 1924 and later Bob Marshall. Perspectives also have a way of changing when conditions are harsh. The old adage "misery loves company" may be
especially true in remote wild places. I'm reminded of my own embrace of Thor
Tingey's group that stormy night near the Arctic Divide. Their voices and laughter were welcome indeed.

FOR MOST OF us Americans—and increasingly around the world—contemporary life provides an abundance of distractions and barriers that magnify the
sense of separateness between humans and the rest of nature. And even among
ourselves. For instance: we spend most of our lives indoors, whether at home,
the office, shopping, or even recreating, and in getting from one place to another.
Many remain insulated when they head "outdoors." Even at our nation's most
famous wilderness parks, most people spend the bulk of their time in cars, buses,
cruise ships, hotels, or gift shops. Consider, for example, Denali National Park,
generally recognized as Alaska's premier tourist attraction. Only a small fraction
of visitors go more than a quarter mile beyond any of the park's roads, trails, or
parking lots. And among the hundreds of thousands who visit each year, the vast
majority "experience" Denali from the inside of a bus. To take it a step further: of
those who are bused along the single, ninety-mile-long road that dissects Denali's
six-million-acre wilderness, an increasing number do so on "natural history" tours
that go less than twenty miles from the park's entrance. The average stay of a
Denali visitor: one day. And most of that is indoors. It boggles the mind.

It can be argued that most people's reluctance to get out and explore tundra, forest, wetland, or desert is a good thing, because it keeps wildlands from being trampled. But there must be some middle ground that gets the masses more in touch
with wild nature. For until we humans feel some bond, some connection, it's all
too easy to imagine other forms of life as "things" to be utilized, overlooked, or dis-
missed. Or worse, to be eradicated, as we "improve" living conditions for humans.
In recent years, I, like many other nature writers, have worked to communicate
the surprising and often spirit-lifting wildness to be found all around us, even in
our yards and neighborhoods. Still, I understand that the possibilities expand in
places like parks and wildlife refuges. If people resist touching and being touched
by nature in parklands, then where?

For all that we wilderness advocates gain from our adventures, its preservation
is not a self-serving elitism, as so many development proponents would argue.
While it's true that wilderness trips are often expensive, especially in Alaska, it's
equally true that most people who visit remote backcountry are neither wealthy
nor among our nation's powerful elite. We are simply willing to scrimp and save

and devote limited resources to our trips into the wilds rather than spend money on high-tech toys, SUVs, expensive properties, or packaged resort or cruise-ship vacations. At the same time, many preservationists work, without pay, to protect lands and waters they will likely never visit, because they believe in the critical necessity of such places.

In the extreme, some wilderness defenders have proposed that there might even be places where *no* human presence is allowed. Edward Abbey, for instance. In *Down the River*, he suggested the possibility of an "absolute wilderness," which would recognize "the rights of other living beings to a place of their own, an evolution of their own not influenced by human pressure." Even in Abbey's time, such an absolute wilderness might have been impossible to achieve. It certainly is now, for as environmentalists like Bill McKibben have pointed out, there is no longer any place on Earth that can totally escape the pervasive influence of humans. That doesn't mean we should stop setting aside wilderness areas, or give up on the possibility of a planet where we are more friendly cohabitants with Earth's other life forms. In the fourth edition of *Wilderness and the American Mind*, partly in response to research and writings that emphasized the global ecological crisis (most notably McKibben's *The End of Nature* and Carolyn Merchant's *The Death of Nature*), Nash proposes a visionary shift in behavior that he calls "Island Civilization," in which high technology *reduces* our species' impact on the world.

"The key," he explains,

> is implosion. A thousand years from now human beings (hopefully fewer of them) could occupy several hundred concentrated "habitats."...The rest of the planet, indeed almost all of it, would be left alone, uncontrolled, and wild. Instead of dominating Earth, people and their works would occupy small niches in an interconnected, wild ecosystem. Instead of islands of wildness (or parks) in a civilized matrix, it is *civilization* that is contained.

Nash further explains, "The beauty of Island Civilization is that it permits humans to fulfill their evolutionary potential while not compromising or eliminating the chances of other species fulfilling theirs." He then calls for an "ecological contract" that extends natural rights to all of nature, thus building on Aldo Leopold's "land ethic."

Given his vision, it should come as no surprise that Nash is among those who wish our species to respect "the existence rights of the other species occupying this planet" while assuring wilderness's preservation and even its growth, rather than diminution.

More openly a wilderness advocate since he retired from academia in the mid-1990s, Nash offers a searing appraisal of humanity's modern place on Earth: "Sure humans are 'natural,' but somewhere along the evolutionary way from spears to spaceships they dropped off the biotic team" to become "cosmic outlaws" who no longer think or act like part of nature. "Right now," he urges,

> we desperately need a "time out" to learn how to be team players once again. We need to learn how to live responsibly in the larger neighborhood called the eco-system, and the first requirement is to respect our neighbors' lives.
>
> What wilderness provides is precisely this "time out" from the civilized jug-gernaut. Its presence reminds us of just how far we have distanced ourselves from the rest of nature. Wild places, remember, are uncontrolled, "self willed."...We didn't make wilderness; it made us....This is where wilderness assumes not only ecological but ethical value....The concept of wilderness helps our kind better understand the rights of other kinds to a place in this planet's community of life; the actuality of wilderness provides that place.

Powerful ideas, well thought out and expressed.

So, yes, wilderness preservation is partly about opportunity. But even more, it's about caring for the wild Earth and recognizing that large expanses of wild-lands are needed to prevent ecosystems from becoming fragmented and provide necessary habitat for large, wide-ranging animals such as grizzlies, wolves, eagles, and caribou. A preservation ethic comes from the understanding that our planet's nonhuman inhabitants have value in and of themselves, regardless of their utility to *Homo sapiens*; and that their homelands, largely diminished throughout most of the world, require whatever protections we can give them in an era of unsur-passed human greed. Perhaps, as Nash proposes, we will someday move beyond that greed toward a greater good that encompasses the entire Earth and all our planet's residents.

IN ONE RESPECT, Gates's planners were at odds with Marshall: the naming of things. There's a certain irony to Marshall's arctic explorations. Here was a man completely fascinated by blank spaces on maps, drawn to the Brooks Range because it seemed on maps to be "the most unknown section of Alaska." Yet by the end of his fourth and last expedition in 1939, he had mapped some twelve thousand square miles that were previously "a total blank." At least to the larger, Western culture. To Nunamiut and Athabascan peoples, much of the Central Brooks range was home, with well-known—and named—places of cultural import. Marshall never seemed to fully grasp or at least recognize that older, oral system of naming and mapping.

By the time he finished, Marshall had officially named 164 geographic features never before printed on maps: mountains, rivers, valleys, glaciers, and lakes. To his credit, he selected old and well-established names when he knew them. And, he emphasized, dozens of other mountains, lakes, and creeks remained unnamed. Still, he compulsively filled up those unmarked maps.

Cultural attitudes towards naming had changed considerably by the 1970s. No longer was it considered necessary or even desirable to fill maps of wild areas with labeled landmarks. In their planning for Gates, Kauffman and his teammates "hoped there would be no more geographic naming, convinced it means more to essay a nameless summit or valley than one tamed by nomenclature." Over time, he adds, this approach has been applied to the entire range.

In the late 1990s, I trekked into an arctic valley enclosed by immense rock walls and towering spires, all of them unnamed. The place reminded me of another spectacular cluster of mountains far to the southwest: the Arrigetch Peaks, or "fingers of the hand extended" to the Inupiat and Nunamiut Eskimos. Those granite fingers are the most famous cluster of mountains in northern Alaska and one of the principal visitor attractions in Gates of the Arctic National Park. Over the years, thousands of people have visited the Arrigetch, and millions more have been mesmerized by their descriptions and pictures in dozens of magazines and books.

Like the Arrigetch, the towers rising before me were within Gates of the Arctic. But they were mostly limestone peaks, not granite. More significantly to anyone who's not a geologist or rock climber, they were—and still are—largely unknown. Anonymous, remote, and difficult to reach, they've attracted few human visitors. And so far, no national acclaim. That was good news for our party of five, because we had this place all to ourselves. We also had few or no expectations when entering the hidden amphitheater. That left room for discovery and surprise.

Such anonymity is also good for the landscape. We found no obvious evidence of human passage here. The Arrigetch landscape, by contrast, shows abundant signs of wear and tear despite its remoteness and expensive airplane access. Repeated and sometimes careless use by backcountry travelers has produced hardened campsites, soil erosion, tundra damage, locally depleted wood supplies, and stretches of well-defined trails in what is supposed to be a pristine wilderness area.

Don't misunderstand me: for the most part the Arrigetch remains a beautifully wild place, one that's both challenging and inspiring to visit. But no longer is it the largely "untrammeled" wilderness it was when Marshall passed nearby in 1931. With few resources to harvest here and no easy passage through the Arrigetch's steep-walled mountains, indigenous peoples seldom visited this rugged terrain, at least for long; and any who came here left little or no evidence of their passing.

Other consequences of the Arrigetch's popularity: visitors are more likely to meet other people than not, which diminishes the sense of solitude that most recreational wilderness explorers desire; and bears that inhabit the area have occasionally harassed backpackers, after learning to associate people with food. Several years ago, park officials killed one such food-conditioned grizzly because they believed the bear posed dangers to Arrigetch backpackers and climbers.

Among my partners on that early-August Brooks Range trip into the hidden and officially unnamed valley were two National Park Service employees: Gates of the Arctic superintendent Dave Mills and subsistence and wilderness specialist Steve Ulvi. The others were Chip and Bucky Dennerlein, both devout conservationists. Given the group's makeup, it was inevitable that we talked about wilderness values, backcountry solitude, the notion of destinations, and the naming of places.

Our group fit decisively within the no-new-naming camp, particularly for remote wilderness areas rarely visited by people, locals included. We found pleasure in walking among nameless mountains and drinking from anonymous creeks; the human imprint seemed somehow smaller, the landscape in some measure wilder, more primitive. Names, we agreed, inevitably attract people's attention. They become reference points or points of interest. "Once you name a place," Dave reflected, "it becomes a destination. And once you have a destination, you face the possibility of overuse."

Even in Gates, a vast parkland the size of four Yellowstones, most visitors are drawn to a few well-known, highly publicized "name" places. The Arrigetch Peaks is one. Walker Lake and the Noatak River are others. Dave considered them "hot spots" that need relief. His goal was to spread out the use, encourage people to choose their own blank spaces on the map, make their own discoveries. Yet it's something most people seem reluctant to do.

It seems a natural human instinct, this desire to name things. Hefting fifty-to-sixty-five-pound packs and slowly picking our way across the wet, tussocky tundra, we found ourselves doing it, time and again. Over there: doesn't that look like a Castle Ridge? That rocky stream might be Boulder Creek. As for the hidden amphitheater, Valley of Spires struck my fancy, while another person playfully suggested Tortured Rocks. This personal naming has its merits, we decided. "You can name a hill or a lake and it stays with you, in your memory," Chip observed. "And the best part is, anyone else can do the same. A place and its features take on a personal significance, maybe even a deeper meaning." The name and meaning then remains with you, not imposed upon the country.

It seems desirable, even necessary, to more fully discuss the naming of places by Alaska's Native peoples, because their approach contrasts so greatly with both Marshall's method of identifying landscape features and my own group's preference for an unnamed landscape. Here I'll defer to Richard Nelson, who spent considerable time studying—and learning from—Alaska's Inupiat and Koyukon people. He beautifully describes the nature of their landscape naming in his essay "The Embrace of Names," while making indigenous perspectives easily accessible to non-Natives.

Both the Inupiat and Koyukon tribes—and, I'm sure, the Nunamiut people—traditionally use place-names to "chart the landscape and color it with beauty and meaning." The country is rich "not [in] empty words but names, filled with memories, filled with the land's beauty, filled with stories from ancient times."

> Many names tell something about the places to which they belong—how the terrain looks, what animals or plants are found there, what has happened there in the recent or distant past. These are names born from the land itself, as much a part of it as the spruce forests, the bedrock outcrops, and the twisting rivers. They are also rich in sound and sometimes aglow with spiritual power that renders the landscape sacred.

Nelson also speaks to the gradual impoverishment of names "as Europeans spread west [and north], knowing too little of the land and its people to realize what was being lost. The continent was plundered of its names, left desolate, emptied of mind and memory and meaning."

Much of the Nunamiut's homeland, too, has been plundered of its names, at least on official government maps of the Central Brooks Range. For all his vision, Marshall, like his peers, only occasionally considered local indigenous names when filling in those "blank spaces" that so attracted him to the Arctic. Still, a few Native names can be found on the maps I carry on this trek, names closely tied to the landscape with either personal or community significance. Thus Anaktuvuk is the place of caribou droppings. The Arrigetch are the fingers of the hand extended.

Mount Igikpak, the Nunamiut name for the Central Brooks Range's highest mountain, roughly translates into Big Mountain or "two big peaks," reflecting its twin summits. Iñupiat Eskimos living south of the range gave it another name, Papiok, or "fish's tail." According to legend, a giant trout had swallowed a child at a large nearby lake. The mother in revenge dropped hot rocks into the lake until the scalded trout leaped out, high onto the mountain. And there it froze, tail up.

To again give Marshall credit, many of the names he bestowed have local relevance. Consider Gates of the Arctic; Valley of Precipices; Graylime, Grizzly, and

Ernie Creeks; and Hanging Glacier, Blackface, Limestack, and Slatepile Mountains, to name a few. Those are certainly an improvement on Alaska place-names that have no relevance at all to the local landscape, the best example being Mount McKinley.

If Marshall returned today, I'll bet that he, like me, would nod his approval at Nelson's call for a renaming of Alaska's landscape:

> I can think of few more worthy endeavors, few gestures that could better show our respect toward the environment that sustains us, than to remove this blight of numb, invading names. Where elders remain to teach us, we could resurrect original names and put them back where they belong. If all memory has faded, we could find names through the land's own guidance and inspiration, as countless generations of inhabitants have done before us.

If that were done, a landscape filled with names could be preferable to—and undeniably richer than—one of unnamed hills and valleys.

FOR ALL THAT they did to ensure the Central Brooks Range would retain its wild, primitive character, park planners made "one great concession to modernity": access by plane. By the 1970s, air travel was already well established in Alaska's Arctic. And visitors would need some way to get into Gates besides boat or foot. "We had misgivings about it," Kauffman admits, "but realized how difficult, politically, it would be to establish a walk-in park so huge that a pedestrian would need more weeks to get into it than he or she could expect to have free."

Because few travelers would be able to explore anything but the park's fringes, a no-fly, no-road park would come close to Abbey's "ultimate wilderness," realistically attainable only by locals and those exceptional explorers who could afford to take weeks, or even months, to wander through Gates. And they would have to do so Bob Marshall style: on foot, perhaps with packhorses to haul food for an extended stay, and certainly the ability to live off the land, always a challenge in this spare land, made even more difficult by hunting restrictions. In a curious way, then, the elimination of aircraft travel in Gates would create the sort of "elitist" parkland that critics so loudly and alarmingly decried.

While trying to figure out how, if at all, airplane travel into Gates should be managed, planners also looked at ways to spread out and control visitor numbers. What they ended up proposing was a reservation and permit system, similar to the one now implemented in Denali National Park, with backcountry campers assigned to a particular valley, mountain, or river drainage. Such a system, they felt, would ensure a greater sense of solitude and personal discovery. It would also prevent the "erosive overuse" of popular destinations. Small groups would be the rule, following low-impact backcountry practices.

"Our hope," Kauffman writes, "was that visitors a century hence would find the same qualities, have the same experiences that thrilled and humbled us, walking in Bob Marshall's footsteps."

At the other end of the spectrum were state politicians, business interests, and even some federal bureaucrats, less concerned with preserving wilderness values than the ways Alaska's new parklands would serve visitors and the state's economy. With such disparate attitudes and visions, compromise was inevitable. The reservation/permit system would be among the casualties.

Another Alaska-specific compromise was the separation of Gates into both park and preserve. About 948,000 of the unit's 8.2 million acres—approximately 12 percent—are designated preserve lands. In Gates, as in certain other Alaska parklands, "sport hunting" and recreational trapping are allowed in the preserve, while only subsistence activities by locals are allowed in the park. And while nearly all of the park is officially designated wilderness, none of the preserve is (although potentially it could be).

BY ALL ACCOUNTS, the 1970s push to pass the Alaska National Interest Lands Conservation Act—more simply known as the Alaska Lands Act, or ANILCA— was the environmental community's largest and most organized campaign ever. Propelled by an alliance of groups called the Alaska Coalition, conservationists inspired a national movement to protect wild lands and waters in America's Last Frontier—the last remaining place in the United States that wilderness preservation could be done on such a huge scale. The effort gained critical political support and momentum in 1976 and '77, first with the election of Jimmy Carter as president, followed by critical leadership changes in Congress, most notably involving two Democrats in the House of Representatives, Morris "Mo" Udall and John Seiberling, both passionate ANILCA advocates.

The campaign was also helped along by the eloquence of activists like Mardy Murie. After Olaus's death in 1963, Mardy had taken on much of her husband's work. As the years passed, she carved out her own legacy while working for the passage of the Wilderness Act (1964) and then ANILCA. By her death in 2003, she would become widely and affectionately known as the "Grandmother of the Conservation Movement."

In 1975, Murie boldly told an Alaskan audience,

I think my main thought is this: that perhaps Man is going to be overwhelmed by his own cleverness; that he may even destroy himself by this same cleverness; and I firmly believe that one of the very few hopes left for Man is the preservation of the wilderness we now have left; and the greatest reservoir of that medicine for mankind lies here in Alaska.

…Man, for his ego, is not the only creature. Other species have some rights too. Wilderness itself, the basis of all our life, does it have a right to live on? Having furnished all the requisites of our proud materialistic civilization, our neon-lit society, does it have a right to live? Do we have enough reverence for life to concede to Wilderness this right?

The notion that wilderness and its inhabitants might have innate "rights" was—and remains—a visionary idea that doesn't compute for most Americans. To even suggest the possibility to an Alaska audience was bold indeed. Equally bold was Murie's 1977 testimony before the House of Representatives' Alaska Lands Subcommittee, which began, "I am testifying as an emotional woman and I would like to ask you, gentlemen, what's wrong with emotion?" After that stunner, she continued, "Beauty is a resource in and of itself. Alaska must be allowed to be Alaska, that is her greatest economy. I hope the United States of America is not so rich that she can afford to let these wildernesses pass by—or so poor she cannot afford to keep them."

How much her words moved the House committee is uncertain, but they earned her a standing ovation from the audience.

For all of that, by 1978—after a half decade of intense political maneuverings—Congress's great debate over Alaska's wildlands still showed no signs of being resolved. With the d-2 land withdrawals set to expire on December 18 if Congress failed to act, President Carter and his secretary of the interior, Cecil Andrus, took matters into their own hands. Using his executive powers, Carter proclaimed seventeen different areas as national monuments, even as pro-conservation leaders in the Senate and House worked for legislation that would provide even greater protections. Alaska's political leaders fought just as hard to stop them.

Carter's loss to Ronald Reagan in the 1980 presidential election forced wilderness advocates to accept a take-it-or-leave-it deal in the Senate. Though not all that they sought, it was mighty impressive, protecting an area larger than California. President Carter signed ANILCA into law on December 2, 1980, one of his last—and greatest—acts as president. Years later, he would call it "one of my most gratifying achievements in public life.…This final victory was especially pleasing because it was also a triumph over a mighty phalanx of greedy special interests who had made a last-minute effort to kill the bill."

In setting aside more than 104 million acres in federal public lands, the Alaska Lands Act doubled the size of the national wildlife refuge system, added forty-seven million acres to the National Park System, and designated twenty-five Alaska streams as National Wild and Scenic Rivers. Three existing Alaska parks were expanded and ten new units were established, including Wrangell–St. Elias National Park and Preserve, which at 13.2 million acres is larger than Maryland, Massachusetts, and Delaware combined. Nearly two-thirds of the parkland—thirty-two million acres—was designated wilderness (by comparison, all U.S. parks outside Alaska include only six million acres).

Planners who had crossed the Brooks Range in search of special places didn't get everything they had hoped and asked for. Still, most of the Brooks Range was protected, in five different units that spread almost continuously from Canada to the Chukchi Sea: the Arctic National Wildlife Refuge, Gates of the Arctic National Park and Preserve, Noatak National Preserve, Kobuk Valley National Park, and Cape Krusenstern National Monument.

While most wilderness lovers and advocates still look upon the Alaska Lands Act as an enormous victory, it is far from perfect. That's not especially surprising, given the nature of political compromise. As Kauffman has written, "Celebrated as a great conservation coup, ANILCA is also now regarded by many as a monstrosity, 180 pages long, that confused its would-be implementers with all sorts of strange new provisions…[that] countermanded the intent of preservation, protected the status quo of a variety of state and private property rights and mechanical access rights, and undermined conservation precedent."

Kauffman paints a rather bleak picture of a degraded Central Brooks Range in his early-nineties epilogue to *Alaska's Brooks Range*, and he warns of an even more dreadful future. I'm happy to report that his dire predictions of a developed, fragmented, and greatly diminished landscape have so far not been realized. Yes, "the freshness has faded." There are places, primarily around Anaktuvuk Pass, where ATV trails mar valley bottoms. And the Hickel Highway still scars the John River valley. More people roam the landscape and they tend to be funneled into valleys where air landings are possible. A few popular and well-publicized destinations have been loved into ill health, though nothing approaching death, by the comings and goings of too many wilderness seekers. And Bob Marshall would probably despair that it's almost impossible to escape airplane overflights anywhere in the range.

For all of that, the Central Brooks Range remains vibrantly wild. Development is largely restricted to Anaktuvuk Pass, the Trans-Alaska Pipeline corridor, a few lodges, and some small-scale gold operations; and all of those but Anaktuvuk village and one lodge are outside the park's boundaries. Even now, fewer than two thousand people visit the park most years from mid-June through mid-September, the prime time for wilderness trips. There are still times and places where you can go days, even weeks, without seeing another group. I've had the luxury of such immense solitude myself, just as I've had the great pleasure of hiking numerous valleys and ridges that bear little, if any, human sign.

More good news: park managers are serious about keeping the human imprint light. No other park in the system places such a focus on solitude and wilderness recreation, just as no other park is to be managed, first and foremost, "to maintain the wild and undeveloped character of the area." (No matter that "wilderness management" is something of an oxymoron.) To that end, limits have been placed on the size of commercial parties, and nonguided visitors are encouraged to voluntarily keep their groups small. And there have been tentative steps toward a new backcountry/wilderness plan (put on indefinite hold as this is written) that might include some sort of zoning system to disperse use and relieve the pressure on popular areas.

Though Gates is inland and mountainous, recreationally it is first and foremost a river park. At first that seems strange. But as Gates wilderness planner Steve Ulvi (now retired) once explained, "Rivers are natural highways through these mountains. You can cover more ground and see more wildlife, and it's easier than backpacking." Only a quarter of the park's visitors travel exclusively overland; the rest combine river trips with day hikes. Because of that, much of the park's updated backcountry plan, when it finally happens, will almost certainly address recreational use of river corridors.

Ideally, a wilderness plan would have been in place years ago. But as Ulvi has noted, "We still have time to do it right. This is our challenge: to take our nation's flagship wilderness park and create a plan that preserves its wilderness character, and opportunities for wilderness recreation, in the long term—before there are any crises, or compromises to be made."

With such a backcountry/wilderness plan still in limbo, we can only hope that visionary leaders will step forward while, as Ulvi put it, "we're still ahead of the game."

SIXTEEN

From Geologist to Writer and Greenie

WHILE STUDYING THE GATES IN LATE-MORNING SUN, I NOTICE A dark speck against milky white vapor in the mostly azure sky. Through binoculars, the speck becomes a golden eagle, wings outstretched to catch the thermals on which the great bird spirals upward. It's calm here along the river, but the sun's reappearance after so many days in hiding has sufficiently heated the atmosphere to create warmed, rising columns of air. The silhouetted bird soars in great arcing swoops, and in these ever-widening coils the eagle's head occasionally flashes golden, in brilliant contrast with its dark body.

A second eagle joins the first. There's little difference in size, at least from this distance, but the second bird has a band of white across the bottom of its tail feathers, revealing it to be a juvenile, perhaps one just getting its wings. While the parent soars without beating a wing, the youngster now and then flaps its huge feathered arms, as if not fully confident it could otherwise remain aloft. Parent and child fly nearer, swing past each other in intersecting loops. I imagine the adult, in example if not words, gently encouraging its offspring, "See, this is how it's done."

Then a third eagle circles in. Another adult. Thousands of feet above the ground, the three eagles gradually drift up valley, toward me, and I must lay my head on the river bar's cobbles to follow their graceful flight. Like so many skills, when mastered this soaring looks easy. Yet the juvenile's flapping shows that is not necessarily so.

Minutes pass—or is it hours?—and the young bird abandons its parents, flies on great flapping strokes back down valley, lands on a craggy hilltop. Has it grown tired from the exercise? The parents slowly follow their offspring south, once more drifting apart. I lose sight of one, then the other. They're gone as suddenly as they joined my day.

Leaving my spot beside the North Fork, I explore my temporary home. The riverbar's outer edges are bare gravel and sand, but sections closer to the forest—and farther from the North Fork's cycles of erosion and deposition—have been colonized by pioneering plants: cottonwood, willow, and spruce saplings; dwarf birch; grasses and mosses; soapberry, whose shining fire-engine-red berries are a favorite of grizzlies but bitter to humans; dwarf fireweed, also known as "river beauty," a fitting nickname for a plant whose fuchsia flowers brighten northern riverbanks and bars; and Eskimo potato, whose roots are also favored by grizzlies. Along the forest's edge, an assortment of woodland wildflowers are in full bloom: tiny, delicate twin flowers, tall magenta fireweed, sweet-smelling wild rose, and white shy maidens, their upper stem and flower "faces" humbly bent toward the earth.

I notice lots of insects, too, perhaps drawn out of hiding by today's warming sun. Grasshoppers, leafhoppers, various beetles, and green caterpillars jump, scurry, and inch their way among the greenery, while moths flap through the air, joined by at least four kinds of butterflies: white ones and lemon yellow ones with a dark spot in the middle of each wing; gorgeous small ones with blue-black bodies and lavender wings bordered in brown; and even one species I can name, swallowtails.

Crane flies, deer flies, cervid flies, and swirling gnats buzz among the flowers, along with fuzzy bumblebees and sleek, aggressive yellowjackets, all of them pollinating as they go. Mosquitoes, too, hover and buzz about, though they haven't been an annoyance here. For all the misery they've brought to me (and other explorers), I appreciate their role as important arctic pollinators. It's something I mention when friends sometimes ask, "What good are mosquitoes, anyway?"

A person could spend an entire summer—or many summers—just getting to know the insect life of this one gravel bar. And I mustn't forget the spiders: web builders and ground hunters carrying egg sacs abound.

Across a wide channel, on a smaller slice of gravel, is some gleaming debris. Hoping that no human is attached to it, I move closer and peer through the binoculars. It's a brass-colored "space blanket," tangled in a bleached tree trunk and partly buried by stream debris. What circumstances might have led to the loss of that protective gear? I also find a small black plastic funnel that's cracked; boot prints; a campfire pit with charred driftwood and semicircle of sitting stones. I wonder how often people camp here, such a lovely, inviting place at the edge of river and forest, surrounded by mountains.

The North Fork is still running high, fast, and murky, but I decide to again try my luck at fishing, only the second time in ten days. I toss spinners into the pools of side channels along the bar's edges. The pools hold promise, but again I'm skunked and I quit in frustration after an hour. My attempts at catching grayling have been pitiful: two tries, one and a half hours total, and only a couple of nibbles by six-inch-long fish. In 1929, Bob Marshall's packing buddy, Al Retzlaf, supposedly caught twenty-four grayling in twenty-five minutes while fishing Ernie Creek. I doubt even he could coax up more than a fish or two here. Or have my angling skills deteriorated that badly? The rod, reel, and spinners have been excess baggage, but to be honest, I haven't made more than a halfhearted effort, given the high, dirty water. At least I didn't lose any lures, though I'd consider tossing them all if not for the litter problem.

As I fish, a distant plane flies somewhere above the range, unseen and heard only briefly, faintly. Overflights have not been the nuisance I expected. I've heard a plane or two most days of this trip, but only rarely have they passed directly over the valleys I've traversed.

The sun's warmth, combined with the day's devotion to leisure, make this a perfect time for more musings on my past and the path that brought me here. I'm again transported to the mid-seventies, a time of great personal turmoil and change.

FOLLOWING MY LIFE-ALTERING DISCOVERY in the Ambler River valley, I finished out the field season and then joined seasonal and permanent WGM staff in Anchorage several months afterward, to help compile data and write annual reports. My bosses were happy enough with my work to offer me a permanent position. But that only fed my mounting insecurities. I felt as if I were fooling people; I wasn't the talented geologist others seemed to think. And my heart wasn't in my work. Other things were bothering me too, outside of my job. I felt unfulfilled and unhappy. Only in my twenties, I plunged into something resembling a midlife crisis.

Hoping to escape the gloom that had settled on my life, I moved to Southern California in 1976. After years of trying to suppress them, I was finally ready to face the demons that had been unleashed from my own Pandora's box while in college.

Talk about culture shock. In six years I never learned to love the Los Angeles megalopolis, and often felt isolated and out of place among its millions of people and freewheeling, freeway lifestyle. But some critically important changes happened there, on many fronts. First and foremost, I got the help necessary to heal some of the deep wounds left by my fundamentalist upbringing, for so long denied or not even recognized. In doing that work I began to better understand myself and what's most important to me. And I came to appreciate the saving graces that both sports and nature had been during my darkest teenage years.

Though still largely apolitical, I started to pay more attention to environmental issues, became friends with conservationists, joined Sierra Club outings. And, after several unhappy months at a geological engineering firm, I began to seek a career that I could love as much as my geology buddies loved their work. What that would be, I had no idea. Many friends and family members thought I must be nuts, to throw away all the years of hard work, the MS in geology, and the opportunity to work in a profession where I'd already had some notable success. But the void beckoned. I had to make a leap into the unknown, because the real craziness lay in doing work I'd found to be either boring or destructive to what I loved.

A series of events led me into journalism. It began while I was still employed as a geologist, by a company based in Pasadena. The firm got a job at Pierce College, a two-year school in the San Fernando Valley, and my bosses assigned me to a drill rig doing soil tests. I can't exactly say why, but the campus immediately appealed to me. The comings and goings of students, the pockets of trees and large grassy areas between buildings, and even the buildings themselves—all seemed welcoming somehow. Maybe it was simply the contrast between my job and the surroundings: engineering geology had proved utterly dull, while college life—or memories of it—seemed delightfully stimulating. Freeing.

I forgot about Pierce until, several months later, I quit my tedious eight-to-five job with its long commute, tiny office cubicle, and ridiculously rigid rules: coffee breaks at exactly ten a.m. and three p.m., lunch hour noon to one, required to stay until five even if the day's work is done. A serious amateur photographer for several years, I decided to return to school and see how photojournalism suited me. Without much savings, I focused on local junior colleges, which seemed ideal for experiments like mine. As a California resident in the late 1970s, I could take a full load of courses for under $20. Among the schools that taught photojournalism, one immediately caught my eye: Pierce College.

I wouldn't learn until later that Pierce's journalism department was nationally acclaimed. Nor could I know that its staff would quickly recognize some raw talent in this serious new student—in writing and reporting, more than photography— and shepherd me toward a new and then-unimaginable life. My three-semester apprenticeship at Pierce led to a real newspaper job at the tiny *Simi Valley Enterprise* and my entry into the life of a professional journalist. But more than that, it led me to something that soon became a passion: writing. All that remained was one final link to a lifelong love, wild nature.

Much like the circumstances leading from grad school to Alaska, this turn of events initially seemed to be a string of coincidences or lucky breaks. But with a quarter century of hindsight, I now hear the words of Joseph Campbell, who in talking with Bill Moyers during *The Power of Myth* series referred to the ideas of the nineteenth-century German philosopher, Arthur Schopenhauer:

> When you reach a certain age and look back over your life, it seems to have had an order; it seems to have been composed by someone. And those events, that when they occurred seemed merely accidental and occasional and just something that happened, turn out to be the main elements in a consistent plot. So, [Schopenhauer] says, who composed this plot? He said, just as your dreams are composed by an aspect of yourself of which your consciousness is unaware, so your whole life has been composed by the will within you. Then he says, just as those people who you met became effective agents of the structuring of your life, so you have been an agent in the structuring of other lives. And the whole thing gears together like one big symphony, he says, everything influencing and structuring everything else. It's as though our lives were the dream of a single dreamer in which all the dream characters are dreaming too and so everything links to everything else, moved out of the will in nature.

WEEKS INTO MY first semester at Pierce, I knew my geology days were ended. But the pull to Alaska remained strong. I traveled north twice more during the late seventies to spend my summers as a field geologist, using my first career to finance my entry into the second. Someday, I knew, I would return for good.

That day came in February 1982: I flew north to join the *Anchorage Times* as a sports writer. Three years later, after much lobbying and shameless pleading, I became the newspaper's outdoors writer. It was then that my green side began to blossom. I gradually became an advocate for parks and wildlife refuges, bears and wolves, howling my opposition to state-run predator-control programs. In my outdoors columns, I offered a counterpoint to the *Times*' staunchly conservative and pro-development editorials. I relished the opportunity to be the newspaper's lone "voice crying out in the wilderness," though it occasionally got me into trouble and, at least once, nearly removed from the outdoors beat.

My new passions also led me into new circles of friends. As time passed, I lost contact with nearly all of my geology coworkers and friends. To a great degree, this came from my inability to bridge the growing differences. Though we didn't talk much about it, some of my buddies and former bosses must have been startled by my transformation and outspoken stances against development activities that threatened Alaska's wilderness and wildlife. In a curious way, I felt I had let them down, after the opportunities they'd presented. And maybe I did, by going over to the "other side" without explanation or discussion.

My relationship with the Brooks Range, on the other hand, has deepened over time. Like Bob Marshall, I have returned there again and again, first as an exploration geologist, later as a backpacker, wilderness lover, and writer. Since 1974 I have spent well over a thousand days in Alaska's wilderness, from the southeast Panhandle to the North Slope, and the Brooks Range remains my favorite place of wildness. It's a landscape I love deeply, one that is always with me, not only in memory but in spirit. When I think about my relationship with the Brooks Range, I'm often reminded of a poem by Nancy Wood that's become a personal favorite:

Never shall I leave the places that I love
Never shall they go from my heart
Even though my eyes are somewhere else.

In part my enduring relationship can be traced to the shift that occurred one summer day in the Ambler River valley. Though I couldn't have known its full implications then, my changed perspective—which really was the resurrection of deep-seated but long-dormant beliefs—deflected me toward the path I follow today, one in which writing, exploration, wilderness preservation, and notions of wildness are inextricably intertwined.

The transformation from geologist to writer and eventually wilderness advocate has been gradual, occurring in bits and pieces over a span of many years. This is another reason I keep returning to the Brooks: to learn what else awaits me. In changing my life, this arctic landscape also reaffirmed my most fundamental values, which include a respect and passion for wildlands and wildlife, and the understanding that their inherent value has nothing to do with human utility.

SEVENTEEN

In the Shadow of Doonerak

DAY TWO ABOVE THE NORTH FORK–ERNIE CREEK CONFLUENCE. I awake to what sounds like a plane taking off, but it is only the river's loud churning and throbbing. The day is warm, the sky mostly blue at noon, and my feet feel much better today, so I head out from camp to visit Doonerak. One of my desires has been to approach—and perhaps walk upon—this mountain, which held a special place in Marshall's heart and imagination and was the central character in two chapters of *Alaska Wilderness*.

On spotting the "towering, black, unscalable-looking giant" in 1929, Marshall guessed it to be the Koyukuk country's tallest mountain. Given its shape and size, he initially named it "the Matterhorn of the Koyukuk," while adding, "it looked less ascendable than its celebrated Swiss namesake." Upon returning home, he would calculate the peak's height at more than ten thousand feet and rename it Mount Doonerak, which he "took from an Eskimo word which means a spirit or, as they would translate it, a devil. The Eskimos believe that there are thousands of dooneraks in the world, some beneficent, but generally delighting in making trouble."

Marshall didn't spend much time reconnoitering Doonerak during his first Brooks Range expedition, but nine years later he returned intent on climbing the giant, which he now figured to be the highest in all of arctic Alaska. On both that count and his earlier height estimate, he was off by a substantial margin. Using more accurate tools, the U.S. Geological Survey later determined Doonerak's height to be 7,457 feet. That makes it substantially shorter than 9,020-foot Mount Chamberlain, 8,975-foot Mount Isto, and other 8,000-foot peaks in the eastern range. Even within Marshall's beloved Central Brooks Range, 8,510-foot Mount Igikpak stands taller. Still, there's no question that Doonerak ranks among the Arctic's most formidable mountains.

Marshall headed for Doonerak confident that no one had climbed the peak or even walked upon its slopes. "Since I had discovered the mountain [which may or may not have been the case], had made the first map of it, and had named it during my trips in 1929 and 1930–31, I wanted to complete the job and also make the first ascent."

Joined by locals Ernie Johnson, Jesse Allen, and Kenneth Harvey, Marshall left the village of Wiseman on August 10, floating an "old tub" of a boat down the Middle Fork of the Koyukuk toward its confluence with the North Fork. For the next six and a half days, the four men and two pack dogs then worked their way up the North Fork, sometimes forced to muscle the boat through roaring whitewater. On the next-to-last day of their river journey, the team passed through the Gates, named almost a decade earlier. To Marshall "it seemed as if we were leaving the world of man behind and were pioneering in a trackless wilderness. This was not far from being true. We calculated that probably no more than twelve white men had penetrated the six hundred square miles of the magnificent Koyukuk country north of the Gates of the Arctic."

As usual, he overlooked or ignored the region's Native residents.

The team established a base camp two miles below Ernie Creek, some one hundred and eighty twisting and turning river miles above the North Fork's mouth, and more than eighty miles from the miners digging for gold along Nolan Creek, near Wiseman. After building a cache to store provisions for a month's worth of exploration, the crew headed overland under thick clouds.

Atop a berry-rich hill, they watched while the clouds lifted and dispersed, to reveal

the goal of our expedition, the summit of Mount Doonerak. What a summit it was! It jutted so pointedly into the air that it seemed quite impossible to ascend. The northwest face, which to our vague recollection from eight years before was the one to try first, now appeared absolutely impossible. Impossible, too, was the west side, while the north face seemed to have a 2,000-foot sheer drop. We knew that the east side, which we couldn't see, was hopeless. The only chances seemed to be (1) a ridge leading up from the northwest which we could only partly see, but which we thought we remembered might be possible; and (2) the south side rising from Pyramid Creek, which apparently had never been visited.

The next day Johnson and Marshall headed up Pyramid's unknown north branch. But rain clouds hid any potential route to Doonerak's summit. "This was the tenth day of rain out of eleven on this trip," Marshall later recounted, "and it began to be almost depressing." Continued overcast and rain prompted the group to leave Doonerak and trek toward the Arctic Divide and the headwaters of the Anaktuvuk River, rather than possibly spend the entire trip waiting for clear skies.

The explorers returned to Doonerak on September 2, only to be hit by a ferocious blizzard. The snow squall passed quickly and gave way to a cloudless blue sky, raising Marshall's dimming hopes. But the next morning, they woke to renewed overcast, fresh snow on the surrounding mountains, and all indications that another storm was on the way. "Doonerak was hopeless for this year," Marshall reluctantly admitted. "It was time to get out."

Descending the rain-swollen North Fork in their tub of a boat, the four men were floating merrily along when they suddenly discovered that recent storms had carved a new channel, passing just beneath an overhanging riverbank. Despite desperate attempts to change course, the crew headed straight for the tunnel.

"There was a frightful crunching of shattered wood as the boat passed under the overhanging bank," Marshall later recalled.

All at once I was deep under icy water where no light penetrated. Immediately I felt the overwhelming certainty of death. There was no reasoning in it and there was no fear, but there was no doubt either....

Suddenly through my closed eyelids the encompassing blackness changed to bright light. I opened my eyes and saw instantly that I was out of the tunnel, on the left edge of the main current.

All four men survived the capsizing, but they lost much of their gear and found themselves on opposite banks, separated by raging waters and soaked, in temperatures that were close to freezing. Wasting no time, Marshall's sourdough companions used their living-off-the-land expertise—and matches protected in waterproof cases—to build roaring fires. Adding to the group's good fortune, enough of their food and gear remained lodged in the damaged boat to complete the journey without additional hardship.

After repairing the boat enough to ferry Allen and Harvey across the still-swollen stream, the men left the North Fork and headed overland, covering the seventy-five miles to Wiseman in three days. Upon their return, they learned that they had endured—and barely survived—the worst rains and flooding since white men had settled in the upper Koyukuk region in 1899.

As he so often did, Marshall looked at the bright side of things: "We had failed in our major objective—climbing the Arctic's highest peak. We had had twenty-seven days of rain in twenty-nine. We had lost our boat, [and] much of our equipment.... Nevertheless, we had explored the upper reaches of the Anaktuvuk; and, for purely a good time, it would be hard to beat our four weeks' adventure in unexplored wilderness."

Unable to resist the call of "unconquered Doonerak," Marshall returned nine months later for one final try, this time strictly by foot. He was joined again by Jesse Allen and Kenneth Harvey, while an Inupiat Eskimo named Harry Snowden (or Nutirwik, in his Native tongue) took the place of Ernie Johnson, who was busy mining for gold. They also brought three dogs to assist with the 285 pounds of gear.

Leaving Wiseman on June 23, the team reached its base camp on lower Bombardment Creek at the end of the month. After sitting out some stormy weather, the team made its first attempt on July 4. But the ridge they chose brought them to sheer limestone faces, only three thousand feet above the valley.

When July 5 dawned cloudlessly blue, Marshall, Nutirwik, and Harvey tried again. Here's his account of the ascent, as they followed a northeast shoulder of the peak:

We continued climbing easily until we were nearly 6,000 feet high. Then we had precarious footing for a quarter of a mile over tumbling slide rocks toward the base of a rocky dome, a thousand feet high, to the north of Doonerak itself, but sitting on the same massif. We called this dome North Doonerak and started to work our way up it in the hope that from there we would be able to see what the chances for a northeastern ascent of Doonerak might be. We proceeded with great caution, the rock being loose and crumbly.

We labored up almost vertical chimneys, crawled around the edges of great cliffs, took toe and finger holds and pulled ourselves up ledges. By slow degrees we worked higher until finally, five hours after leaving camp, we reached a knife-edge ridge which dropped precipitously on one side toward the North Fork and on the other toward Bombardment Creek. It was a short and easy climb on the crest of this ridge to the summit of North Doonerak. Here was a most comfortable little flat, about ten by six feet, covered with reindeer moss, *Dryas*, and heather. We sprawled out in comfort and leisure to enjoy mountains everywhere under the blue sky.

Dominating the scene, of course, was the great black face of old Doonerak, less than half a mile away and jutting straight up for nearly 2,000 feet. I did not believe that any climber, however expert, could make that face. The northeast shoulder which had been our one remaining hope, we could now see plainly.

Some day, probably, people with years of rope-climbing experience will succeed in reaching the top by this route. We all knew that we never could....

Thirteen years after that wistful summer day, a team of three scientists/rock climbers would finally reach the top of the "unscalable-looking giant." Starting at Wiseman as Marshall had done, George Beadle, Gunnar Bergman, and Alfred Tissieres carried seventy-pound packs to Bombardment Creek. Though from a distance the peak looked "steep and dark and forbidding," the ascent proved easier than expected and the team reached Doonerak's summit on June 30, 1952.

Several days after turning back from Doonerak, Marshall completed his last trek through Koyukuk country. And only four months after that, he would die while riding a passenger train from Washington, D.C. to New York City. Marshall's death, likely from a heart attack, shocked his friends, particularly given his youth and vigor. Still, he had packed more into his thirty-eight years than most people do in twice that span. And he had found true happiness in his beloved Brooks Range wilderness. Marshall's special connection to this place is wonderfully expressed in the notes he wrote at the end of his last arctic adventure:

Now we were back among people in Wiseman. In a day I should be in Fairbanks, in two more in Juneau, in a week in Seattle and the great, thumping, modern world. I should be living once more among the accumulated accomplishments of man. The world with its present population needs these accomplishments. It cannot live on wilderness, except incidentally and sporadically. Nevertheless, to four human beings, just back from the source streams of the Koyukuk, no comfort, no security, no invention, no brilliant thought which the modern world had to offer could provide half the elation of the days spent in the little-explored, uninhabited world of the Arctic wilderness.

TO REACH DOONERAK'S FLANKS, or even see the peak, I must first hike to Bombardment Creek, about three and a half miles east of camp. The North Fork's braided and meandering channels would likely require crossings, so instead of following the valley bottom I sidehill through open spruce forest, gradually ascending into a subalpine patchwork of tundra meadows and alder-willow thickets.

Morning's blue sky has gone gray and sprinkles patter lightly against my sweating head. The light rain is refreshingly cool, but it heralds more serious precipitation. To the south, an ominous black shroud sweeps quickly across the mountaintops toward me. Soon I'm being splashed with big drops of water. I put on my rain gear, but that only delays the inevitable full-body soaking. It's not just the rain shower, which is mercifully brief, but the thickets I must pass through. Every bush and tussock now oozes water. Soon my boots and rain jacket are oozing too. Beneath my outer shell, rain and sweat combine to soak my capilene shirt; my pants fare better, only becoming damp.

Much of my enthusiasm washes away in the unexpected downpour. Doonerak is still hidden behind this hillside, but I'm sure the mountain's upper reaches are wrapped in vapors. And though warm enough now, once I stop hiking I'll quickly cool. Even with the extra layers stuffed into my pack, I resign myself to an uncomfortable, perhaps chilling, hike, knowing I'll return to dry clothes, a hot meal, and, if necessary, a warm sleeping bag.

Continuing to traipse across the tundra, I come to a brush-lined gully. From a distance it appears much like others I've crossed today: a narrow, shallow, rocky channel. But at its bushy edge, this gully is revealed to be a slot canyon, with steep-walled sides and sudden drop-offs. Bouncing down a series of cascades and waterfalls, creek water rushes over rock that is polished smooth and slick, a treacherous trap for careless hikers. I'm fortunate to enter the gulch at a bench; but both above and below me the creek plunges over sheer rock faces, twenty or more feet high. Just a few yards wide, this slot hardly shows on the one-inch-to-one-mile map I'm carrying, though the contour lines hint of its presence if you study the map closely enough. I carefully navigate the gulch only to discover another one a few hundred feet beyond. These hidden canyons, and heavy bushwhacking between them, drive me uphill several hundred feet to an alpine tundra bench.

Stopping to catch my breath on the rain-slickened slope, I turn to the north and see a rainbow has formed, its faint bands arching across the North Fork. Doonerak can wait, I tell myself, then take a seat and sip some water while savoring the beautiful aftermath of the passing shower.

The clouds are quickly breaking apart to reveal blue patches and bursts of sunlight. Best of all, there's a wide swath of blue up ahead, where Doonerak should be. My prospects, like the late afternoon, are brightening. The only downside: the day's increased warmth and my heavy sweating reinvigorate the area's mosquitoes. Under heavy attack, I liberally apply repellent, which I've hardly used for several days.

Back on the move, I get my first glimpses of Doonerak's upper reaches at thirty-five hundred feet (eighteen hundred feet above camp). It's enough of a tease to keep me stepping quickly. I round one bend after another, expecting a full view of the mountain each time, but there's always another spine to block the peak. Then, finally, I angle across one last hump—and I'm greeted by the face of God. Or at least one of His more spectacular faces.

I shrink in size, a mere mote on the mountainside, while hushed by the stark magnificence before me. Never before—not in Yosemite, the Grand Canyon, the Arrigetch, the Alaska Range, or the St. Elias Mountains—have I been graced by such an immediately overwhelming presence. Part of it is the surprise, coming over that final rise in the tundra. Though enticing, the earlier glimpses gave me no hint of this.

Even after reading and rereading Marshall's enthusiastic descriptions, I wasn't prepared for such a landscape. Desolate, yet sublime. The word, the idea that keeps coming to mind, is *transcendent.* I've been lifted into an extraordinary realm. It's not only Doonerak that overwhelms me, but also its neighbor, Hanging Glacier Mountain, and the chasm, Bombardment Creek, that both separates and connects the two. A deep gash between looming, steep-sided rock walls three thousand or more feet high, this narrow gorge is unlike any I've seen. In its shadowed, bare-rock bottom are remnant snowfields, cascading whitewaters, landslide and avalanche debris, and, near its head, a stair-step waterfall fed by gleaming snowfields and corniced, knife-edge ridges south of Doonerak.

Beyond the waterfall, out of sight, is Marshall Lake, which the explorer sighted during his 1939 attempt on the peak, and the team of rock climbers named thirteen years later after ascending Doonerak. Getting to the lake would be a hike and climb worthy of Marshall himself.

I'm not sure that summer fully touches Bombardment's upper reaches, or that sunlight ever warms its darkened depths. Yet as desolate and uninviting as the gorge appears, a game trail crosses a talus slope not far above the creek bottom. Dall sheep must have made it. I've seen some in the neighboring hills; and caribou wouldn't travel up this dead-end valley. Or would they?

East of Bombardment Creek, gray and tan limestones form Doonerak's lower reaches (any notions about walking upon those limestones during this visit have been erased by the chasm below me). The limy rocks give way to a succession of dark spires and pinnacles that ascend to Doonerak's ultimate heights, with a final black tower as its throne. The mountain's flanks are whiskered by green tundra plants to a height of perhaps five thousand feet, but its upper slopes are bare rock, blanketed by recent snows that accentuate the sharply angled, erosion-sculpted rock forms.

Uphill from me, Hanging Glacier Mountain thrusts skyward on massive rock walls and great towers, weathered and broken into the shape of arrowheads and pyramids. From here, Hanging Glacier's monolithic northeastern face is every bit as impressive as Doonerak's steep walls, if not more so. Like Doonerak, its dizzying faces are dissected by deeply incised couloirs.

There's a constant clattering and banging of falling rocks. Rockfall, talus piles, and landslide debris all hint at the persistent, ongoing erosional processes wearing down these grand mountains. Yet there's even a greater sense of tectonic uplift. The combined effect of mountains and gorge is one of extreme verticality. The landscape sweeps sharply upward, thrust more than a mile into the sky from the bottom of Bombardment Creek to the top of 7,457-foot Doonerak, over a distance of some two and a half miles. From Bombardment to Hanging Glacier's summit is an even more vertiginous uprising: four thousand feet in less than one mile.

I can easily understand why Marshall estimated Doonerak's height at more than ten thousand feet. It seems such a soaring mountain must be at least that tall. It's as if somehow I've been transported to the edge of the Alps or Himalayas and now stand at the entryway to what Galen Rowell called the "throne room of the mountain gods." This sense of being on the threshold of a more transcendent realm is accentuated by the gentler, greener landscape below me to the north: the broad, forested valley of the Koyukuk's North Fork and the rounded, more subdued mountains across the valley. I bow to Doonerak and Hanging Glacier, the Koyukuk's dark king and queen, god and goddess.

I take all this in, try to memorize the landforms, while standing on one of the tundra-covered rock fingers that project from Hanging Glacier's northeast flank, as warming sunshine and a steady but gentle breeze dry my drenched outer clothing, spread across the tundra. I've heard that Doonerak can be ascended without technical climbing gear or expertise, but like Marshall I can't imagine how, unless it's possible along some face or ridge that I can't see from here. For today, simply being in the looming presence of these two peaks is enough to meet my desires.

Stomach growling fiercely, I end my mountain reverie and begin gathering my gear. The hike to this bench has whetted my appetite for more than food, however; so before descending to camp for a late-night dinner, I promise myself I'll return some day, with enough time to at least explore Bombardment Creek and Doonerak's lower slopes.

I'M RAMBLING THROUGH lushly green alpine meadows, wildflowers of almost every possible hue sparkling brightly as raindrops on leaves and petals catch the evening sunlight, when a large animal appears higher on the hillside, maybe one hundred and fifty yards away and heading toward me. At first I think it might be a wolf. But my binoculars show the animal to be a heavily muscled, full-bodied grizzly. The bear's honey-colored coat glows in the back lighting, as if surrounded by a halo. The grizzly, like me, seems to be out for a leisurely stroll.

Where they still exist, grizzlies—like humans—can be found in the most out-of-the-way places, including the ice-covered slopes of Denali and the barren, barely vegetated volcanic landscapes of Alaska's "ring of fire." So I'm not overly surprised to see one high on this mountain, near the upper limits of plant growth. But I'll bet the last possible thing the bear would expect to meet here is a human. If he's even encountered our kind before.

The wind blows toward me and the bear's casual demeanor suggests he hasn't seen or heard me, though once the grizzly hesitates slightly and raises his head. Is he looking my way? We won't meet if both of us stay on our present paths, so I see no reason to alert the bear. I take another look through binoculars, just to be sure that "he" isn't a mom with cubs. Seeing none, I move ahead, but drop behind a knoll that hides us from each other. After several hundred feet I look back uphill, hoping to spot the grizzly, maybe even watch him awhile, but see nothing. No sense risking the chance that he's altered his route, so I keep angling downhill toward camp. I turn several more times to look, but don't see the bear again.

A short while later, I'm delighted to find sparkling clear water bubbling out of the tundra. If there's ever a spot to drink untreated water without fear of giardia, this spring is it. I take several gulps of the deliciously cold and sweet water, then fill my empty water bottle and offer a word of thanks for this surprise gift.

Back in the open forest, I get another surprise: in a clearing a few hundred feet above me is a blocky, dark brown form. At first I think it's an animal, maybe even another bear, but it's not. As to what it really is, I can't say, though it doesn't strike me as a rock or tree stump. Its upper part has a headlike shape, with what could be horns. Perhaps because I'm tired and famished, my mind begins playing tricks. I'm reminded of the mythical Greek god, Pan. Could it be one of the Arctic's doon-eraks? Whatever it is, the object is eerie enough to give me goose bumps. I think about checking it out, but don't feel like trekking back uphill, or so I tell myself.

I reach camp after seven hours away, the valley awash in golden evening light. The sun dips below the western ridgeline at 9:38 p.m. just as I'm finishing my chicken-noodle-with-broccoli pasta dinner. Except for some wispy clouds, the sky is blue. It could be a cold night, maybe even frosty.

EIGHTEEN

Wilderness Music

THIN WISPS OF CLOUDS MOVE IN DURING THE NIGHT, CUTTING the chill. The sun makes another brief appearance at dawn but by late morning high overcast blots out all sign of the orb. At midday, a steady, light rain again falls gently upon river, forest, tundra, and my rain gear.

On a midmorning walkabout, I briefly glimpse one of the snowshoe hares that have left piles of pellets all over this riverbar. The hare bolts and I try to track it down, but fail. The hare is likely watching me, safely hidden in plain view by the natural camouflage that is the animal's chief defense against its many predators. These include most northern meat eaters: wolves, foxes, marten, weasels, owls, hawks, and especially lynx. Brownish gray in summer, the fur of snowshoe hares becomes snow white in winter. They survive that harshest season through stealth and a diet of willow bark. Hares have chewed the tops and stripped the bark from many of the willows on this bar. That stripping begins one to two feet above the ground, a good indicator of winter's snow depths.

After my wild hare chase, I return to a favorite spot along the North Fork. Then, placing my head beside the river's churning aqua waters, I listen closely to its fluid play of sounds. I've heard beautiful Celtic-like chanting, off and on, for the past few days. The songs seem to come from outside me, from the forest and tundra and especially the river, but I suppose it could all be in my head. I've even put words to some of the music: "*Holy, ho-o-o-ly, holy....*" I wonder what combination of landscape and wind sounds mix with my own memories and thought processes—and several days of solitude—to produce these voices, this music.

My musings are interrupted by an unmistakably "real" voice: a howling comes from the forest, behind my tent. A loud, clear, resonant wail rolls across the valley, of alto key. The howl triggers an immediate physical and emotional response. My heart races, pulse quickens, spirit lifts. I instinctively turn from the river, binoculars in hand, and face the wooded hills above camp. With all the tracks and scat on this riverbar and across the North Fork, I've anticipated—and sometimes imagined—wolf howls throughout my three-day campout here. Each morning and night I've swept the hillsides with binoculars, hopeful of a miracle. Now one has come to me.

I peer at two tundra knobs a few hundred feet above camp, then scan the spruce forest below. Even as I do, the howling resumes. The first baleful voice is joined by a second, higher pitched. This one is more of a soprano. The trembling howls blend and shift key. Are there more than two wolves? Hard to tell. Wolves are known to mix their voices in a way that produces a magnified sense of numbers. I wonder if the wolves have seen me on the open gravel bar, or noticed the tarp or tent. Are they protesting this intruder? Announcing my presence, or theirs, to other wolves?

The rain is falling harder now, but I barely notice. Or care. The wolf songs last a minute or two but resonate much longer. This is what I dream about: to share the wilderness with howling wolves. I wonder which is more desirable, to see wolves or hear them sing? There's no simple answer, but there is this fact: over the years I've seen wolves a half-dozen times, yet heard them howling only once. Those songs came from a distance my first summer in these mountains, though miles to the west.

I don't think the wolves would disturb anything in camp; they're not notorious camp raiders like bears and squirrels and jays. But I go over to the tarp, where I've placed my food cache for lunch, just to be sure. Then back to the water's edge for more looking. Even before I reach my lookout, I see her: a whitish-gray animal, upstream from camp and halfway across the braided North Fork, not far from where I crossed the river three days ago. Maybe two hundred yards away.

If I had to name a color, I'd say white wolf. But that ignores the subtleties of her coat. Bringing her into focus with my glasses, I see she has a mostly white face, with some gray atop her head and on her neck. Her flanks are a light gray, legs are white, tail a very light gray, becoming darker at the tip. In her wettened coat, the wolf appears lean but not skinny, and I assume, for no sure reason, that she's in good health.

The wolf skulks across the midriver sand and gravel bars, crouched low as if to avoid detection. She glances now and then in my direction. I'm sure she sees me. Moving slowly, she reaches the final, deepest channel. She steps gingerly at first, splashing as she angles downstream across the milky green river. Then, for the final few feet, she plunges and swims across. The wolf stops at the forest's edge and looks back intently, but this time not toward me. I've already swung the binoculars back and forth across the river two or three times, expecting another wolf to appear. But none follows. Was I wrong about two wolves howling?

The she-wolf melts into the forest and as she does, a large brownish bird is flushed from a spruce: another predator, a northern goshawk. I assume our encounter is over, but the wolf reappears, walking slowly along the woods' margin. Once she steps into the open, bends, and smells something on the bar. Then back under the trees. She takes one last look across the North Fork and turns away. Her walk becomes a trot and she's gone, melted into the forest's shadows.

Minutes later, there's more howling—from my side of the river, though farther downstream. Perhaps the second wolf was unwilling to cross the stream within sight of me or the camp. The white wolf sings back, briefly. Then silence returns to the valley, except for the rushing, rattling, humming North Fork and tapping of rain. In a growing downpour I stand still another thirty or forty-five minutes, maybe an hour. I listen and look, upstream and down, along the forest's edge and up higher, along tundra terraces. I wipe the lenses of my binoculars. It's become a cold, hard arctic rain but today I don't mind being out in it. Finally I give up my watch, grab shelter under the tarp. I notice I'm shivering; from the wet chill, yes, but also from the song of *Canis lupus*.

I love grizzly bears. They are one of my primary totem animals, maybe my most important. To share the landscape with grizzlies is always an honor and a delight. But to be with howling wolves in the arctic wilds—well, there is no greater magic. Beneath the tarp and later in the tent, I imagine distant, intermittent howling throughout the afternoon and evening. It's amazing how much a river or the wind can sound like wolves.

I've had a feeling about this place since first seeing all those wolf tracks by the Ernie Creek–North Fork confluence. I'd still bet there's a den not far away and would love to stumble upon it, or even see wolf pups from a distance while scanning the landscape. But I'm satisfied now. I've had my communion. Both body and soul have been stirred by songs that tell, without words, of mountains, rivers, and the hunt, of mysteries as ancient as music.

THROUGHOUT THIS TRIP, my most memorable times have come as moments of surprise: sudden (even if anticipated) encounters with the Valley of Precipices, Doonerak, grizzlies, a bear skull, now wolves. Animals have been the best example of this. For all the looking and "hunting" I've done, the wildlife I'll remember most have come to me. It seems I'm being given new opportunities to let go of expectations and, at the same time, be open to possibilities. Both ideas, and the practice of them, have become important guideposts in my middle years.

After spending much of my life trying to keep things under control, I'm learning to surrender to life's experiences, while also embracing the opportunities that come my way. It's not easy, as demonstrated on this trip by my worrying, my off-and-on watch monitoring, and my efforts to stay dry and cozy in my overly large and weather-resistant tent. Yet I've remained flexible and taken some risks, both here and generally. It still sometimes seems amazing to me that a person so drawn to comfort and predictability would take the leaps of faith I've made, from geology to journalism and then to freelancing. And settling in Alaska, of all places! Not many of my childhood friends—or family members—would ever have guessed that the small, shy, sensitive boy of long ago had the potential to become an author, wilderness lover, and activist, or that he'd some day ascend the continent's highest peak or trek alone across miles of untrailed arctic wilderness.

The sun briefly returns in the evening and I hike to a rocky knob above camp. From here I get a better sense of how the landscape sweeps out and away from the Ernie Creek–North Fork confluence and the two streams' large gravel bars, first to lowland forest and then upland tundra meadows and willow thickets, and even higher to encircling tundra-topped foothills and mountains with bare, jagged ridgetops. Beyond those hills and mountains are more waves of peaks and hidden valleys.

I feel so lucky, so happy, to be in the heart of this vast wilderness, where wild places still mostly free of human influence span dozens of miles in any direction. I need these trips for so many reasons: to refresh my spirit, test my limits and stretch my horizons, embrace solitude, expand my sense of what's possible, encounter "the other," renew my bonds with wildness in its many forms, and see more clearly what's important, both here in the wild and back at home. Still, I can't imagine making a home here (if it were allowed), so far from other people and the conveniences of modern living. I don't try to fool myself: this northern wilderness is a harsh, demanding place, and to live here year-round would require skills I haven't acquired.

Thinking about the trials and perils of arctic homesteading, I again recall Ernie Johnson, "the most famous trapper of the North Fork," for whom Marshall named Ernie Creek. According to Marshall,

Although [Johnson] had come north on a gold rush, he had also been drawn by his love of the woods in this greatest wilderness on the continent. Here he spent all but about two weeks in the year out in the hills, away from the "cities" of Wiseman (population 103) and Bettles (population 24)....He trapped and hunted, averaging a yearly income of about twenty-five hundred dollars. "I can make better money as a carpenter," he said, "but I am staying out here because I like it among these ruggedy mountains better than anywhere else in the world."

Here was someone who'd chosen the hermit's life I once talked about pursuing while fed up with people and relationships during my grad school days; someone who actually chose to spend most of his adult years in seclusion. What revelations and understandings did Ernie find here among the sheep and grizzlies? As much as I desire and seek out solitude, I can't imagine a life so empty of people.

From the perch above camp I trace much of the route I've followed along Ernie Creek, from the Precipices to the North Fork. Then I look downstream, where I'll be walking tomorrow. It appears I'm bound for "the dark forest." Thick stands of spruce press close against the meandering river. I will likely cut through the woods in places, either to shorten my route or where pushed into the trees by steep, river-eroded cutbanks. I hope it's not too dense or brushy for easy path finding.

While plotting my route, I hear more howling, downriver. The wolf song is loud and clear, but brief. I wish for more, but instead hear only the rush of river. And gradually, more chanting voices. These are less pleasing, more eerie. My mind imagines a chorus of "*Sorry...sorry*" sung in a mocking, almost malevolent tone. Is the darkness in this chant tied to my worries about tomorrow's route?

The chanting unnerves me and I'm unable to get the words out of my head as I descend back to camp. Can such things come from too much solitude? Again I wonder how much I'm "hearing" and how much imagining. The presence of these landscape sounds and voices has been among the stranger aspects of this trek.

NINETEEN

Middle-Aged Discoveries

ALTHOUGH BOB MARSHALL GREATLY RESPECTED ERNIE JOHNSON and the life choices the trapper had made, I doubt he seriously envied Johnson's life, given Marshall's love of the human community. Like him, I've remained a "city boy" all my life, even in Alaska. Yet the state's urban center—like its wilderness—has taught me essential lessons about larger, wilder nature, especially in my middle years. The community and landscape of my adopted home have been instrumental in the long, meandering journey back to my wild roots.

Besides knowing almost nothing about Alaska when I came north from grad school, at age twenty-four, I didn't clearly understand the importance of wild nature to my life. Or, perhaps better put, I'd gradually forgotten its importance, something I'd intuitively understood as a young boy. In Alaska I have rediscovered my early passions and reformed primal bonds that connect me to the more-than-human world. Along the way, I have redefined and continue to explore what *wildness*—as opposed to wilderness—means to me, and its relevance to my life and the larger American culture.

Because as a nation we are ever more separated from wild nature, our relationship with the Earth and our planet's other beings is increasingly ruinous. How do we stay connected, whole? One answer, given by many others before me but worth repeating over and over, is that we need to pay more attention to the nature—the essence—of the places we inhabit: the seasons and weather, the shape of the landscape and its waters, the natural and human history, the animals and plants. And we must do so wherever we live, from remote backcountry to inner city. Paying attention is an essential step to becoming a true inhabitant, a native; it's part of the practice that poet-essayist-philosopher Gary Snyder so beautifully describes in *The Practice of the Wild.*

Most Americans seem to believe that true wildness is only to be found "out there," in the remote backcountry. By and large, our culture equates the two: wildness equals wilderness. Looking back, that's pretty much how I saw things for much of my young adulthood, especially while living in Tucson and Los Angeles in my twenties. Yet as a young boy I innately understood that wildness was right outside the back door. Sometimes it even infiltrated our house.

As Jack Turner points out in *The Abstract Wild,* this popular misconception helps to explain why people so often misquote Henry David Thoreau, erroneously substituting *wilderness* in his famous saying, "In wildness is the preservation of the world."

Of course wildness and wilderness are not at all the same, a point that Snyder, Turner, Paul Shepard, Wendell Berry, and many other American nature writers have emphatically made in their works, sometimes at great length. (I use the term "nature writers" loosely, to include all those who've written about humans and our relationship with larger nature; some would shudder at being defined this way.)

Wilderness is a place. And, some would argue, an idea. Wildness is a quality, a state of being. Perhaps that's why wildness and its root word, *wild,* are so hard to define, or pin down. I love Snyder's discussion of the two in *The Practice of the Wild.* "The word *wild,*" he writes, "is like a gray fox trotting off through the forest, ducking behind bushes, going in and out of sight." Later he compares its various definitions to "how the Chinese define the term *Dao,* the way of Great Nature: eluding analysis, beyond categories, self-organizing, self-informing, playful, surprising, impermanent, insubstantial, independent, complete, orderly, unmediated, freely manifesting, self-authenticating, self-willed, complex, quite simple. Both empty and real at the same time. In some cases we might call it sacred."

Wildness, he continues, "is everywhere: ineradicable populations of fungi, moss, mold, yeasts and such that surround and inhabit us. Deer mice on the back porch, deer bounding across the freeway, pigeons in the park, spiders in the corners.... Wilderness may temporarily dwindle, but wildness won't go away."

Even in our high-tech, polluted world of the early twenty-first century, wildness is all around us. And within us. Our bodies, our imaginations, our dreams and emotions and ideas are wild. But in going about our busy, modern lives, we consciously or unconsciously suppress, ignore, deny, or forget our wildness. In adapting to the human-dominated, civilized environment we've built, Paul Shepard argues, we become tamed.

Still, the wild animal remains, waiting for release. And—naturally—it's most easily set free in wild surroundings free of artifice and development. Free, largely, of the human touch. That's why the feeling of wildness most deeply resonates within us when we enter wilderness. And for many of us, the longer we stay in the "wilds," the more connected, refreshed, invigorated, and even healed we feel. There's a sense of being at ease, and sometimes even of "being one with nature." Something shifts *inside*.

That's what happened, I think, when I came to Alaska in the mid-seventies and spent several summers working deep in the wilderness. Something shifted and opened. Feelings and understandings I'd had as a youngster were subtly resurrected. Even when my life took a necessary detour to Los Angeles, I knew I would return to Alaska. I had to return. After moving back in 1982, I naturally resumed my wilderness explorations. But, perhaps more importantly, I also began to pay more attention to my new homeland: Anchorage and its surroundings. At the same time, I began to explore a literary genre that I'd largely ignored—or, more to the point, that I hadn't been aware of: nature writing and the literature of place.

In my fourth and fifth and now sixth decades, I've rediscovered how much wondrous wild there is to be found right outside my door, or even inside it, though I live on the edge of Alaska's urban center. It seems that for me, entering the wilderness was a necessary step to recovering this lost, or buried, recognition. And living in Anchorage, I have the advantage of being an urban guy surrounded by wildness.

A CITY OF some two hundred and eighty thousand people, Alaska's largest community is rarely lauded for its wild nature or frontier aesthetics. Many rural Alaskans consider Anchorage a northern incarnation of Lower 48 excesses. They derisively call the city Los Anchorage, a not-so-subtle comparison to Southern California's smog-enshrouded, freeway-infested, urban-sprawl megalopolis. Other Alaskans, including some locals, ridicule Anchorage as Anywhere USA and claim its only saving grace to be the close proximity to "the real Alaska." Outsiders— anyone living beyond the state's borders—too get in their digs. John McPhee took perhaps the most famous swipes at Anchorage in his best-seller *Coming Into the Country*: "Almost all Americans would recognize Anchorage, because Anchorage is that part of any city where the city has burst its seams and extruded Colonel Sanders....It is virtually unrelated to its environment. It has come in on the wind, an American spore. A large cookie cutter brought down on El Paso could lift something like Anchorage into the air."

The truth stings: Anchorage deserved McPhee's late-1970s jabs. It still merits them and, to some degree, those of rural critics. Poor municipal planning has led to haphazard development and ugly architecture. Much of the city is an appalling mix of malls, fast-food restaurants, boxlike discount stores, massive parking lots, and steadily enlarging service stations and quick-stops. More than ever, the city's credo seems to be, Develop, develop, develop. Too many of the country's mega-chains have heard our politicians' declaration that Alaska is "open for business," turning sections of Anchorage into versions of Miracle Mile.

Yet for all of this laying down of asphalt and mushrooming of boxy buildings, pockets of wetlands, woodlands, and other wild areas remain scattered through-out the Anchorage Bowl, a roughly triangular piece of land that is bounded on two sides by the waters of Cook Inlet's Turnagain and Knik Arms, and on the east by the Chugach Mountains. You just have to know where to look. Those natural areas continue to sustain a wide diversity of wildlife and native plants: the bowl is seasonal home to 230 species of birds, five types of Pacific salmon, and forty-eight different mammals.

Anchorage's patchwork of greenbelts and municipal parks is threaded together by a network of bike trails and walking paths. From Anchorage's much-beloved Coastal Trail, bicyclists, joggers, and walkers can occasionally spot pods of ghostly white beluga whales, chasing fish through the inlet's murky waters. Along that trail and others, people may also meet moose, lynx, great horned owls, black bears, and even the occasionally grizzly. Beyond the Coastal Trail is a state wildlife ref-uge, a place of surprising wildness and solitude on the city's western flanks, inhab-ited in spring and summer by all manner of songbirds, shorebirds, and waterfowl, from savannah sparrows to arctic terns and sandhill cranes.

Also threading through the bowl are several creeks, which connect hills to low-lands to saltwater. Some are filled in, paved over, or polluted before they reach the inlet, but others are large and pure enough to have natural or rebuilt salmon runs. In Anchorage's most industrialized section, anglers pull forty-pound king salmon from Ship Creek. The bowl is also rich in lakes and bogs, which serve as important avian nesting grounds. Anchorage, in fact, is the largest U.S. city to support nest-ing populations of loons. And wolf packs roam the city's eastern edges, sometimes sneaking into homeowners' yards to kill domestic fowl or dogs.

Though I've resided here since 1982, only since the mid-nineties have I truly delighted in Anchorage's greener, wilder side. In part that reflects changing desires and priorities: once a newspaper sports reporter tied to newsroom desks and indoor arenas, I've metamorphosed into a nature writer who chooses woodland trails and alpine meadows over noisy, sweaty gyms. I now prefer watching birds and bears to TV sports. And I've relearned the value of paying close attention to my home grounds, something I did as a boy but somehow forgot in my early adulthood.

Another reason for my new perspective: relocation to the hills on Anchorage's east-ern edge in October 1993. That move, as much as anything, clarified what my friend

William calls the "power of place." From 1982 through 1988, I lived the mobile life of a renter. Then I became a first-time homeowner. But like my earlier rentals, that cul-de-sac property failed to draw me into the local landscape. Needing solitude or a renewal of spirit, I would invariably go "out there," to the wildlands beyond Anchorage.

On the Hillside that wasn't necessarily so. I continued to love my forest and mountain walks in neighboring Chugach State Park and I certainly relished my longer backcountry trips deep into Alaska's wilderness. Yet I also began to find joy, surprise, connection, and, yes, even solitude on Anchorage's Hillside, an area of town that mixes modern suburban neighborhoods with older homesteads on the wooded foothills of the Chugach Mountains.

Everything wild seemed closer on the Hillside: the clouds, the mountains, the animals, the weather. It became easier, somehow, to slip outside at night and stargaze, stand in the eerie light of a full moon, or look for northern lights. Easier to go walking and exploring. Winter comes earlier and stays longer. There's more snow. More wildlife. More frequent and stronger gales. Born along Alaska's Gulf Coast, high winds called chinooks come roaring out of the southeast and through the Chugach Mountains, then tumble down the Hillside as warm, dry, turbulent air, in gusts of fifty to one hundred miles per hour.

Once I'd settled into the Hillside, all manner of things began to grab my attention in new ways: the chinooks; the pleasing rush of springtime creek water; the winter commutes of ravens, which fly daily between their nighttime roosts in the Chugach Mountains and the scavenging-rich environs of mid- and downtown Anchorage; the spruce bark beetle and its infestation of local forests. Nothing, however, grabbed me as deeply as the neighborhood's black-capped chickadees, whose bright presence drew me into bird feeding and watching and along the way transformed my world, showed me some of what I had been missing.

I have since moved from the Hillside back to Anchorage's lowlands, near the city's western, coastal border. There's still plenty of wild nature in my new neighborhood, manifested in moose and fox, merlin and goshawk, chickadee and waxwing, spruce and birch, on and on. The opportunities to encounter wildness and learn more about my homeland are endless.

IN RECENT YEARS I've come to believe strongly that this sense of connection, this love for wild nature, is a crucial part of our humanity. It's alive in us when we're born, no matter where that is. The question, then, is how do we nurture our wildness, rather than subdue and tame it?

In *The Abstract Wild*, Turner argues that "in many inner cities, here [in the United States] and in the developing world, people no longer have a concept of wild nature based on personal experience." I agree wholeheartedly with that. But I also believe it is possible to have "raw visceral contact with wild nature" wherever we live, if we take the time, make the effort, and leave ourselves open to wonder and mystery. Then the challenge becomes: how do we reinforce and encourage this wild awareness in each other, in our children? I don't have any easy answers. But my life in this far north metropolis has offered some hints of what's possible.

At first glance, my choice to settle in Anchorage may seem a strange one for someone who claims to be so passionate about the natural world. But in living along the city's eastern and western edges, I've gotten the best of both worlds, natural and man-made (though of course the two are connected). I love the amenities that come with living in an urban center, with its coffee shops and restaurants, movie theaters and performing arts center, universities and libraries and sports programs. Here I've found intersecting circles of writers and outdoors enthusiasts and earth- and peace-loving activists. Yet I also have easy access to parks, trails, greenbelts, a coastal refuge, and a nearby mountain range, the Chugach, whose remotest valleys and peaks are seldom visited. And I reside in a landscape also inhabited by chinook and coho, goshawk and owl, coyote and lynx, moose and bear.

Living in Anchorage, I'm constantly reminded that wildness is all around us, all the time, even in the city. It's just that most of us humans don't notice the "wild side" of our busy urban lives (some, it's true, are simply trying to survive their urban lifestyles, which leaves little, if any, opportunities for wild connections). Of course, in many a metropolis you have to look hard to find even hints of the wild behind the elaborate layers of human construct that shield us from the rest of nature. Anchorage's juxtaposition of malls and moose, brewhouses and bears, libraries and loons makes it easier to notice urban wildness here than in cities like Los Angeles or Tucson or even Lewiston, Maine, all places that I've lived. This city, more than any other, has opened my eyes and enlarged my awareness of wild nature in a way the wilderness couldn't.

EVEN AS I'M traversing one of North America's greatest remaining wildlands and reflecting upon my own relationship to wilderness and wildness, a growing number of activists, historians, philosophers, and environmental scholars are debating the idea of wilderness that has guided the preservation of parklands, refuges, and preserves throughout the United States and, increasingly, around the world. I will remain blissfully unaware of that largely academic dispute for several more years. But eventually I'll be pointed to a book that explores *The Great New Wilderness Debate*. Edited by two philosophy professors, J. Baird Callicott and Michael P. Nelson, this "expansive collection of writings" presents the perspectives of some three dozen people (nearly all of them male), including several who've substantially influenced me: Bob Marshall and Roderick Nash, of course, and also Aldo Leopold, Jack Turner, and Gary Snyder. But I'm more interested in the perspectives that challenge the American idea and ideal of wilderness.

Up front, the editors explain that this raging new debate turns on a concept that they call "the received wilderness idea—that is, the notion of wilderness that we [late-twentieth and early-twenty-first century Americans] have inherited from our forebears." Just who are those forebears? They're the philosophers, naturalists, wilderness lovers, and writers of the nation's colonial and postcolonial era, for instance Ralph Waldo Emerson, Henry David Thoreau, John Muir, Teddy Roosevelt, Aldo Leopold, and yes, Bob Marshall. And the received idea? The editors say it is crystallized in none other than the Wilderness Act of 1964 (parts of which I've already quoted): "a wilderness, in contrast with those areas where man and his own works dominate the landscape, is hereby recognized as an area where the earth and its community of life are untrammeled by man, where man is a visitor who does not remain."

Callicott and Nelson further argue that the wilderness idea that's come down to us has religious roots; it reflects the Christian—and especially Puritan—dichotomy between humans and nature. Rather than being joined, the two are separate. (Nash, it should be noted, makes much the same case, though he, ironically, is considered a wilderness advocate, not a naysayer.)

Several of the criticisms leveled against the modern idea of wilderness have great merit and in fact parallel some of my own recent thinking and that of my contemporary influences. At the core of the debate is this reproach: the modern idea of wilderness perpetuates the separation of humans from nature, which in turn contributes to our species' environmental irresponsibility; while wilderness has become something of a sacred place to be kept in a pristine, unspoiled condition, everywhere else is open to rampant development or even trashing, commonly in the name of progress. Equally important, the wilderness idea ignores the longtime presence of indigenous peoples on landscapes that we Westerners have deemed to be places "untrammeled by man." This notion has contributed to the oppression—and in some cases, the extermination—of original inhabitants in much of the world colonized by Euro-Americans.

In short, the editors and many of the contributing writers conclude that the modern idea of wilderness is largely an artificial construct that needs replacing or at least reshaping, if we Westerners hope our culture to be more earth and life friendly. More appealing to them are concepts that recognize "people are a part of nature." Thus they prefer notions of wildness to wilderness.

One often-cited critic is environmental historian William Cronon, whose 1983 book *Changes in the Land* was instrumental in sparking the new wilderness debate (though that wasn't the book's intent). Cronon's more recent essay, "The Trouble with Wilderness, or Getting Back to the Wrong Nature," succinctly summarizes many of the issues, including wilderness as a cultural invention. Though prepared to dislike Cronon's ideas (and those of editors Callicott and Nelson), I've found myself nodding in agreement with many of his arguments and criticisms. He too decries the "central paradox" of wilderness, that it preserves the Christian conceit that humans stand outside nature. Worse than that, "to the extent that we live in an urban-industrial civilization but at the same time pretend to ourselves that our real home is in the wilderness [in which, paradoxically, we are now defined as visitors], to just that extent we give ourselves permission to evade responsibility for the lives we actually lead."

At the same time we idealize remote, pure places, we perhaps unconsciously denigrate or otherwise belittle our homelands. Because of their diminished status, it becomes easier to treat them disrespectfully. "The majority of our serious environmental problems start right here, at home," Cronon writes, "and if we are to solve these problems, we need an environmental ethic that will tell us as much about *using* nature as about *not* using it. The wilderness dualism tends to cast any use as *ab*-use, and therefore denies us a middle ground in which responsible use and non-use might attain some kind of balanced, sustainable relationship."

Cronon goes on to share a belief that largely matches my own: "[O]nly by exploring this middle ground will we learn ways of imagining...a world better for humanity in all of its diversity and for all the rest of nature too. The middle ground is where we actually live. It is where we—all of us, in our different places and ways—make our homes."

I say a loud "Amen" to that. And I believe many wilderness advocates would wholeheartedly agree with Cronon that "wilderness gets us into trouble only if we imagine that this experience of wonder and otherness is limited to the remote corners of the planet, or that it somehow depends on pristine landscapes we ourselves do not inhabit....

"We need to honor the Other within and the Other next door as much as we do the exotic Other that lives far away."

I still have much to learn about this new wilderness debate, but it seems a desirable and necessary discussion, and one in which I've been participating without realizing it. The ideas of Cronon and Nash, Callicott and Snyder (and many others) are helping me to better crystallize my own, evolving credo: let us protect and celebrate the Earth's remaining wilderness areas and their inhabitants, human and otherwise. *And* let us celebrate and honor the wild nature that is all around us and within us, all the time.

TWENTY

The Journey Ends

JULY 31. IT'S A BEAUTIFUL MORNING TO PACK UP CAMP: CLEAR blue sky, gentlest of breezes. Warm after a chilly night, yet remarkably mosquito free. I'm able to dry out anything that's damp or soggy, air out my down-filled sleeping bag. My spirit, like the day, is bright and calm, though I'm sorry to be leaving this spot, which has made such a terrific base camp. Adding to my cheer is a festive send-off by a flock of chattering boreal chickadees and later, the sweet warbled notes of a solitary robin.

By late morning a stiff southerly wind has kicked up and tendrils of clouds rush up valley. Signs of yet another weather system moving through, likely bringing rain. But at least I'm blessed by a warm, dry start.

About a mile below the North Fork–Ernie Creek confluence I come to a large opening in the forest. Huge mounds of rock debris have been piled in the clearing, much like a dump truck—or dredge—might leave. So much for my untouched-by-man musings of last night. The rocks are gray to green phyllites and schists, the sort that might contain veins of gold-bearing quartz. These must be the workings of a gold-mining operation, perhaps from decades ago. It appears the forest was cleared and the streambed reworked. Over the years, willow and alder thickets have taken over much of the space between the piles. There are also numerous muddy, meandering channels of water that eventually feed the North Fork.

I'm working my way through this maze of rock mounds when another wolf appears. This one is tawny colored, a mix of tan, gray, and white, and smaller than the she-wolf I watched yesterday. We spot each other at almost the same moment and I think I see a surprised look on the wolf's face. Shocked or not, the wolf quickly lopes into the forest. I imagine him wondering, in his wolfish way, *What's that crazy guy doing here?*

With symphonic and choral tunes again playing in my head, I pack six miles in just under six hours, mostly through forest or along the forest edge. Today's musical interlude is highlighted by orchestral strings and some sort of blended Celtic–Native American chanting. There's also increased birdsong: boreal chickadees, juncos, and robins all serenade my passage, while gray jays and ravens squawk and caw. Much of the way I follow game trails used by wolves, moose, bears, and who knows what else. Some sections of trail are well defined, for instance where they cross bluffs that overlook the North Fork; elsewhere they branch out and sometimes disappear. Even with the trails, I am forced to do plenty of bushwhacking and tussock hopping.

I'm nearing the end of my day's march, resting on a riverbar, when four people approach from the south. We wave greetings and they come over to chat, my first conversation with people (other than myself) since July 23. Part of a ten-member British expedition, the three women are from England, the guy from Germany. Their ages range from late teens to early thirties.

The oldest (and fittest-looking) of the bunch is named Liz. One of the expedition's co-leaders, she tells me their party has been marching nonstop for about a week, along an ambitious route that's taken them across a steep mountain pass, through rugged and thickly brushed country. They're hauling so much food and gear that they've had to make multiple carries from one camp to the next. Right now they're headed back for another load. Like me, they're headed for the Gates. From there, they will float the North Fork to Bettles. To keep to their travel schedule, expedition members have had to pack excessively heavy loads for exceedingly long hours. One recent move lasted fifteen hours, through often-thick brush. I'm the first person they've seen outside their expedition, which prompts one woman to pull out her camera and take my picture.

All four are wearing small, jingling bear bells, so I playfully mention that they're known to Alaskans as "dinner bells," because so many end up in grizzlies' stomachs. That draws a few uncertain chuckles, but one woman frowns at the joke. Like me, they're unarmed, except for pepper spray. Of course there is added safety in numbers. And as Liz reminds me, they come from a culture with highly restrictive gun laws. Passing through Fairbanks on their way to the Brooks Range, team members were appalled to learn you can buy handguns in Alaska's grocery stores. Such is life in the Last Frontier, I explain.

It's early evening when I part company with the Brits. Now only a few miles from the Gates, I could reach my rendezvous point late tonight. But I'm already bushed and Liz reported that a small tent city has formed at the site, the only gravel bar on which planes can safely land in this part of the Brooks Range. Choosing solitude over crowds and rest over ambition, I stop at a sandbar for one last night of solo camping. A good decision, it turns out, because I escape the deluge. Well, almost. Clouds racing in from the south unleash a driving, pounding rain just as I'm setting up camp. Both the tent's exterior and I get drenched, but good ol' Stephenson stays dry inside. Actually all my gear stays dry, except for my super-saturated rain jacket, boots, and socks.

A second, even heavier downpour hits as I'm finishing dinner. Beneath the tarp, I savor coffee and Baker's chocolate while watching and listening to the splattering rain. I pity the Brits, packing in this miserable, soaking rainstorm.

Yet a third tropics-like outburst strikes shortly before midnight, after I'm curled inside my sleeping bag. The rain is still falling hard as I drift off to sleep. Side channels of the North Fork surround my tent site, but all have meager flows. There seems little chance that I'll get flooded out, as Marshall and Retzlaf did in 1929 while camped on an island at the North Fork–Clear River confluence, some twenty-five miles to the south. Still, I wake a couple times during the night and check things out, just to be sure.

THE FIRST MORNING of August brings sunshine, mostly blue skies, and steady, dry winds to the North Fork. Who knows what else will blow my way today? A plane with friends, I hope.

The rising sun reaches my part of the valley shortly after nine, bathing me in warmth and light. After last night's raw, torrential rain squalls, the sun's soft caress is profoundly stirring, a gift from heaven. At this moment I can easily understand why many cultures have worshipped the sun and its life-giving energy. Such an ordinary yet marvelous event, the sun's appearance from behind the peak has raised my spirits and renewed my hopes, added joy to an already glorious morning.

Packing up camp, I am closely watched by a family of forest predators: two northern goshawk adults and this year's offspring. Among the largest of Alaska's hawks, they tend to stay within the forest or along its edge while hunting birds and small mammals such as squirrels and snowshoe hares. Like owls they have remarkably quiet wing beats, and show great agility while maneuvering among close-spaced trees. These three have taken up positions atop spruce trees, from which they sometimes launch themselves in fast, plunging attacks. Perhaps alarmed or annoyed by my presence, they've voiced their disapproval with piercing whistles. With my departure they can ease their vigilance until the next group of packers comes along.

I walk along the river when possible, but the North Fork's meanders occasionally push me into the woods, where game trails again ease my passage across the forest's often boggy, hummocky floor. The Brits, too, have been following the game trails as they ferry loads through the forest, and much of the route I follow is marked by boot prints, stripped branches, and trampled ground cover. At one point the path heads into heavy alder, along a steep slope that drops toward the rushing North Fork below. I should know better than to follow it, but I do. When it's too late to easily turn back, I find myself in a dreadful maze of nearly impenetrable alder, growing downslope at angles nearly perpendicular to the direction I need to go. Clambering over and under alder as thick as a tree, slipping on wettened mosses and getting snagged on branches, I stumble and fall too many times to count.

No animal in its right mind—except, perhaps, a bulldozing grizzly—would attempt to plow through this worst of green hells, when only ten to fifteen feet higher the alder gives way to more open forest. As awful as it is, this *must* be a human detour. Finally at wit's end, my body sweating heavily and bruised by alder bashing, I climb up and away from the so-called trail. Later, the Brits will insist they were following a game trail, but I can't imagine that's so. None other that I've followed took me through such a brutal, almost impassable thicket. And where they did weave through willow and alder, animal trails followed a path of least resistance. Here, maximum exertion is required, accompanied by much tumbling and cursing.

Maybe it's because I know the end is near, but my pack seems heavier and my muscles feel achier today. As the hours pass I grow weary of the frequent detours, from riverbars to forest and then back again, simply to avoid cutbank channels and soaked feet. Finally I decide the most direct route works best, even if it's the wettest. Alternately slogging through slow-moving side channels and crossing riverbars, I see more and more signs of a human presence. Dozens of boot prints have been pressed into the sand and increased numbers of aircraft roar through the sky. By day's end I'll count five planes, the most I've seen or heard on this trip.

I'm forced to make one final detour into the woods where the North Fork's main channel swings east and cuts a steep bank. There's no way I'll try to wade its deep, fast-moving waters. I follow an old, dry channel bed for a while, but it takes me ever farther from the stream. I cut back through the forest, stumble through a mass of willows. And there before me, on a large gravel bar, are two tents and two people.

Even from a distance, I recognize Patti and Nancy. Friends from Anchorage, they've come to float the North Fork. Hallelujah! My endless last-day trudge is over, except for one final channel crossing. I wander into camp, beaming and waving.

I've survived my two weeks alone in the wilderness. It's time for some hugs and stories and food. As Bob Marshall, the great wanderer himself, once put it, "Adventure is wonderful, but there is no doubt that one of its joys is its end."

I throw off my pack and begin sharing stories, but my tales are interrupted by the surprising—and alluring—smell of bacon. Excusing myself, I leave Patti and Nancy and wander over to the Brits' camp, where several members of the expedition are gathered around a fire. Having lugged far too much food into the wilderness, they're having a banquet before beginning the next, waterborne stage of their adventure. I offer to help them get rid of their sizzling bacon and they happily oblige me with a bacon bagel, followed by a buttermilk pancake, eight inches across. Yummmm!

At the risk of being an ungracious guest at their table, I tease them about their meal choices and warn of the dangers that come with cooking bacon in grizzly country, given its smell and greasy leftovers. I'm surprised that their leaders would haul such food into the backcountry; and I'm even more shocked to learn that Alaska-based outfitters were responsible for arranging their supplies.

Paul and Liz don't take offense at my needling; in fact, they admit they've made some embarrassing mistakes and agree they goofed by not questioning the supply of bacon, eggs, sausage, pancake batter, biscuits, bagels, cheese blocks, and tins of salmon when presented with the foodstuffs back in Bettles. Not only is their food smelly, it's heavy and bulky, and one reason the group has had to do so much hauling of gear. Well, things should get easier on the river. And the group, which Paul has compared to Outward Bound, has gained some valuable lessons along the way, without harm to either humans or wildlife.

My wife, Dulcy, and another Anchorage friend, Michael, arrive a couple hours after me, flown in from Bettles by bush pilot Jay Jesperson. Dulcy jumps out of the plane bringing big bear hugs and sweets she's hauled from Anchorage: orange, tomato, roast beef sandwich, Pepsi, fudge brownie. More food, more hugs, more stories. Words pour out of me. It seems I can't stop talking—about the weather, Doonerak, encounters with wolves and bears, the magic of river songs, the splendid solitude, the terror of stream crossings. No more worries now about rendezvous points to reach, miles to go, or rivers to cross. No more need to be alone. I am a happy pilgrim.

TWENTY-ONE

Joined in Community

AFTER TWO WEEKS OF SOLITUDE, THE GATES GRAVEL BAR OVERLOADS my senses, in many ways: the abundance of fat- and sugar-rich foods, the loud (and real) human voices, the constant comings and goings of people, the rumbled landings and takeoffs of planes, the opportunity for conversation and human touch.

With no nearby lakes, airstrips, or other riverbars suitable for airplane landings, this wedge of sand and gravel has become the chief entryway into the Brooks Range's Koyukuk country, at least for airborne travelers. In the two days I'm here, I meet at least a half-dozen other parties, and exchange hellos with twenty to twenty-five people, either entering Gates of the Arctic or on their way out. And planes seem to land or fly over this spot every few hours. The noise and busyness swallow any sense that this spot is deep in the wilderness, more than thirty miles, as the Cessna or raven flies, from the nearest settlement and nearly forty miles from any road. By foot, it's a much longer trek than that, as I know firsthand.

Surprisingly, I'm not put off by any of this, except the mechanized roar. I'm ready for human company, ready to trade stories and join a tent city, ready to indulge myself with junk food. As much as I consume in calories, I release in steady conversation. Everyone is surprised by my loquacious behavior, including me. As Michael marvels at one point, "I've *never* heard you this talkative." Details keep pouring out; there's so much to share. I can now better understand why solitary miners and trappers so eagerly embraced Bob Marshall and the Muries and often poured out their stories as if they were bursting.

Though unusual, my almost nonstop jabbering reflects another major change in my life. Once a loner with few friends, I've become a person who enjoys—and sometimes revels in—human company. For much of my life I felt anxious, uncertain, even wary around people. I felt distrust of my own kind, largely because I'd learned not to trust my own instincts, feelings, and thoughts. In recent years I've occasionally joked that "I'm learning to like people as much as I like nature." Sure it's an exaggeration, but not far off the mark. I can thank the shift to decades of healing work, and much of the healing has come through a sense of belonging.

I recall what a friend once said while attending the Sitka Symposium, a summertime gathering in southeast Alaska that explores the interconnections of nature, culture, and story: "I've finally found my tribe." That's often how I feel now. I began life as part of a community joined by family ties and religious beliefs; and for a while, I belonged. But for reasons of my own choosing—some of them clear to me then, others to be discovered much later—I left my original tribe and went on something of a quest, though unsure of what I was seeking.

In his *Power of Myth* discussions with Bill Moyers, Joseph Campbell describes the "hero's journey" as a series of trials and revelations. He also emphasizes that every human, in his or her own way, experiences some aspect of that journey simply through the act of living. That's why stories of heroism resonate: they represent an archetypal experience. Well, I've had my trials, just like every other human. And I've been blessed with my share of revelations. Some of the most important ones have come in the wilderness. But others have come in the company of humans, or through the arts, especially that of storytelling, both oral and written. My guides along the way—my mentors, teachers, and healers—have come in many forms. The most cherished have been nature writers, activists for environmental and human justice, leaders of what's been labeled the mythopoetic men's movement, spiritual mentors, friends, and lovers. And in my middle-aged years, family once more.

So again I find myself part of a human community, this one of my own choosing. It's a community of intersecting circles, people I've come to know through shared interests and loves: love of writing (and other art forms), love of wilderness, love of the wild Earth and larger creation, love of nature and spirit, human and otherwise, love of the greater mystery that informs and shadows our lives.

WHEN PLANNING MY solo journey, I'd rounded up some buddies and convinced them to join me for a couple of additional weeks in the Brooks Range. This is why Dulcy and Michael have come here. In a few days, two more friends will join us. We've expected to stay along the North Fork and explore the area on day hikes, to avoid heavy packing. But three days at the Gates airstrip and transfer station change our minds, for reasons that include the wet, forested terrain and the over-abundance of planes and people. We want more solitude and drier alpine tundra for easier rambles through the mountains.

Fortunately for us, pilot Jay Jesperson is agreeable to a shift in plans. Dulcy, Michael, and I fly to Bettles, where I give my newly slimmed body its first hot shower in nearly three weeks. Next I discover that the local store owner has added an espresso bar, and celebrate with their biggest mocha. Then I gobble down syrup-saturated pancakes and yet more bacon at the Bettles Lodge, which has changed lit-tle since my first visit a quarter century earlier. The main difference is a café add-on and gift shop where the kitchen used to be. Once again I share tales from my trek, this time prompted by Dale and Ellen, newly arrived from Anchorage, though by now my flood of words has slowed to more of a trickle. With Jay's help, our now-completed group picks its revised destination: a remote lake along the Arctic Divide, west of Anaktuvuk Pass and the John River in an area I've never visited.

"You won't be disappointed," he assures us.

It's August 6 when we fly out. And we quickly discover Jay to be right. The area is perfect: the lake sits in a wide-open tundra basin, enclosed by hills and ridges that we can scramble up and easy-to-reach perches from which we can look in any direction and see nothing but mountains and river valleys, as if they extend forever. Within an hour of landing we also see more wildlife than we did during our four-day stay at the Gates: ravens swooping above the tundra, sparrows in the willow thickets, loons and ducks on the lake, and fifty or more caribou scattered on the hills.

It turns out that this valley is one of the Western Arctic Caribou Herd's migra-tory paths; over the next eight days we'll see at least two to three hundred, usually in groups of a dozen or less. We'll also share the surrounding valley, hills, and sky with a couple of grizzlies, a fox, a long-tailed jaeger, a golden eagle, and a group of Dall sheep ewes with lambs.

A family of short-tailed weasels also stops by and checks out our camp. An entertaining mix of bold curiosity and wariness, they appear one day out of the willow thickets that edge our group shelter (a three-sided, high-tech thing that we christen "The Dome," it helps block the wind and rain when we gather for meals or conversation). The weasels approach to within a few feet, skitter away, and slowly return. Fiercely beautiful hunters, they have sleek chestnut brown and creamy white bodies, and long black-tipped tails. When startled or chasing food, they are extremely quick and agile. They also seem quite playful as they hop and prance among themselves, large black eyes gleaming brightly. They stay a while, then leave, perhaps out on a hunt.

Fall arrives during our stay, with winter surely not far behind, and the alpine tundra slowly comes afire with golds, russets, and purples. Daytime temperatures range from the thirties into the fifties and we wake one morning to a skim of ice on the lake. Still, we find some hardy summer remnants in winter's looming shadows. Late-blooming wildflowers brighten protected swales and our tundra passages: purple monkshood, blue Jacob's ladder and mountain harebells, pink plumes, magenta dwarf fireweed, white arctic sandwort. Less pleasing are the mosquitoes that occasionally swarm us when the wind dies and temperatures warm.

The chill disappoints Dulcy, who isn't ready for the early onset of winter. Though she joins some of our shorter outings, the cold air in combination with some sort of viral bug keep her largely in the tent. She assures me she's a contented cocooner, cozied up in the comfort of her many layers of clothes and heavy sleeping bag, with books to keep her company when the rest of us are out exploring.

We go on long hikes nearly every day and even playfully "bag" one of the higher peaks near camp. It's nothing more than a hard workout, a scramble to a rounded summit nearly a mile high and some two thousand feet above camp. The peak is already officially named on maps but we rename it "Coughing Lady Peak" in honor of Ellen, who's been coughing loudly since the start of our ascent; the leftovers of a chest cold, she explains, aggravated by the rigors of the climb.

It's cold and blowing on top, so we only stay long enough to pose for pictures, nibble snack food, and identify neighboring landmarks. Nahtuk is a dark chocolate kiss to the south while 6,188-foot Sillyasheen is dark, massive, and monolithic. Much farther to the west, and hazy in the distance, are the Arrigetch Peaks, rising sharply into the sky. Memories of my 1984 trip—my first backpack into the Brooks Range after returning to Alaska as a writer—are inevitably stirred. Some day I'll return to those rocky "fingers of the hand, extended," I'm sure of it. In the lowlands are Lonely Lake and Easter Creek, which inevitably raise questions about the people and circumstances involved in their naming. And all around us are scores of anonymous mountains, ridges, lakes, ponds, creeks, and valleys. Though people have wandered these lands for generations, there must be hills and ridges out there that have never been walked. It's almost a certainty that others have stood here, but we wonder how many—or how few—have come before us. Not many, is our guess.

One evening after dinner, Dale, Michael, Ellen, and I head north from camp toward the Arctic Divide. We high step through ankle-grabbing sedge-tussock tundra, and pick our way through and around willow thickets, dwarf birch, and boggy pools of flesh-numbing water, gradually stripping off wool caps, fleece gloves, and rain jackets as our bodies warm in the gradual ascent. In no hurry, we stop now and then to graze on small but juicy and sweet blueberries and to admire piles of drab gray slate that wear bright beards of orange lichen. Finally at the top, we peer down at streams carrying water bound for the Arctic Ocean. Michael is jubilant. "This is way better than the Arctic Circle Club," he exults. "This is the Arctic Divide Club."

"Yeah," Dale chimes in, "this is much more exclusive."

While we pull back on layers earlier discarded, three caribou approach. The two cows and a calf check us out, then skedaddle down the ridge, headed north. Dale too wants to keep walking, to the next highest point, and then the next, on and on, as long as it takes. Golden beams shoot down from dark rolling masses upon mountains that glow as if lit from within.

There's no obvious sign of humanity besides our tiny speck of a camp, no human sounds beyond our small voices. The ridges and valleys belong to caribou and bear, wolf and raven, sparrow and squirrel. Though we stand upon the crest of an immense mountain wilderness, I am once again struck by the sense of vast, open space. These mountains don't enclose but open up; they invite both eyes and imaginations to more distant realms. They draw us out of ourselves, expand our awareness, and shrink the ego.

This is the first time that Ellen, Dale, and Michael have entered the Brooks Range wilderness and it's a joy to share this special place with them. Their words, but even more the tone of their voices and expressions, tell me they too are enamored of this place. And now, I suspect, they better understand my own passion for these arctic wilds.

These days spent with good friends in my favorite place of wilderness are deeply fulfilling. We share laughter, walks, stories, and moments of grace and delight in the presence of grizzly and weasel and caribou. We take turns making dinner, grumble playfully about the cold, and get goofy with each other. We give each other nicknames: Dulcy and Ellen are the Basecamp Babes; Michael becomes Caribou Man after lugging some huge bleached racks back to camp; I'm the trip-organizing Scoutmaster (an interesting choice since I never joined the Scouts); and Dale is tagged Bagel Man, for all the bagels and other heavy foods he hauled out here. We give Dale grief about the Dome, but appreciate its small comforts. Michael sits upon his much-envied Throne—a portable backcountry lounger—while sharing real coffee he's brewed in his French-press-style cup inside the Temple of the Bean, a.k.a. the Dome. When not sipping on the real stuff, I'm content with my coffee bags, but Ellen swears them off forever.

Ellen, an anthropologist, finds what she thinks might be stone tools (one a finished spear point, the other a broken worked piece); if so, they could be up to nine thousand years old. Her discoveries raise the question of whether our campsite and some nearby knobs might have been hunting camps in the distant past. From our lakeshore camp we have a sweeping view of a basin traveled by migrating caribou. Ellen also discusses the ethical dilemma of removing such pieces (she leaves them be), even if only to take to an expert familiar with this region's prehistory. And we wonder: has this valley been previously studied?

Among the many highlights, one of my favorites is the night we five adventurers sit inside the Dome, sipping our drinks while we share readings from the journals we've been keeping, a delightfully intimate glimpse into one another's experiences out here.

After two weeks of solitude, this time together has also given me the chance to move more slowly back into the modern, high-tech world of humans, with all its complexities and paradoxes and puzzles. Like Marshall so many years ago, I understand that the vast majority of people have no desire to spend time deep in the wilderness, far from the comforts that make modern life easier in many ways, but also more disconnected. And harmful to the planet. Given this reality, those of us who seek out the wilderness—whether in the Arctic, the desert Southwest, or tropical forests—need to keep sharing what we've learned about its nature, its power and magic. To have such vast natural landscapes is critical, not only for our species' present and future, but for wilderness and wildness itself.

If I were never to return, it would be enough to know this place exists.

During one of our many walkabouts, I'm lagging behind when Ellen glances back at me and then wonders aloud, "Why the big smile?"

I haven't realized I've been smiling so. "No special reason," I say. After brief reflection, I add, "I think it's just that I love being out here so much." That's reason enough, we agree. I feel no need, right now, for epiphanies or revelations. It's enough simply to be immersed in wilderness and touched, moment after moment, by wildness and a community of friends that open the senses, open the heart.

EPILOGUE

Marble tower, Valley of Spires.

Return to Gates

MY MIND REELS IN DISBELIEF, MY SPIRITS PLUMMET. LESS THAN an hour into a ten-day, solo wilderness journey I face a crisis of my own making. The problem may in fact be minor and easily resolved, but for the moment (and hours afterward) it feels huge and dreadful: one of the tent's three aluminum poles has cracked and splintered, making it appear—in my panicked state, at least—all but useless.

It doesn't help that wintry weather has settled on the Central Brooks Range. Though it's only August 3, surrounding peaks are dusted with fresh snow and temperatures hover in the thirties. The cold complicates things. Right now scattered, gauzy clouds float through an azure sky and the landscape glows in far north light. But a ferocious wind hurtles down this valley north of the Arctic Divide. And, I've been told, this summer in America's northernmost mountain range has been marked by plentiful rain and snow. How the hell am I going to get through ten days of cold and likely wet arctic weather with a damaged tent?

Staring at the pole, I wonder how I could have missed the crack during pre-trip preparations, even if then it was a hairline fracture. Now the curved, segmented pole is broken at the joint where one piece slides onto another. It dangles limply at the end, a broken limb. I accuse myself of complacency, laziness, recklessness. My custom-made tent has performed so well for so long that I've come to take it for granted.

I also curse my shortcomings as a jury-rigger and fix-it guy. The son of a talented carpenter and brother of a highly skilled craftsman, I've never been adept at building things or doing makeshift repairs, whether at home or in the field. And until now I've given little thought to my dependency on properly functioning gear.

Fighting panic—what will I do if I can't fix the damn pole?—I search through the first-aid kit and pull out a small wad of duct tape. I habitually carry it on back-country trips, but only once before (after smashing a Klepper kayak onto a river boulder) have I needed duct tape to make emergency repairs.

I wrap the break, but it's clear the mend is weak. The gnawing in my gut resumes and my racing mind picks up speed. I next craft a crude splint, first with a small willow branch, then the thin brush (much like those used in paint-by-numbers sets) that's part of the tent's repair kit. Shell-shocked with worry, I bind the splint with medical and duct tape. The rush job seems to stabilize the break, but the pole still bends at a frightening angle and I wonder how it would hold up in a gale. What if it snaps and rips the tent's fabric? Could the tent function with only two poles instead of three? A reliable shelter is so critically important in these arctic mountains.

I LATER MAKE a second *Oh, no!* discovery: I've forgotten the stove's windshield. That will complicate its operation. But at least I've brought my high-tech tarp; it will provide a windbreak when cooking.

One more scare awaits me. When firing up my stove, I can't get it to light. This doesn't make sense. It worked fine during a pre-trip check. Inspecting the fuel bot-tle that connects to the burner, I notice a hairline fracture in the bottle's plastic top. Can that be the problem? Again my spirits plunge, my pulse quickens. What if I can't repair the stove? Will I have to abort my trip before it's even started? I've brought along a satellite phone, so calling for help would not be a problem. But how humiliating, to get rescued right at the start.

After fiddling with the stove for several minutes, I figure out the problem: I sim-ply forgot to turn the fuel-flow lever to the proper spot. When twisted to the "hi/light" position, vaporized fuel squirts into the burner.

Huge relief floods my body and I allow myself an embarrassed chuckle. Maybe I can blame this awful, clownish start to being out of practice. I haven't gone on an extended trip deep into Gates—or any wilderness area—since 2001, the year before I became the primary caregiver for my mother, an eighty-year-old widow no lon-ger able to live alone, her bones and joints and flesh aching daily with advanced degenerative osteoarthritis and a weak spine.

Living alone since my father died in 1990, Torie Sherwonit had remained an active and self-sufficient woman, albeit slowed by nearly eight decades of life. But in the months following her seventy-ninth birthday she'd gradually become housebound and required ever-more assistance from neighbors and friends. It was a tough transition for someone who'd been the family's primary caregiver all of her adult life. Besides her weakened, pain-wracked body, she'd had some loss of memory. She confused dates and sometimes names, forgot where she put things or whether she'd taken her medications.

As she approached her eightieth year, it became clear that Mom's three children would have to assume responsibility for her care. We recognized this situation was hardly unique to us. More and more of our middle-aged friends have been faced with the challenges of aging parents, as our mothers and fathers move into their not-always-golden years. Parents move in with their kids, or into assisted-care facilities, or nursing homes. For as long as possible, we agreed, we would try to keep this in the family. Of all her kids, I seemed most able to take on the challenge; after all, I worked at home and was married to a woman who was newly retired and who had become a great friend to Mom. In short, my mother wouldn't be so lonely.

And so in summer 2002, Dulcy and I traveled to Virginia and brought Mom back to live with us in Anchorage. It marked a major shift for us all, but was an especially huge upheaval for Mom, yet a necessary thing if she were to remain with family.

Six years later, my marriage to Dulcy has ended but I'm still responsible for Mom, who remains remarkably positive and gracious despite her slow but steady decline and endless pain. I seem more closely tied to home than ever, despite lots of help from agencies and individuals in the Anchorage community. But this year, after far too long away, I've been determined to return to Gates. And it's worked out, thanks in large part to my sister, Karen, who's come north from Chicago to be with our mother while I'm in the Arctic.

MY CAMPING WOES get me thinking about legendary wilderness travelers I've met in person or through reading. Contemporary Alaskans Dick Griffith and Roman Dial immediately come to mind, along with historic American figures like John Muir, Meriwether Lewis and William Clark, and, of course, Bob Marshall. I imagine Marshall and the others shaking their heads in amusement at my worried mind and fumbling antics and a voice whispers in my head: *C'mon Sherwonit, get your act together. You can do better.* Then, more calming, *Buck up, things are going to be* OK.

Wherever it comes from, that advice and a hot pasta dinner seem to settle me down. Occasionally I look up from the meal to scan the surrounding valley and hills. Once I notice a large bull caribou prancing beside the lake where I'd been dropped off. There's no sign of other caribou and I wonder if this one is a straggler or simply off on his own adventure. Whatever the case, he's a welcome presence on a mostly fretful evening.

I enter the wind-whipped tent around nine p.m. and settle in for the night while a light rain begins to fall. Now comfortably cocooned in my sleeping bag, with the pole holding up well, I'm more at ease, even content.

My plan is to backpack six or seven miles and establish a camp near the unnamed valley of marble towers that I visited in 1998 with four others. Their tight schedules allowed us only five days and I vowed to return for more leisurely explorations. Now, alone and with ten days to play around, I have plenty of flexibility. Whether I move camp in the morning will depend largely on the weather.

MY SECOND DAY in the mountains is mostly rainy and gusty, so I stay inside the tent except to cook and stretch muscles on a short ridge climb. The hike is exactly the tonic I need. Step by step, my worries wash away while I gently slip into the wonder of these wild and ancient mountains. It's as if this harsh, rugged place somehow eases me into a more tranquil state of being. It's a subtle shift, until finally it hits me: *Wow, it's great to be back.*

Night brings a change in the wind from south to north, colder temperatures, and a snow squall. A skim of slush covers the tent when I awaken from a deep sleep. A quick look outside convinces me I'm not going anywhere yet. Mountains and valley are veiled in soupy grayness and sheets of wet, wind-driven flurries rush by.

The tent and its damaged pole have held up well during two nights of steady and sometimes fierce winds and I'm much more relaxed. It also helps that I've caught up on much-needed sleep. I'm not yet itching to pull up stakes and carry my heavy load across the tundra in wind-whipped wetness, so I allow myself the luxury of daydreams, reflection, journal writing, and naps. Now and then I study my maps, though I know exactly where I'm going and how to get there. I'm curious to see how this area links up with other parts of Bob Marshall country that I've explored on previous trips, particularly my solo trek from Anaktuvuk Pass to the Gates in 2000.

The valley I'm in is nearly two miles across, with the classic U-shaped form of glacially carved drainages. Its many unnamed rivulets and creeks feed a clearwater stream that will eventually join the much-larger Colville River and empty into the Beaufort Sea. The bordering mountains rise three thousand to four thousand feet above the valley floor, their brown, gray, and black forms tufted by green alpine tundra. Enough plants cover those hillsides to sustain a large population of Dall sheep. Aided by binoculars, I've counted more than thirty, including sixteen in the hills above camp. All that I've seen are ewes, lambs, and adolescents, but mature rams also inhabit these parts, drawing trophy seekers to the preserve, which is open to sport hunting. Right now I'm camped near the park/preserve border, but for most of my visit I'll be in designated wilderness, where only subsistence hunting by residents of the region is permitted.

An afternoon lull in the storm again pulls me out of the tent for another tundra walk. The landscape has already begun its seasonal shift. Summer's lush greens are patched and streaked by the faint but deepening reds of bearberry leaves, the oranges of dwarf birch, and the yellows of various willows and wildflowers. Summer's wildflower bloom peaked weeks ago, but several late-blossoming species still brighten the landscape and my mood. I begin to make a list that will eventually grow to nearly twenty species. The most common flowers near camp are purple gentians, many still in their prime. Also sprinkling the tundra are magenta dwarf fireweed—a mountain as well as a river beauty—yellow tundra rose, fading purple monkshood, creamy prickly saxifrage, and frazzled-looking wooly lousewort. I also find a single pink plume and, huddled behind a rock, a solitary forget-me-not, its still-vivid sky blue petals glowing amid the grayness.

The wildlife isn't nearly as varied, but assorted whistles, chirps, and chatter also liven the somber day. Ground squirrels are everywhere; they scold me while I filter water, cook my meals, explore their neighborhood. A hoary marmot whistles a warning before ducking inside a pile of rocks. Ravens and mew gulls squawk and screech around the edges of the nearby lake, which is also patrolled by long-tailed jaegers, handsome with their black heads, white breasts and "collars," charcoal gray backs and wings, and long, streaming tails.

Even more abundant than the squirrels are American pipits, sparrow-sized tundra birds with grayish backs, beige undersides, and striking white tail feathers that they display when flying. A mix of curiosity and shyness, they fly in close as if to check me out and wag their tails while flitting from boulder to tussock to boulder, then rush off while talking among themselves with characteristic "pipping" calls.

I'm not one who likes high-technology aids when trekking through the wilderness, but I'd agreed to bring a satellite phone to ease my sweetheart Helene's anxieties. Even rentals are expensive, $150 for two weeks, plus $1.75 per minute of use. Unless faced with some dire emergency, I didn't expect to even take the thing out of its case. But now, missing Helene and feeling a little playful, I decide to surprise her with a phone call.

Having never used a satellite phone before, I'm amazed both by how easily it connects me to Ashland, Oregon, and how crisp Helene's voice sounds. She could be right around the bend.

"Hi, Helene, it's Bill . . ."

"WHAT? BILL?"

It's understandable she sounds a little freaked out. We'd had no plans to talk unless something went wrong. So I make it clear, "Everything's OK, I just wanted . . ."

Then the phone cuts out. I redial and impatiently wait for the satellite to reconnect us, hoping she heard my reassurance. Finally the phone rings.

"Hi, me again."

"Bill, wow, what a shock. How are things going?"

Not wishing to worry her, I don't mention the broken tent pole, but describe the wintry weather and assure her I am doing fine.

"Oh, that's great. I've been worried about you. You know how I need something to worry about . . . I know it's only been a couple of days, but already I miss you."

"I miss you too."

We talk only a few minutes, then send long-distance hugs and exchange I-love-yous.

So technology (of course) does have its merits. Happy and hopeful of moving camp tomorrow, I slip back into the tent and sleeping bag and fall quickly into a dream-rich sleep.

MORNING BRINGS A heavy frost and an early wake-up. Fog drifts through the valley but overhead patches of blue sky peek through the grayness. And the air is calm. By nine thirty I'm ready to go. The pack doesn't feel as heavy as I feared, though it must weigh close to sixty pounds. Going light is still not my thing. I'd rather carry extra food and clothes and suffer the pounds that they add. Plus there's the tarp, satellite phone, camera, water filter, pepper spray, on and on.

By the end of my day's packing—six hours, seven miles, and a thousand feet of elevation gain—my body is weary and achy, my feet carry a few blisters, and I've been stung by a yellow jacket while picking blueberries. But I'm a happy camper, now within a couple of miles of the areas I've come to explore, especially the narrow, steep-walled amphitheater that ten years ago I nicknamed the "Valley of Spires" (which I now shorten to Spire Valley). Even from afar, it's clear that something extraordinary lies ahead. Some great force has compressed the main, broad valley into a tight ravine, scraped away the tundra, and squeezed its mountain walls into a chaotic mass. Jumbled spires and huge, overlapping plates of bare rock hint of a gateway to another world.

My hike to this spot had its share of surprises. The presence of tall fireweed, a tundra slump, dense willow thickets, and mixed songbird flocks that include robins, tree sparrows, and varied thrushes all have me thinking about global warming and how it's changing this landscape.

It's difficult to say how much has changed here since my 1998 visit, because I wasn't paying close attention to such things then. And documenting changes would likely be just as tough ten years from now, unless someone were to do baseline measurements. Maybe a series of landscape images? Perhaps this trip I'm noticing surprising details—patches of tall fireweed, woodland birds—I might have missed before because I know the arctic landscape is shifting. The thrushes, especially, seem out of place, because I associate the species so closely with forests. On returning home, a check of my Alaska bird guide will confirm that varied thrushes are rarely seen in the Arctic. Is that changing?

My awareness of human contributions to global warming is also heightened, yet I flew north anyway. Of course I can rationalize the trip, my first to the Arctic in seven years, but any nonessential travel—especially by an avowed Earth-friendly person—is open to criticism. I wonder what sort of guilt-assuaging carbon credits would adequately compensate for the series of flights that brought me from Anchorage to the Brooks Range, especially the air-taxi flight on which I was the only passenger.

Another surprise: a grizzly family. Not that grizzlies should be unexpected here. On my previous visit, we didn't see any bears, but today I saw enough sign—mostly scat and uprooted tundra—to stay on high alert. Still, the presence of a female and her two cubs shook me up a bit, especially while bashing my way through head-high willows. Fortunately, they were a good distance away, a hundred yards or more.

The bears must have seen me first, because mom already had her cubs on the move when our eyes met. The female paused briefly, which led to an uh-oh moment: will she charge or will she flee? Flee she did, after the briefest hesitation.

Heading uphill, the grizzly mom barely stopped until she reached the ridgeline, pausing only now and then to check on her cubs. I watched enthralled while the family of bears ascended a thousand-foot slope in a matter of minutes, the female's muscles rippling as she climbed, the cubs only slightly slower. The grizzlies had to negotiate one final steep, rocky gully to reach the ridgeline and it hardly slowed them down. After watching the effort that female put into removing her family from danger, it is easy to understand the severity of attacks by grizzlies protecting their cubs.

AUGUST 7. Happily, I'm losing track of the days, but now and then I still check my watch for the time and date. An old habit that's tough to break and another inconsistency for one who wishes to be immersed in the wilds and "wilderness time." So it goes. I've learned to accept the fact that I, like other humans, am a bundle of contradictions.

It's a cold, frosty morning. And gloriously clear. Waking at six, I'm tempted to rebury myself in the sleeping bag, but the cold—and memories of last night's opening of clouds to reveal blue skies—prompt me to peek out the tent's front flap. Lower body still wrapped in down-filled bag, I'm treated to a dazzling sight: early-morning sunlight warms and brightens the uppermost reaches of the marble amphitheater I've come so far to see. I quickly bundle my torso in several layers of clothes, add wool cap and fleece gloves, and join the day.

Backlit by the sun, a dense and glowing fog bank moves up valley, though only a few faint wisps will reach this high. Still in shadow, the tundra around camp is white with frost, tiny fragile needles of ice growing on every leaf and limb and berry. It's hard to imagine these crystals grew in the hours I slept, transforming the tundra into a miniature, if ephemeral, world of ice.

I climb higher on the bench that is my temporary home, to gain a more expansive view of the marble spires and walls, which rise brightly into pale blue sky. A soft, diaphanous cloud grows around the front spire, casting shadows and adding depth and texture to the landscape. I enter a photographic frenzy, something that rarely happens to me anymore, and take picture after picture. As much as anything, I want to capture images of Spire Valley to share with Helene, a photographic record to complement my journal jottings.

Wishing a different slant, I walk to a neighboring knoll. The earth and mountains move, too, giving the sun room enough to flood nearly the entire basin with its light. The landscape now flashes with uncountable sparkles, ice crystals reflecting the sun even as they begin to slowly melt. Though my attention has largely been focused on the bigger, more dramatic rock drama before me, I stop now and then to marvel at the equally wondrous frost crystals and the myriad plants they've grown upon, an infinity of shapes and textures hugging the ground. A person could spend hours, a week, a lifetime, meditating on those small beauties.

It's a blessing to be here for this morning's spectacle, one that's been repeated an untold number of times across the ages and yet never quite the same as today's. I think that's one of the things I love about this wilderness, the immensity of scale that's revealed, both across the landscape and through time.

I'm reflecting upon all of this and more, breathing in the light and grandeur of the place, when it hits me: the same sort of earthly wonders that once inspired me to become a geologist have now inspired my return to Spire Valley. And they're a big part of what keeps bringing me back to Gates of the Arctic. Not just the spectacular rock towers of this place or the Arrigetch, but the many landforms—the peaks and valleys, the rivers and ridges—I've spent time among. Decades have passed since I mapped a landscape or tried to figure out its history, since I collected rock samples or sought natural riches for their economic value. But now, once again, I've been drawn back by the complex and contorted nature of immense rock formations—and the inconceivable forces that have formed the steep-walled amphitheater that rises before me.

It also appears that I've lost much of the discomfort and defensiveness I once felt about being a "failed"—or at least inadequate—geologist and can now more fully appreciate these landforms as naturalist and nature writer, a generalist rather than one schooled in the earth sciences.

Through binoculars I look at some of the limy strata that were once deeply buried and are now thrust high into the air, revealed in all their magnificent complexity. Though the marbles are layered, it's impossible—at least for a nonspecialist—to follow any one bed for long, while gazing upon the more vertical and deformed towers. The rocks have been squeezed and squished, fractured, slid along faults, uplifted and eroded, to now form fantastically curved and broken shapes.

How long have these spires stood here, revealed to grizzly, wolf, and human? How have their shapes shifted in the thousands of years that people have inhabited Alaska's Arctic? In the millennia that humans have inhabited the Earth? I love coming here as naturalist, writer, explorer to revel in the landscape's mysteries and majesty, without having to figure out the geology. Or even try.

TAKING A ROUNDABOUT route to stay on the driest, firmest tundra, I reach Spire Valley's portal in a little more than an hour. Then I follow the one easy route into it, up a narrow chute that's regularly traveled by local inhabitants as well as the occasional visiting humans. Scat and tracks show that caribou, sheep, grizzlies, and wolves have all passed this way.

An initial steep ascent brings me to a small meadow, but there's still one passageway to go, a narrow seam between marble bedrock and a huge pile of rubble. Stepping out of that, I enter a place that has the feel of a hidden, magical realm. Immediately before me is a lush marshland whose sedges, cotton grasses, and other plants form a bright mosaic of greens and yellows. A gently moving stream meanders through the marsh, connecting a half-dozen milky aquamarine ponds, their surfaces mirror smooth. A delight in itself, this alpine wetland is made even more memorable by the stark, soaring rock walls that enclose it. Dark gray marble slabs form the valley's northern flanks; one stacked upon the other, they slant steeply and uniformly to the south, with huge piles of rock debris heaped at their bases.

While the north rim is eye-catching, the valley's south face is mind-boggling. Still and lifeless by human standards, the towering spires nevertheless embody a strong sense of movement. Once-horizontal rock strata have been violently tilted until standing on end. Their precipitous faces rise two thousand feet high from base to top. The tilted layers, in turn, have been folded crosswise, transforming the rock walls into sharply angular shapes with vertical striations. It's easy to envision giant fangs, dark and ominous. Or, like the Arrigetch Peaks, they can be imagined as the clawed fingers of an outstretched hand, clutching for the sky.

I have wondered, over the years, if the magic of this place would be dimmed on a return visit. Though the surprise of my earlier entrance can't be repeated, the place continues to hold great power. Again I shrink in size, humbled by the landscape and the gigantic forces it suggests.

Last time, I stayed near the ravine's entrance, so one of my goals is to explore its upper reaches. The valley bottom is strikingly flat for several hundred yards, as if a long-ago lake has been filled in to form the marsh. Gradually the floor begins to rise and the marsh gives way to wet tussocky tundra, then to an area that resembles a braided river, with multiple channels, gravel bars, and fields of dwarf fireweed, river beauties now largely faded. The fireweed fields in turn give way to a rubbly outwash plain of gravel and cobbles and an occasional boulder.

I stop my wanderings near the tundra's margin, at about five thousand feet, close to five miles from camp and fifteen hundred feet above it. Here the valley bends to the south; a quarter mile away is a dark brown "rock glacier." The map shows its icy parent to be higher in the basin, but all I can see is more rock debris, streaked in places by recent snow. If there's ice above, it's buried by thick deposits of rock and dirt. More evidence of warming.

Though the day has been mostly calm, a fierce wind begins to roar out of the north as I make my way back to camp. It smacks full force into the side of my tent, which I aligned with the east–west-trending valley. Again I worry about the damaged pole, and again it holds up admirably.

I GO ON one more long hike, to the south of Spire Valley, but for much of the next week I choose to go on shorter forays and spend hours in camp or nearby it. Initially I criticize myself for not being more ambitious. But in fact I'm enjoying this more leisurely approach to wilderness "exploration" and once more I gradually embrace my way of getting to know this part of the Arctic. And my place in it.

On one of my sleep-in mornings, the urge to pee finally pulls me from the sleeping bag. As I open the tent door I find myself looking directly at a bear—which is also looking at me. Fortunately it's a young grizzly, an adolescent, at least fifty yards from camp and headed away from me. In a couple of seconds, he's out of sight. If I'd been just a bit slower, I likely would have missed the bear's passing. I'm calm, but there's an inevitable surge of adrenaline, to see a bear so close to camp. Did the grizzly hear me zip open the door? Or already know of my presence?

Eager to get a second, longer look, I quickly put on my clothes, grab binoculars, and walk uphill. I scan the upper basin and its tributary valleys for at least half an hour, gradually making my way farther up the drainage, but the bear has disappeared.

Returned to camp, I put up the tarp and make myself breakfast. More like brunch, actually, since it's early afternoon. I love my flexible wilderness days, so different from the busy, often harried schedule I keep in town.

Now that my initial trip anxieties have passed, I'm more relaxed. And spontaneous. I can sleep until midday or leap out of the tent at what in Anchorage might seem an ungodly hour. Here I have plenty of time to meditate and reflect on life's ups and downs, its challenges and blessings. I can muse in my journal or read Loren Eiseley (more weight, but worth it when the book is *The Immense Journey*). I can sip coffee and nibble dark chocolate while studying the landscape or, when the spirit moves, grab my pack and go tramping around the countryside.

Time like this is good for the spirit, good for the soul, whether in the wilderness or some inner-city retreat, but somewhere, somehow, some way. I know I'm lucky to be able to do this. And I've arranged my life so I can have these times of grace, the opportunity to recharge the self. And, I think, grow.

NOTIONS OF WILDERNESS inevitably weave through my head during these long, contemplative days. I think about the "great new wilderness debate" that continues to seethe in some quarters, particularly among thinkers and activists. Before leaving on this trip, I learned that Michael P. Nelson and J. Baird Callicott have followed up their original *Great New Wilderness Debate* tome with an even bigger (723 pages) work, *The Wilderness Debate Rages On.* Even if it were available (which it won't be, until October), I wouldn't have lugged the bulky, heavy book out here. But I wonder what new angles the editors will present.

Months later, I'll find out.

Besides aiming zingers at some "good-old-time-wilderness-religion zealots" (chief among them Gary Snyder and David Foreman) who've had the temerity to lash out at their own ideas, Nelson and Callicott expansively—and, one might argue, a bit self-righteously and self-servingly—explain the importance of the debate that they continue to fuel and why their sequel "is mandated."

Of more interest to me, the editors argue that America's conservation movement chose a path that "for better or worse" led to the idea of wilderness they have
chosen to assail, a path in which the "received wilderness idea…coalesced from
three main sources." The first of those was wilderness preservation for recreational
purposes; the second, for aesthetic and spiritual values; and third, to preserve "big,
dramatic, awe-inspiring, monumental scenery." Callicott and Nelson contend it is
time to pursue a different route, in which wilderness is set aside for scientific purposes; for the protection of threatened and endangered species; and for the preservation of "representative landscapes and ecosystems" whether they inspire awe or
not. In short, they argue for the need to preserve the Earth's shrinking biodiversity.
And because, in his view, the idea of wilderness carries so much baggage, Callicott
proposes instead "biodiversity preserves."

I don't know any Earth-and-life-loving person who would argue against the
need to preserve the world's remaining wild landscapes, habitats, ecosystems, and
life forms, whether in areas designated wilderness or preserve. In fact, some of the
people who Callicott and Nelson appear to dismiss as wilderness zealots also argue
for biodiversity, Snyder among them: "Wilderness is the locus of big rich ecosystems, and is thus (among other things) a living place for beings who can survive in
no other sort of habitat. Recreation, spirituality, aesthetics—good for people—also
make wilderness valuable, but these are secondary to the importance of biodiversity. The protection of natural variety is essential to planetary health for all."

Callicott himself couldn't have put it better.

Unfortunately, while they push for what they perceive to be a new and better
world-conservation movement, Nelson and Callicott appear to have created—and
continue to build—unnecessary schisms and tensions that needn't exist within
the environmental/conservation community. I will find myself nodding agreement, over and over, while reading "The Not-So-Great Wilderness Debate…Con-
tinued," penned by environmentalist and educator David Orr and included in the
collection of forty-one writings.

Orr, like me—and presumably many other wilderness advocates—believes that
this debate has its merits:

> I think it can be said that, under provocation from Callicott, Cronon and
> others, a stronger and more useful case for wilderness protection [has]
> emerged.…The conjunction of older ideas about wilderness providing spiri-
> tual renewal and primitive recreation with newer ones concerning ecologi-
> cal restoration and the preservation of diversity offers a better and more
> scientifically grounded basis to protect and expand remaining Wilderness
> Areas in the 21st century.

On the other hand, Orr points out,

The world now more than ever needs better ideas about how to meld society, economy, and ecology into a coherent, fair, and sustainable whole. The question is whether environmentalists can offer practical, workable, and sensible ideas—not abstractions, arcane ideology, spurious dissent, and ideological hair-splitting.. . . . In this regard, the most striking thing about the ongoing "great wilderness debate" is the similarity of positions that have been cast as either/or. There is no necessary divide, for example, between protecting wilderness and sustainable development. To the contrary, they are complementary ideas.…Since all participants profess support for the place called Wilderness, as distinct from the idea of it, we are entitled to ask: what is the point of the great wilderness debate? If we intend to influence our age in the little time we have, we must focus more clearly and effectively on the large battles that we dare not lose.…

As Aldo Leopold pointed out decades ago, we need well-kept farms and home places, well-managed forests, *and* large Wilderness Areas. None of these needs to compete with any other.

There's plenty of other provocative, stimulating essays, articles, and rants in *The Wilderness Debate Rages On*, but of the pieces I've read as of this writing, Orr's take on the debate resonates the most with me. It's time to move on and do the good work that's needed to preserve more wild landscapes, ecosystems, and species, whatever name we give to protected areas, while also preserving the rights and lives of indigenous peoples who maintain traditional relationships with their wild homelands.

MY RENEWED CALM and enjoyment of the Arctic is tempered one afternoon when I return to camp and discover the tarp has been damaged. When away from camp, I pull the tarp tight against the ground and place rocks along its edges, to keep it from blowing around (or away). There's been no strong wind this day, yet two stakes have been pulled out, several rocks have been tossed aside, and the tarp itself has been flipped over. Taking a closer look, I find two gashes, one about eighteen inches long. Near the tears are a few small holes, suggestive of bite-puncture marks.

All the evidence suggests a grizzly has ripped the tarp, perhaps the same adolescent I saw earlier. I swirl around, looking for the intruder, but see no sign of bear. Though rattled by the damage and what it suggests, I'm greatly relieved the tent is still standing. From a distance it looks untouched, but a thorough inspection reveals two small, parallel tears near one of its zippered entryways. I imagine the same bear swatting at the tent. What could have possessed the grizzly to enter camp, then strike or nudge the tent and tug on the tarp? And what possessed it to stop before doing more damage? Again I swirl around, consider other possibilities. Human? Wolf? Some mythical arctic trickster? It had to be a grizzly. Young "teenage" bears are notorious for their curiosity. And, sometimes, boldness.

Next I check my food, cached apart from both tent and tarp. It's untouched. At least the bear didn't get any reward. I whisper a prayer of thanks, even while trying to imagine what must have happened. A part of me wishes I could have watched the bear move through camp, though if I'd seen the grizzly I would surely have tried to drive it off.

Pulling out the duct tape, I again make temporary repairs. My senses remain on high alert for several hours and I periodically scan the area with binoculars. I doubt the grizzly will return, but I do keep the pepper spray close at hand when I settle into my sleeping bag. And I wake a couple times during the calm, quiet night, listening for footsteps or breathing outside the tent. All I hear is the soft, guttural growling of a willow ptarmigan somewhere on the tundra.

TOWARD THE END OF MY STAY, I realize it's no coincidence that I brought the writings of Loren Eiseley—a scientist who believed in miracles and embraced mystery—on this latest venture into the Brooks Range wilderness. No accident, either, that life's circumstances forced Helene to bow out of the trip at the last minute, leaving me alone in the arctic wilds for ten days. That's not much when compared to Christ's forty days or any number of contemporary solo journeys. But it's enough time, certainly, to do some serious soul searching and shed enough of my urban skin to more openly embrace the wondrous wild.

Going solo into the wild raises the stakes; it magnifies and intensifies experiences, whether unnerving (a river crossing, a broken tent pole, a bear in camp) or sublime (Doonerak, howling wolves, the Valley of Spires). There's nothing like a wilderness sojourn, especially when alone, to renew or enlarge one's sense of wonder and awareness of life's miracles—and the greater miracle of creation. Or the universe, or all-that-is, or whatever you prefer to call it.

Is it not a miracle to watch Dall sheep lambs gambol across steep slopes that would paralyze a human mountaineer? Or to watch a yellow spider, no bigger than a sesame seed, crawl across the back of the hand before disappearing back into the tundra, where it somehow survives arctic extremes? And isn't it a marvelous thing to walk among huge, contorted, leaping walls of marble, formed over great expanses of time and then squished, fractured, and thrust upward into the sky and finally sculpted by glacial ice? Or to stand in a valley sparkling wildly as ice crystals are lit up by the sun?

I know: not everyone can get into the wilderness yearly. Or would want to. But of course that's not necessary. While the wilderness may more easily open us to the miracles of this world, there's plenty of wondrous stuff going on around us— and inside us—all the time. *Yeah*, you may be saying, *I know that*. But how often do you *feel* it with your whole being?

As Eiseley and other wisdom keepers have reminded us across the years, life itself is a miracle—as are the parts of creation that our Western culture tends to consider "dead" or lifeless. And to be part of that spectacle is a miracle that needs to be regularly honored.

While it's important that we be educated and warned about global warming, toxins everywhere, the dangers and potential cruelties of industrial farming (or industrial anything), we humans also need reminding that simply to be alive and part of this grand experiment—or whatever you wish to call it—is a mysterious and astonishing thing.

This matters because we behave differently in the presence of the miraculous. We act more respectfully and generously. We're more open to being joyful, playful, and, perhaps most importantly, hopeful, essential ways of being in these anxious, destructive, scary times, when it's so easy to be overcome by despair, hopelessness, and paralysis. I'm not suggesting a retreat from harsh realities. We need to keep working for the greater good, a healthier, more just, and peaceful world. But we need to stop now and then to praise and embrace life.

Firsthand experience of the miraculous is always best. But when that's impossible, we need reminders. I get them from people like Loren Eiseley, Wendell Berry, Robert Bly, Matthew Fox, Terry Tempest Williams, Chet Raymo, Michael Meade, Scott Russell Sanders, Kathleen Dean Moore, James Hillman, Gary Snyder, Thich Nhat Hanh.

Above my desk is a quote attributed to the latter. In his own way, he says much the same thing that Eiseley does. I return to it often, especially when things seem darkest: "People usually consider walking on water or in thin air a miracle. But I think the real miracle is not to walk either on water or in thin air, but to walk on earth. Every day we are engaged in a miracle which we don't even recognize: a blue sky, white clouds, green leaves, the black, curious eyes of a child—our own two eyes. All is a miracle."

Amen and hallelujah.

* * *

THE MORNING AIR is damp and clouds hang low over the mountains when I awake on August 12, but there's almost no wind. And no rain, no snow. I wipe moisture from tent and tarp, eat a leisurely breakfast, then take down the tent and marvel, one more time, at the damaged pole that's held up so well, and pack my gear.

By eleven a.m. I'm ready to head back down valley to my pick-up spot. One more day of heavy packing, one more night of camping, and I'll be headed out of the mountains and back to town, body lighter by a few pounds but stronger, spirit lightened and strengthened too. Journal and mind are filled with stories and ideas, heart carries renewed passion, and I intuit a refreshed sense of well-being, a renewed sense of purpose.

The day is warm and still enough that mosquitoes harass me for the first time this trip. I douse myself with repellent, pull on my pack, and begin sloshing my way across the tundra, wettened by last night's rains. Coming to a thicket of willows, I start my bear chant. I will shout it out, off and on, throughout the day.

"YO BEAR, HELLO, HELLO. HUMAN PASSING THROUGH. I MEAN NO HARM."

Hello...and goodbye.

Ten days in the wilderness and the company of bears were just about right this time around. I'm ready to rejoin the world of humans, ready to go home, while carrying new memories and a renewed appreciation for the power of this northern wilderness and the way it has enlarged my sense of the world and life's possibilities.

References and Suggested Reading

Blackman, Margaret B. *Upside Down: Seasons Among the Nunamiut.* Lincoln: University of Nebraska Press, 2004.

Brower, Kenneth. *Earth and Great Weather: The Brooks Range.* San Francisco: Friends of the Earth Foundation, 1971.

Brown, William E. *History of the Central Brooks Range: Gaunt Beauty, Tenuous Life.* Fairbanks: University of Alaska Press, 2007.

Callicott, J. Baird and Michael P. Nelson, editors. *The Great New Wilderness Debate.* Athens, Georgia: The University of Georgia Press, 1998.

———. *The Wilderness Debate Rages On.* Athens, Georgia: The University of Georgia Press, 2008.

Campbell, Joseph, with Bill Moyers. *The Power of Myth.* New York: Doubleday, 1988. (Note: this book is based on the video and audio series of interviews that Moyers conducted with Campbell. I recommend either the audio or the video version.)

Catton, Theodore. *Inhabited Wilderness: Indians, Eskimos, and National Parks in Alaska.* Albuquerque: University of New Mexico Press, 1997.

Cooper, David. *Brooks Range Passage.* Seattle: The Mountaineers, 1982.

Crisler, Lois. *Arctic Wild.* New York: Harper & Row, 1958.

Eiseley, Loren. *The Immense Journey.* New York: Vintage, 1959.

Glover, James A. *A Wilderness Original: The Life of Bob Marshall.* Seattle: The Mountaineers, 1986.

Helmericks, Constance and Harmon Helmericks. *We Live in the Arctic.* Boston: Little, Brown and Company, 1947.

Kauffman, John M. *Alaska's Brooks Range: The Ultimate Mountains.* Seattle: The Mountaineers, 1992.

Lopez, Barry. *Arctic Dreams.* New York: Charles Scribner's Sons, 1986.

Louv, Richard. *Last Child in the Woods: Saving Our Children from Nature-Deficit Disorder.* New York: Algonquin Books, 2005.

Marshall, Robert. *Alaska Wilderness: Exploring the Central Brooks Range* (originally published as *Arctic Wilderness*). Berkeley: University of California Press, 1970.

———. *Arctic Village.* Fairbanks: University of Alaska Press, 1991 (originally published in 1933 by H. Smith & Hass in New York).

McGinniss, Joe. *Going to Extremes.* New York: Alfred A. Knopf, 1980.

McPhee, John. *Coming into the Country.* New York: Farrar, Straus, and Giroux, 1976.

Milton, John. *Nameless Valleys, Shining Mountains.* New York: Walker and Company, 1969.

Murie, Margaret. *Two in the Far North.* New York: Alfred A. Knopf, 1963.

Nash, Roderick Frazier. *Wilderness and the American Mind* (fourth edition). New Haven, Connecticut: Yale University Press, 2001 (originally published in 1967).

Nelson, Richard. *Make Prayers to the Raven: A Koyukon View of the Northern Forest.* Chicago: The University of Chicago Press, 1983.

Snyder, Gary. *The Practice of the Wild: Essays.* San Francisco: North Point Press, 1990.

Staender, Vivian and Gil. *Our Arctic Year.* Anchorage: Alaska Northwest Publishing Company, 1984.

Storr, Anthony. *Solitude: A Return to the Self.* New York: Ballantine Books, 1988.

Turner, Jack. *The Abstract Wild.* Tucson: The University of Arizona Press, 1996.

Wright, Billie. *Four Seasons North.* New York: Harper & Row, 1973.

Wright, Sam. *Koviashuvik: A Time and Place of Joy.* San Francisco: Sierra Club Books, 1988.